Nietzsche

Lou Salomé

NIETZSCHE

edited, translated
and with an introduction by
Siegfried Mandel

BLACK SWAN BOOKS

For Theo and Edie

First English translation of Lou Andreas-Salomé's *Friedrich Nietzsche in seinen Werken* (Vienna: Carl Konegen, 1894).

Published by

BLACK SWAN BOOKS Ltd.
P. O. Box 327
Redding Ridge, CT 06876
U.S.A.

ISBN 0-933806-31-0

CONTENTS

Lou Salomé

Friedrich Nietzsche (1873)

Introduction

THE NEW SURGE of interest in Nietzsche makes it timely to translate into English this first and rare closeup view of the Nietzsche who entrusted his thoughts and deeply subjective philosophizing to Lou Salomé during their veiled or chaperoned encounters from April to November of 1882. Until the end of their lives, neither quite forgot the other. Quite startling to Nietzsche's friends was his recorded assertion at the Jena psychiatric clinic in March 1889 that his wife Frau Cosima Wagner had brought him there; with that they also saw the unfolding of riddles in his writings through a cryptic note earlier the same year to Cosima—"Ariadne, I love you! Dionysus." These revelations overshadowed some other fascinating documentation of how Nietzsche's unhinged mind swung back to events of earlier years. During a week in the Basel asylum, he made a somber drawing of two persons embracing. Identifiable is a shield with a heraldic cross which matches that of the famous "lion memorial" at Lucerne's Gletschergarten. At his urgings Salomé had agreed to a rendezvous there on May 13, 1882, and according to her diary, she turned down his marriage proposal. Her objective was not to capture his heart but to come in contact with a great mind. She underestimated his emotionality because she did not fully know his previous biography.

During his lifetime, most of Friedrich Nietzsche's monographs and books barely covered the cost of printer's ink for lack of sales, and his name was far from being a household word either in academic or public circles. His elation therefore was boundless when the influential Scandinavian critic Georg Brandes wrote to him in May 1888 about newspaper reports that recorded an ovation by a large audience for his final lecture on Nietzsche: "Such ovation is attributable almost entirely to you." Brandes aimed to enter "the workshop" of Nietzsche's thoughts, in agreement or dissent, and to present a psychological portrait of their author: "Your name now, I can say without exaggeration, is very *popular* in all intelligent circles of Copenhagen, and *known*, at least, in all of Scandinavia." Brandes understood Nietzsche's professed aim of a relentless "revaluation of all values" held by society and he forwarded Nietzsche's polemic, *The Case of Wagner*, to "the greatest Swedish author, August Strindberg, whom I have completely won over to you. He is a true genius, only a bit crazy like most geniuses (and non-geniuses)." Strindberg, too, wrote to Nietzsche saying that he ended every letter to his friends with the injunction: "Read Nietzsche."

Months later, Nietzsche declined into madness—until he died in 1900—and could not hear the din that began to surround his iconoclastic writings, nor could he enjoy his own prediction that the dynamite in his writings would explode in European circles. Amid the groundswell of Nietzsche adulation and criticism, Lou Andreas-Salomé's book *Friedrich Nietzsche in seinen Werken* was published by Carl Konegen in Vienna in 1894. It was the first full-length attempt to ferret out the man in the midst of his works, and the book contributed to the verbal bloodletting in progress. Her provocative diagnosis showed Nietzsche's madness to have been the inevitable result of psychophysical factors ostensibly mirrored in his writings. Graphic support was lent to her thesis by one of the two Nietzsche photographs reproduced in her book. It was a head-and-shoulders blowup—badly cropped and retouched—from a May 1882 photograph in which she was shown kneeling in a cart and wielding a whiplike lily stalk as her two friends, Nietzsche and Paul Rée, posed at the cart handle. The photograph's caption—"Friedrich Nietzsche, *formerly* professor and now a wandering fugitive"—was mischievously snipped and transposed from a letter to Rée by Nietzsche in 1879, referring to the severance from his ten-year position at the University of Basel. The self-description "*fugitivus errans*" had nothing to do with the idea of madness. It suggested Nietzsche's statelessness; he had to relinquish his German citizenship in 1869, but because of "continuous residence" requirements he never became a Swiss citizen either; instead, he was pleased to call himself a "good European."

Parts of Salomé's book had formerly appeared in widely read newspaper serializations. Erwin Rohde, drawing upon his long acquaintance with Nietzsche, wrote that "nothing better or more deeply experienced and perceived has ever been written about Nietzsche. . . . One can hardly wish for a better overview. . . .

Now it is clear to me that the madness began with *Thus Spoke Zarathustra*, but what a madness and what fire and illumination he casts over the world!" Nietzsche's only personal disciple and voluntary part-time secretary, Peter Gast, noted with disdain that Salomé tried to give an impression of longer familiarity with Nietzsche in correspondence and person than was the case and that she glossed over the sudden break in their relations. Astonishing, he said, is the fact that although Salomé was a rare phenomenon—a female intellectual—who had come in close contact with Nietzsche, she remained a cool observer and a scholarly reporting-machine rather than a person enflamed by the master. Salomé's bitterest enemy, Nietzsche's sister Frau Elisabeth Förster-Nietzsche, entered the fray through a hired underling in her Nietzsche Archive who trumpeted her views in a mass media magazine: Salomé's fantasies misconstrued Nietzsche's writings through the devious "artifice of neurotic female psychology." Nietzsche's old friend Carl von Gersdorff, who had not read Salomé's articles nor even intended to read her Nietzsche book, cheered delightedly that now the "evil Amazon" has been lifted out of the saddle. Indeed, Nietzsche partisans made no bones about their conclusions that Salomé's book was "a female act of revenge."

One French critic thought it a cruel irony that Nietzsche "who consistently misesteemed women was now most intimately understood by a woman." Others complained that Salomé made mythical monstrosities out of Nietzsche and his concept of the *Übermensch*, the superior man. Nevertheless, after Salomé's friends had launched the book with accolades, her reputation and own writing career gained momentum despite detractors. However, her Nietzsche book slowly faded from view, translated only into Danish in 1911, French in 1932 and Japanese in 1974, but it occasionally reappeared in German language reprints in 1911, 1924, and 1983. Quick to capitalize on the situation in the 1890s was a Swiss playwright—unsympathetic to Nietzsche—J. V. Widmann, who dramatized *Jenseits von Gut und Böse* (*Beyond Good and Evil*) and found a popular audience intrigued by the promise of its title.

At first, the reading public's curiosity about writings by a man who had deteriorated into madness set publishing wheels into motion with books that displayed sensationalized hostility, but then the tide turned with books intended for the more serious reader. Some readers probably would have liked to see more personal revelations in Salomé's book; yet they had to be satisfied with discreet descriptions and expository discussions of Nietzsche's thematic ideas.

Since the time of Nietzsche's first publication of her Nietzsche book, many writers have drawn upon her portrait of Nietzsche and quietly—and with little acknowledgement—have either accepted or dismissed her systematized approach to Nietzsche's artistically disguised life-experiences in his books. In 1954, the respected historian of philosophy Karl Löwith in his book *Nietzsches Philosophie der ewigen Wiederkehr des Gleichen* began to redress matters. He expressed astonishment at the care and maturity of Salomé's characterizations, which appeared before Nietzsche's posthumous self-portrayal and assessments of his own works in *Ecce Homo.* "During fifty years subsequent to Salomé's book in 1894," wrote Löwith, "there has not appeared a more central and contributive study. . . . Already evident were clearly worked out lines of a 'system'—and, indeed, without ignoring Nietzsche's teachings of the eternal recurrence, which exclusively gives his philosophy its focal point."

Up to her death in 1937, Salomé refused to answer publicly— either in rebuttal or verification—the questions raised about personal matters relative to the so-called "Nietzsche-Lou affair." By the Thirties, moreover, it would have been very risky to air her recollections of a distant past, in view of Elisabeth Förster-Nietzsche's high standing with the Nazis; besides she was already in hot water with Rilke heirs about her disclosures of Rainer Maria's last difficult days. Some answers surfaced, however, in her diaries (*Lebensrückblick*), edited by her literary executor Ernst Pfeiffer, in 1951. By and large, her reconstructions have been taken in good faith and at face value; not always so, however, for Rudolph Binion in his massive psychiatric biography, *Frau Lou: Nietzsche's Disciple,* attempts literally to shred her reputation and motivations: "Nearly all of Lou's fables in *Friedrich Nietzsche in seinen Werken* come under the double head: heiress pose and Nietzsche romance."

* * *

WE DO NOT KNOW which of the many versions of his life Nietzsche gave Salomé, for often he suited them to different occasions. Recurrent, however, in them is his deep and abiding affection for his father—a person "sensitive, kind and morbid." Pastor Karl Ludwig Nietzsche came of a line of Protestant clergymen, as did his wife Franziska Oehler. Their son Friedrich was born in 1844 in Röcken in the Prussian province of Saxony, and two years later his sister Elisabeth—whose later distinction in life was to promote aggressively the publication of her brother's works, although she either did not understand his main ideas or indeed profoundly abhorred them. Personal tragedies struck early and quickly. Nietzsche's father died agonizingly in 1849, and the attending physician attributed it to softening of the brain. Franziska protested such a socially unacceptable diagnosis and attributed her husband's lingering illness to an earlier fall from the stone stairs of their home. But his father's colleagues noted that even a year before his death he was progressively unable to carry out his duties because of nervous debilitation and epileptic types of attacks. It appears that extreme despondency also had overtaken him upon the political events of 1848 that saw social discontent rise in revolutionary waves and break over the European continent, threatening to replace the old, cherished monarchies with new democratic orders. Nietzsche was haunted by what he knew of his father's mental illness and the fear of dying at the same age as his father; he always memorialized him for the gentleness of his character and his musical improvisations at the piano. Then too, he inherited his father's disapprobation of democratic mediocrity; he later was enthusiastic about Brandes' typifying his political convictions as "aristocratic radicalism," after he had sent Brandes a short autobiographical sketch that inventively also linked his ancestors not to German commoners but to Polish nobility.

The six-year-old Fritz—as Friedrich was called by his family—suffered another shock when his infant brother died of convulsions. Some eight years later, he put to paper a dream he had shortly before this fatality:

> . . . I heard the sounds of the church-organ, as if at a burial. When I noticed what the cause was, there suddenly appears a grave and out of it emerged my father in a death-shroud. He hurried into the church and soon returned with an infant in his arms. The mound of the grave opened; he stepped into it and the cover once again sinks back over the opening. At the same time the upsounding organ tones subside and I awake. The day after, little Joseph becomes unwell, has cramps, and dies in several hours. Our anguish was immense. My dream fulfilled itself completely.

This recollected anticipatory-dream undoubtedly has as much psychological significance as the hallowed aural vision of God during the time of Fritz's confirmation. About a decade later, for New Year's Eve of 1864, he recorded a willed disembodiment of his "self" during the waning hours before midnight as he played the *requiem* from Schumann's *Manfred* on the piano and then sank into a trance and let his spirit roam through places of the past. His spirit returns to his room and Nietzsche sees the dying year "on my bed," surrounded by shades who express their feeling about the old year:

> Suddenly everything lit up brightly. The walls of the rooms flew outward and the ceiling floated aloft. I looked for the bed. The bed was empty. I heard a voice: "You fools of time which exists nowhere except in your minds! I ask, what have you done? Do you wish to be and possess that for which you hope and wait? Well then, meet the test set by the gods if you wish to gain the battle's prize. When you have matured, the ripened fruit will fall, and not sooner!" Above me the clock's hand moved, everything disappeared, it sounded twelve, and in the streets people cried loudly, "Long live the new year."

Here we find a key dream-parable that with variations repeats itself in Nietzsche's works, and most profoundly in his eventual Zarathustra figure—the disembodied alter-ego who messianically looks to the awakening of the superior men, the *Übermenschen*, in the ripeness of time. Twice Zarathustra repeats a song of dance and intoxication during which he awakens from a dream, and with the insights gained he awaits the midnight strokes of an old, heavy growl-bell and "the ring of recurrences." One such dream or vision he first confided to Lou Salomé, as his awesome intimation of the "eternal return of life" and the essence, as Salomé saw it, of his teachings of an eternal recurrence of the same events, presaging the heaviest psychological, self-imposed burdens and fears he could conjure up.

Nietzsche also thought of dreams as having organic sources in daily life and compensating for lack of satisfaction; or, far in advance of archetypal interpretations in our time, he speculated that dreams are a means of recapturing man's deep-layered, somatic and recessed archaic experiences.

The early loss of a benign and loved father forced a move from the small town of Röcken into the somber quarters of relatives in the city of Naumburg. "God in heaven," the young Nietzsche wrote, "was our sole solace and protection," echoing his mother's pious assertions. Naumburg's terrifying bourgeois conventionality, conformism, and religious conservatism seeped into his being as afflictions he called "*Naumburger Tugend,*" a superficial decorum or respectability against which he was to rebel strenuously or meekly accept all his life. The young, early-widowed mother devoted herself energetically to a pietistic, dietetic, and athletically programmed upbringing of her son and daughter in a socially "correct" and unambitious way, aided by her mother-in-law and two maiden sisters-in-law. The physical bond and overt conventional etiquette between son and mother rarely slackened but the emotional and intellectual distance steadily widened. Toward his sister he assumed a courteous, dignified, educative attitude with bible quotings galore, earning him the nickname "little pastor" from schoolmates as well. Retrospectively, the nineteen-year-old Nietzsche saw himself as a "stick-in-the-mud Philistine." Though companionless at the public school, he later made friends at the Gymnasium with youngsters who brought him into contact with their families of high social standing. His intellectuality quickened and his predisposition for music—composition and performance on the piano— grew apace. Like many a budding young scholar, he entertained hopes of attending the exclusive imperial and Protestant university-preparatory school at Pforta which boasted such alumni as the distinguished brothers Schlegel, Fichte, Novalis and Klopstock. A Pforta examiner was impressed with Nietzsche, and soon the young man was offered a full scholarship. Roused by the heavy strokes of a monastery bell at the break of day, 180 students would begin with assembly prayer, bread and butter breakfast, before launching into eleven hours of class, lectures, recitation, and study. From 1858 to 1864, Nietzsche thrived on a curriculum—concentrating on theology and philosophy—that would make many scholars blench. With a pretended matter-of-factness he wrote to his sister: "At the moment, I am even studying Italian, on my own though. Latin, Greek, Hebrew—reading the first book of Moses—the original German of the *Nibelungenlied*, French . . . and in Latin, concurrently, Vergil, Livius, Cicero, Sallust; in Greek, the *Iliad*, Lysis' oratory, and Herodotus." But his readings and curiosity branched out into other directions as well: Shakespeare, Goethe, Byron, the "mad" poet Hölderlin, whose heroes stimulated in him an urge for independence of thought. The concept of "fate" he welcomed because it required strength to overcome, while he began to regard the talk of "will"—especially the will of God—as a rationalization that allowed people to submit cowardly to inaction.

Nietzsche craved intellectual action and adventure of the boldest sort. But first he allowed himself to be completely immersed in some theological and philosophical system in order to master it during a period of gestation and then to rebel against it with explosive force. Throughout his career, it was to be theology first and then philology, philosophy, scientific positivism that were to submit to that pattern. However, during his last years at Pforta and the years at the University of Bonn from 1864 on, his mind was engaged primarily with problems of Greek culture and history through scholarly philological research; theology was to take a back seat. Because his mother continually had to scrape the bottom of the barrel to provide Fritz with schooling, books, bread and board, he had to be temperate in explaining to Franziska his turn from anticipated vocational theological ministry to philology and music. His mother lost no time in emphasizing *her* expectations: "Give your heart over to the dear God and Lord, and all the worldly wisdom you find in thick tomes will then be revealed to your heart and eyes as desecrations. . . . Your life's responsibility later will be to become a good provider for your mother and perhaps also for your sister. . . ." Her letters habitually carried pietistic reminders to her dearest son: Daily and hourly every Christian must battle his way to the realization that "life is a gift of God and that our borrowed time is to be used and paid for by woeful humans in a dignified and Christian way, so that after this preparatory life we may enter our eternal home though the grace of God . . . and with the help of his Son and the Holy Ghost." His mother became the hidden model for the religious sentiments against which overtly he was to turn with bitter contempt, but in his return letters he donned one of the many masks he learned to create and with persistent, though half-way measures, outlined his new direction.

Nietzsche had adopted cultural relativism. In educative notes, he chided his sister Lisbeth for the naïve, girlish tone and content of her letters and suggested that if she wanted to follow her dear brother into higher intellectual realms, she would have to make an unforced and serious choice between habituation to deep-rooted views about the world, God, and atonement held by family and society, and the difficult, convention-defying search for beauty, the good, and truth—"even if it were to be most repelling and ugly." And lastly:

> Suppose that since childhood we had believed that all salvation flows from someone other than Jesus, perhaps Mohammed; would it not be true that we would have gained the same blessings? Certainly, belief alone and not the objectification behind belief blesses us. I point this out to you, dear Lisbeth, only to disprove the most common means of evidence relied upon by orthodox people who derive the infallibility of their belief from subjective, inner experience. Every true belief is indeed infallible; it achieves whatever the particular believing person hopes to find in it, but faith does not in the least offer support for establishing an objective truth.

Here, people's paths diverge: Do you wish tranquillity of soul and happiness, well then, believe; do you wish to be a disciple of truth, well then, search for it. . . . On this serious foundation I will build an edifice that will be all the gayer for it. (June 11, 1865)

Indeed, the revaluation of norms and the relativism of religious faith gave evidence in Fritz's letter of his "search." He thought a day to be wasted if he had not lopped off at least one belief. (Later he honed this observation further: "Wherever the strength of a belief strongly steps into the foreground, we must infer a certain weakness of demonstrability and the *improbability* itself of that belief," (*Toward a Genealogy of Morals: A Polemic*, III, 24, 1887). Until her personal rebellion some twenty years later in the 1880s, Lisbeth would submit to his benevolent intellectual tyranny without being able to enter the spirit of his work and without ceasing to shower him—the only male figure in her world—with sisterly admiration and affection. In turn, he did not hesitate to hold himself up to her as a paragon of virtue and to exploit her sentiments. He idealized her pert and plump femininity while jibing at her "llama-like" affability. She accepted the German nickname *"Lama,"* at first reluctantly, as a term of affection; her young brother drew that name from a book on natural history, which described the llama as a peculiar and sensitive voluntary beast of burden, also capable of defending itself by spewing saliva and half-chewed cud at any tormentor. That description was in part uncannily prophetic.

In a decision that was both unforeseen and fateful to his career, Nietzsche followed Professor Friedrich Ritschl to the University of Leipzig in 1865, and at his suggestion actively helped to organize a philological society. At his suggestion, too, he wrote a learned monograph on the transmitted texts of the Greek oligarch Theognis of the sixth century, although he already resisted the confines of such painstaking scholarship as "woodchopping philology." Theognis' elitism attracted Nietzsche, for the Greek writer praised the moral values of his fellow rulers as "good" in distinction to the "bad" morality of the commoners. Nietzsche, too, was to make a distinction between the morality of the powerful few and the morality and mentality of the herd and mass-man.

The features in Judeo-Christian tradition which favored the latter in an attempt to revolt against and emasculate the natural superiority of the strong rulers, Nietzsche saw as pernicious. He found parallel support for this view in his study of Greek civilization, as he formulated his basic philosophy: Christianity under the influence of Judaism fostered a slave mentality and timidity, while paganism with its master mentality fostered strength and intensity of life. While he cautiously kept his philosophy from public view temporarily, he continued his personally unsatisfying, though craftsmanlike, scholarly works which were published under the auspices of Ritschl. At the same time, his readings and thoughts penetrated to every corner of Greek literary, dramatic, and philosophic culture, forming rich resources for the future.

Intellectually and emotionally he lived a double life—characteristic for him in each of his working phases. He practiced what he was to call "dissimulation" (*Verstellung*—an activity Salomé discusses) in an ironic adoption of masks, much as an actor uses them on stage and enjoys the artistic deception. Nietzsche found stimulation in the tension created by the dual activity and eventually craved and willed that tension as a necessary condition for his creativity. A perfect antithesis to his philological work was his heady and overwhelming discovery of Schopenhauer's *World as Will and Idea*. Schopenhauer's personal ethics, crystalline style, and audacious philosophizing acted like a magnet; he has "removed the blindfold of optimism from our eyes," Nietzsche wrote to a friend, "so that one sees life more sharply, more interestingly, though it reveals life as ugly." In the mirror of Schopenhauer's "healthy pessimism," Nietzsche saw his world and his own nature depicted "with frightful grandeur," as every line of Schopenhauer "loudly cried out for renunciation, denial, resignation." Schopenhauer raised the pursuit of knowledge and wisdom above the sensual, materialistic, anti-intellectual, and noncultural life of the Philistine. Nietzsche readily agreed with the attack on mediocrity; yet he was not about to raise material deprivations into absolute virtues. A universal, pervasive "will," a thing or force supreme in itself, Schopenhauer argued, can be transcended by an objective intellect possessed by geniuses—the aristocracy of mankind—whose loneliness often results in madness. Nietzsche was intrigued by Schopenhauer's idea that music, unlike all the other arts, is like the "will" with its independent and nonverbal power to direct our emotions. If Schopenhauer granted talent but not genius to women, so did Nietzsche. As for Schopenhauer's views of paganism, Judaism, and Christianity, they were not far from Nietzsche's own; but Schopenhauer's thought that the unifying intuition of Buddhistic religions was directed toward the destruction of the "will" also spurred clarifying ideas in Nietzsche's mind. Eventually Nietzsche sloughed off the skin of Schopenhauer's pessimistic attitude, but was indebted to Schopenhauer's teachings in developing or even rejecting them in the brilliant shaping of his own insights into Greek civilization and his own philosophy of living.

Nietzsche's impoverished circumstances, illustrated for instance by having to send his laundry home to Mama and Lisbeth, limited his participation in the roisterous life of a graduate student fraternity. He invited a fencing duel and proudly carried away a wound and permanent scar on his nose. Moving from Bonn to the University of Leipzig, he seceded from the Franconian Society, with a politely disparaging letter. In all, however, it may have been the lessons of medical treatment for venereal disease that tempered his urge for the sexual outlets common to young men of his environment. It was a period in which his energies were to be sublimated to work and music. A further challenge to his maleness came with his military service induction—despite Nietzsche's severe nearsightedness and slight corpulence—in October 1867 at Naumburg and official dismissal a year later. Service with the cavalry detachment of a field artillery unit was a not unpleasant Spartan experience until he fell from a horse. Torn chest muscles, a protruding bone, and months-long suppurations would have made surgery necessary except that his robust constitution and a persistent self-healing restored him to health and good spirits. Retrospectively, there was a measure of joy and vanity in the military experience, as well as a sense of relief when it was over; later he would on occasions refer to himself proudly as an "old cannoneer" and master of the saber. The militant man as hero remained for him more than a figure of speech.

Nietzsche's musical talents in performance and composition were of high amateur, rather than professional, standing, no matter how hard he tried to cross the line during his life, so that his constant discipleship to music was to prove fruitful to his personal needs and of course to his philosophizing. He knew the classical and romantic repertoires intimately but was slowly and with critical reservations drawn to the music "of the future" as it was sounded in Richard Wagner's *Tannhäuser* and *Lohengrin*. A concert performance of the *Tristan* introduction and the *Meistersinger* overture which "caused my every fiber and nerve to quiver . . . with prolonged rapture" converted Nietzsche to Wagner, who already was a living legend in his time. Fate brought Nietzsche an invitation to meet Wagner at the salon of Professor Hermann Brockhaus, Wagner's brother-in-law and a friend of the Ritschls. Frantic sessions at a tailor, straight out of a Gogol scene in the "Overcoat" story, prepared Nietzsche sartorially for the red-letter evening of November 8, 1866, when Wagner was to arrive incognito to shield him from Leipzig newspaper reporters.

Leading up to the *soirée* invitation, the wife of Dr. Ritschl, Sophie, the first of Nietzsche's motherly friends, had mentioned to Wagner that she had become familiar with some of his compositions through a musically gifted student of her husband. Wagner wanted to meet the young man. Nietzsche reported the evening in glowing letters to his friends, suiting Wagner to Schopenhauer's definition of genius. Wagner, in fact, had written Schopenhauer that he was the only philosopher who understood the essence of music, and during the first evening with Nietzsche the ice was broken with a shared admiration for the atheistic philosophy of Schopenhauer who valued the self—with its unconscious and conscious activity—as worthy of exploration and exploitation for the sake of creativity. Wagner was the only genius Nietzsche had ever met, then or later, who lived that challenge and displayed a formidable will to power which intimidated Nietzsche. If Wagner's and Nietzsche's personalities were incompatible—one was a tyrannical extrovert and the other a more subtle thinker inclined to introversion—what was the hypnotic attraction for Nietzsche toward the signorial figure during a decade of correspondence and visits? The pattern which Lou Salomé saw points to one answer. Nietzsche perennially craved stimuli, challenges, and threatening fatalities that would immerse and expose him to new experiences and test his ideas and emotions. Gorged with the experience and revolted by what he called sickness, he would slough it off like a snake's hardened skin. Schopenhauer and Wagner were eventually to be overcome during Nietzsche's periodic self-conquests, but the after-effect was a bitter-tinged nostalgia.

By 1869 Nietzsche was also surfeited with scholarly work— "devil fate"—and was ready to abandon it by escaping to Paris with his friend Erwin Rohde or changing his studies from the humanities to the sciences; but unexpectedly he was to ride on the tail of an academic meteor. In a search to fill its chair for Greek language and literature, the University of Basel found Nietzsche to be the most highly recommended among its list of candidates. Professor Ritschl pulled out all the stops in describing Nietzsche as the most mature young man he ever saw during 39 years of his academic career in philological disciplines—an energetic and healthy person capable of accomplishing anything he might set out to do. Although the required teaching curriculum went against his grain, Nietzsche could do nothing less than accept the prestigious offer. The faculty of Leipzig chose to regard Nietzsche's published philological monographs as equivalents for a dissertation—although Nietzsche was ready to present new research work—and awarded him a doctorate without further examinations, an unusual step that brought Nietzsche envy and damaging hostility from some academicians. He responded modestly to admiring congratulations, but unsatisfactory tribute from an old friend, Paul Deussen, prompted him to send a professor's visiting card with a notation that their friendship was at an end, blaming Deussen's temporary "mental derangement." The friendship was resumed later, and Deussen was to play a role in Nietzsche's intellectual life with the publication of a brilliant orientalist book. A year after Nietzsche's death, Deussen published a well-intentioned reminiscence that however opened dark corners in Nietzsche's life and imagination.

In keeping with his new position, Nietzsche asked his mother to find a suitable man-servant for him, but she talked him out of this extravagance, even though the economic clouds had lifted. More pressing was the promised task to index the 24-year-old journal issued by the Rhine museum, under Ritschl's editorship, and Lisbeth helped to finish the onerous business. Although Ritschl had assured Basel officials that Nietzsche was of "non-political character" and not inclined to Prussianism, the neutral Swiss wanted clarification. Since Nietzsche could be called up as a reserve cavalryman in time of war, he requested and received an official expatriation document and no longer was a Prussian or German; from then on he was a stateless émigré.

One of the advantages Nietzsche looked forward to by living in Basel was the nearness to Lucerne, where Wagner presided on the Tribschen estate with Cosima Bülow (Franz Liszt's illegitimate daughter) and her four daughters (two of Wagner's paternity). Cosima was estranged from her husband Hans Guido von Bülow, the well-known conductor, pianist, and journalist, and as one wag put it, he had the double bad luck of worshiping Wagner while Wagner adored Bülow's wife. Wagner and his entourage had to leave Bavaria for Switzerland when the Wagner-Cosima scandal forced "mad" King Ludwig of Bavaria to exile his favorite composer, though continuing his royal largesse. After one month in Basel, Nietzsche made his first pilgrimage to Tribschen and then marked off 23 more on his calendar for three years into 1872 when the Wagners, now married, moved permanently to Bavaria's Bayreuth where the Wagner opera-theater and cult were to flourish.

At Tribschen, two rooms were furnished for Nietzsche's visits, but cordiality was never mistaken for real intimacy as the Professor was addressed with the formal "*Sie*" and Wagner with the obligatory honorific "Master." Nietzsche was not exempted from the lifelong criteria Wagner applied to everyone: absolute loyalty and usefulness to the Master. So long as Nietzsche was dutifully submissive, his stock was high with the Wagners; when in a few years Nietzsche reluctantly distanced himself, Wagner forbade the mention of Nietzsche's name in his own august presence. Nietzsche's early letters to the Wagners swelled with awe and stilted obsequiousness, and he even offered to give up his professorship to embark on a lecture tour that would seek proselytes for Wagner. The Master declined, for he felt that Nietzsche was too valuable a showpiece among the academicians he despised; later when he asked for that sacrifice, Nietzsche had begun to assess matters objectively and wormed out of compliance.

With its expanse of soft grass sloping into the clear blue waters of the Vierwaldstättersee which mirrors the violet hues of surrounding mountain peaks, the Tribschen estate was for Nietzsche an "Isle of the Blest" in contrast to the workaday reality of Basel. Yet both worlds fused in his first major work *The Birth of Tragedy from the Spirit of Music* (end of 1871) as Nietzsche refigured the ancient Greek world in imaginative dimensions; it did not contain the scholarship that philologists demanded in resolving the origin of Greek tragic drama, but through intuition he opened up subterranean strata of Greek civilization. Nietzsche destroyed widely held æsthetic views, inspired in 1755 by the archæologist-historian Johann Winckelmann, about the "noble simplicity, calm grandeur," "sweetness and light," harmony and cheerfulness (*Heiterkeit*) of the ancient Greeks and posed instead the dark Dionysian forces that had to be harnessed to make possible the birth of tragedy. In discernible outline the grand design of Nietzsche's æsthetics took shape as he moved from Schopenhauerian-Buddhistic and Christian "negation of the will and world" toward pagan affirmation (exclusive of Plato), and ultimately his own ideal—the ennoblement of the will and the world in a sublime acceptance of the tragedy and suffering within human existence.

As insider and outsider of "court" life at Tribschen, Nietzsche's private fantasies thrived on fertile ground. To the hallucinatory visions and realms already registered belongs one that occurred in Leipzig during the time he first stepped into the magic circle of Wagner, and it has eerie resonance. An autobiographical note, that somehow escaped destruction by Lisbeth, betrays considerable agitation through its hasty handwriting. It reads, "What I fear is not the terrifying figure behind my chair but its voice, and yet not its voice but the ghastly inarticulate and inhuman tone from that figure; yes, if it would only talk like a human." It was an indistinct Dionysian voice. The "symbolical dream image" and unmediated vision which reveals "the inmost ground of the world"—as Nietzsche phrased it in *The Birth of Tragedy*—came to visual concreteness in the pictorial, mediumistic figures and atmosphere of music at Tribschen. Nietzsche thought of art as *mimesis* and the artist at work as an "imitator" of unconscious "art-states of nature" but that the model—especially the dæmonic-ecstatic Dionysus—was the true possessor of artistic energies.

Related to this burgeoning notion was an original watercolor by Bonaventura Genelli (1798–1868) of Dionysus being educated by the muses of Apollo. It hung in the Tribschen Salon, and the pictorial rendering impressed itself upon Nietzsche's mind when writing about Dionysus in *The Birth of Tragedy from the Spirit of Music*. Wagner had written King Ludwig that through Genelli's *Dionysus* he had received the "first lively impressions of Greek ideals of beauty and æsthetics." Yet, like his appreciation of Greek culture, Wagner's view of Genelli's picture was quite superficial. He saw only the idealized young Dionysus surrounded by gracious and musical muses, nymphs, and a winged Eros. Nietzsche, however, was somberly drawn to the disfigured sculpture-torso, placed in the background and over the idyllic scene. It is a phallic Hermes or a Dionysian alter-ego, whose grimacing face is distorted with mad laughter and resembles a mask; the god of the torso carries the allegorical significance of man's chaotic inner nature and Dionysian impulse to life, and beneath the torso—the cult object of worship—lolls an intoxicated, gross satyr. Wagner not only was intrigued by Nietzsche's dæmonic and artistic interpretation but he appropriated it as well, and perhaps with a touch of playful sarcasm: "Now, my gaze sweeps with pure astonishment from Genelli's *Dionysus* to a suddenly illuminated oracular inscription over your last work [*The Birth of Tragedy*]. . . . That presents me with a curious and even marvelous connection, embracing the entirety of my life, through your thoughts about Genelli's picture."

Nietzsche silently glossed over Wagner's unattributed incorporation of his ideas about the Apollonian and Dionysian relationships and complimented Wagner on the similar ideas expressed in the *Beethoven* essay and in Wagner's book *On the Destiny of Opera* (1871). Then Nietzsche even rewrote parts of *The Birth of Tragedy* to suppress ideas Wagner did not want to publicize and to implant references to Wagner's music that would propagandistically extol the glory of the Master. Nietzsche's concept of history portrayed a struggle from Greek antiquity to modern times as waged between the radical, aristocratic spirit of Dionysian creativity and the mediocre political power-brokers of the establishment. And so, Nietzsche wanted to pit "the cultural renewer of German"—Wagner, the musician of the future—against the "literalistic" statesman Bismarck. But Wagner became alarmed over Nietzsche's intended politicizing of art and music because he was campaigning for the patronage of high-establishment persons. With the help of Cosima, he cooled Nietzsche's hot political brew.

At first, Nietzsche envisioned a father-role for Wagner when he sent him twelve long-stemmed roses on his birthday in 1870 and a long, effusive letter that began with the salutation *"Pater Seraphice"* and signed with *"Einer 'der seligen Knaben'"* ("one of 'the beatific boys,'" an allusion to the boys' choir that leads Goethe's Faust to heaven). Wagner was born the same year—1813—as was Nietzsche's dead father. The ghostly substitute, however, would not do, for Nietzsche already had a protective figure he referred to as *"Vater,"* among friends, or as he would write to his mother and sister, photos of "Papa Ritschl and Schopenhauer" are hung in the Basel apartment.

When Wagner appropriated the model of Dionysus to represent "the entirety" of his own life, he unwittingly triggered a role-contest fateful for Nietzsche, a contest that Nietzsche alluded to in riddles. In the Fall of 1870, Nietzsche roughed out a plan for a drama that now is known as the "Empedocles Fragment." Here is one revealing excerpt. "Third Act: Theseus and Ariadne. The chorus. Pausanius and Corinna on stage. Deadly hysteria among the people at the announcement of a rebirth. He is worshiped as the god Dionysus, while he again begins to empathize with the people. (The actor Dionysus falls ludicrously in love with Corinna.)" Finally, Dionysus and Corinna are united in a stream of lava. The elaborate private fantasies overlaid real persons with mythological figures: the "actor" Dionysus = Nietzsche, Ariadne/Corinna = Cosima, and Theseus = Wagner. In the Tribschen drama Nietzsche not only saw himself as an actor but the others as acting out projected roles as well. Wagner, particularly, was costumed for a stage drama, with his huge velvet painter's beret, silk shirts with lace frills, velvet jacket, and ribboned fancy knickers—all of which drew attention away from his short stature; but the bills from Venetian and Viennese tailors were beyond his budget. Wagner was tailored to fit the Theseus prototype. In the 1830s he had triumphed over a swarm of suitors and married the belle of Langstädt, Minna Planer, who was young enough to pass off her illegitimate daughter as her sister. Mutual infidelities and forgivings marked their tumultuous partnership which ended when Cosima became his new objective. Wagner justified his overpowering need for sexual possessiveness—often directed toward women married to friends and acquaintances—by writing to his mistress, Frau Mathilde Wesendonck, about the "sacred path" of real love that "springs from sexuality, the attraction of man and woman." His mistresses were metamorphosed and immortalized in the "stolen" heroines of his music dramas, notably Isolde, Brünnhilde, and Kundry. That Wagner actually was sacralizing and sensualizing sexuality would eventually dawn upon Nietzsche. But just as these women lent intoxication to Wagner's creativity, some of their husbands' purses proved useful for Wagner's extravagances. Cosima von Bülow was his greatest prize, and although she ambitiously served her divine Master with absolute dedication, Wagner even then was not sexually faithful.

Nietzsche's psychosexual eroticism was channeled into identification with Dionysian life, while Wagner's found outlets both in his life and art. Wagner's mother and sister fixation took the form of velvet clothing and silk bedding fetishism, and to Cosima he admitted his erotic predilection: "I have never had a woman who was a virgin." Nietzsche was intimidated by Wagner's sensuality, yet envied its free expression; his horror of his own mother's possessive crush and his dependent exploitation of it were to keep Nietzsche in perpetual bondage. He looked for surrogates for his austerely pious mother and clinging sister—

instead of making clean breaks—and found himself a perpetual third party to marriageable or married women, awkward in his wooing of women he believed to be suitable partners, and tormented by having to seek satisfaction with women outside the pale of respectability, by social double-standards. Nietzsche's ambivalence in print, with touches of arrogant maleness, belied the timidity in his behavior that was often praised as chivalrousness toward the fair sex. Not even Lou Salomé in her search for the man in his writing could talk of such matters—the taboos of the times prohibited frankness in publishable discussions. Yet an understanding of Nietzsche's psychological constraints are indispensable to observations on Nietzsche's writings and to his relationship to Wagner in life, with its compulsive periodic revaluations of the Master in print.

Wagner readily appeared in Nietzsche's imagination to be an incarnation of the mythic Theseus, the wife-stealer. Theseus abducts Ariadne who, as Nietzsche well knew from Hesiod and Euripides, was the wife of Dionysus. (A variant version describes Ariadne as perfidiously accepting Theseus' love.) Her adventures are sorrowful until Dionysus hears her laments and raises up the forsaken woman to be the queen among women in his realm. Dionysus, above all, was a role—or a mask, as Lou Salomé would see it—into which Nietzsche would slip at will, until the mask became the man. "Who except me knows," Nietzsche was to note privately, "who Ariadne is?" At Tribschen he took great pleasure in discussing his works in progress, and his admiration for Ariadne-Cosima took the form of "Five Prefaces to Unwritten Books," given to her as Christmas presents in 1872, but her response was almost indifferent amid more important tasks for the Master. Lisbeth Nietzsche describes the rapt attention to intellectual and personal matters in conversations between her brother and Cosima during a stroll at Tribschen. Cosima wore a rose cashmere gown with decorative lace down to the hem, and on the crook of her arm hung a large Florentine hat with a rose-wreath (an image that became imbedded in Nietzsche's mind as we note in the last page of Salomé's book). Cosima, twenty-four years younger than Wagner and only seven years older than Nietzsche, was the centerpiece of the Theseus-

Ariadne-Dionysus triangle. On one occasion when the Wagner Society congregated in droves toward midnight in 1871 in anticipation of the conductor-celebrity's arrival in Mannheim for his own opera performance, there stepped from the train "a small, distinctive figure with exceptionally expressive agility." Amid resounding cheers, Wagner joked in the local dialect, "Lord Jeesuz, I'm no prince." A short time later, a train arrived from Lucerne, and the mistress of Tribschen stepped to the platform, supported by the hand of a companion: "He is of middle-size, about 27-years-old, with dark brown hair and a bushy moustache, and a distinguishing high, broad forehead. His glasses suggest an academician, while the meticulousness of his clothing, the near-military bearing, and his bright, clear voice say otherwise. Frau Wagner introduces him to the officials of the society as Friedrich Nietzsche." Nietzsche was the Wagners' prize exhibit for a world that needed conversion to the Master's music of the future.

That had been the main cause of Cosima's distress in August 1870 when she learned that Nietzsche had gained leave from the University of Basel to serve in the German medical corps during the Franco-Prussian war. To her esteemed friend, she wrote that it was more important to remain a live professor; the well-organized and conquering army did not as yet need his help. Nietzsche had been undecided until his sister and a patriotic friend appealed to his manliness and sense of duty. From the field of battle, Nietzsche wrote with sadness of French and German wounded, of the stench of death, gangrene, and dying, of protecting the sick and maimed from inclement weather. He empathized with the agony of combat soldiers he could not join. Soon he came down with dysentery, diphtheria, and migraine headaches; though weakened physically, he returned to teaching in a few months. Some forty years later, and after the death of her brother, Lisbeth in publishing her edited Wagner-Nietzsche correspondence wishfully mythologized Nietzsche's war experience as being the source of his "battle courage" and as his "highest will to life, not as an expression of pitiful scrounging for existence, but as a will to battle, as a will to power and over-power," as well as his admiration for the military Germans, "a race that wants to be victorious, to dominate or to perish." As a matter of fact, it did not take Nietzsche long to subdue patriotic intoxication and military self-puffery and to take a dim view of the Prussian victory over France; it is madness to see it as a triumph of German culture, he was to note in his *Untimely Meditations*. Once back in Basel, he advised an old confidant, Erwin Rohde, to escape from the fatal and anticultural Prussia where sanctimonious clerics and serfs sprout like mushrooms. To a close Prussian friend, Count Carl von Gersdorff, he had earlier railed against French effeteness, but now he wrote, "Confidentially, I regard Prussia at present as a power highly dangerous for culture." Culture ("the unity of the artistic style of all expressions in the life of a people," as Nietzsche defined it) must be fought for intellectually. In that respect, Walter Kaufmann surely makes a valid observation: "one may generalize that in most of his notorious remarks about 'war' . . . the word is used metaphorically," in the sense of combativeness and attack upon popular ideologies in one's search for knowledge and truth. The soldier pose and the fictitious "officer" title he gave himself betray Nietzsche's need for admiration and his insecurity about his maleness.

Nietzsche's brief wartime service gave him respite from philological work and teaching, and he was able to avoid the select invitation to attend the Wagners' August wedding in Tribschen. Cosima's letters, however, provided details of life at Tribschen, including the five-year-old Siegfried's baptism: "Siegfried was not at his best behavior during the baptism. At first he babbled and finally—when the Holy Ghost descended—he cried. But now he is a Christian, and if he did not give the priest much joy, I hope that he will be true to the Savior unto the cross." Such pious sounds Nietzsche was accustomed to hearing from his mother, and he ignored them and preserved decorum, despite his freethinking. But Lisbeth tells how offended he was when Wagner heaped ridiculing and atheistic remarks on Cosima's pathetic pieties. Nietzsche was still "courting" Cosima with barely concealed, dreamlike reverence, and although he had not composed any music for six years, he was inspired in 1871 to write a piano piece for four hands, with the long title "Lingering Sound of a New Year's Eve, with Processional Song, Peasant

Dance and Midnight Bell." He called the piece a "Dionysian manifestation." And indeed, we see the links in the title's chain of words, each tolling deep associative meanings—the New Year's Eve dæmon, song, dance, midnight, bell. The composition was intended as a birthday present for Cosima. This "Dionysian composition," as well as the others he was to play for the Wagners, were greeted with evasive courtesy, which Nietzsche for a long time mistook for enthusiasm. Privately Wagner laughed at Nietzsche's "underhanded music score."

The year 1872 marked an end and a new beginning for everyone. Tribschen had become Cosima's "lost Paradise" and Nietzsche had to abandon his "Isle of the Blest" when Wagner had no choice but to move to Bayreuth, near Munich, where, during his birthday, the foundation stone was laid for his new theater; Wagner called his villa *"Wahnfried"*—"peace from delusion"—which was to be his and Cosima's last home. For the Wagners, the existence of the theater and home meant a constant struggle into which they threw every available friend; and yet, without the subsidies of King Ludwig—whose homosexual attraction to Wagner never waned—everything would have foundered. Wagner's operatic fantasies coincided with Ludwig's kingly delusions.

It has been commonly assumed—even by Lou Salomé in her Nietzsche book—that the later falling out between Nietzsche and Wagner occurred over *Parsifal* (an opera long on Wagner's drawing board but first performed at Bayreuth in July 1882), whose libretto Nietzsche thought to be a hypocritical catering to cultural Philistines, Christian sentimentality, as well as to Cosima's piety. That was but the tip of the iceberg. Nietzsche worked hard on behalf of the Bayreuth cause until he saw it as false, self-serving, and exploitative, but he had nothing to blame except his habit of creating impossible ideals and then being forced—as Salomé so perceptively noted—to conquer himself and his illusions, attacking them with the same fervor that he had formerly espoused them. The chores exacted were endless, ranging from trivial errands that he would delegate to Lisbeth to time-consuming writings on behalf of Bayreuth subscription campaigns.

During the Tribschen days when Nietzsche's enthusiasm showed signs of flagging, Wagner would write with mock seriousness: "Not another word; you are becoming problematic to me." Or he would write: "Well then, be of good courage, like a true Prussian cavalryman!" Wagner wanted to spur him along with the copy and illustration preparations for a privately printed edition of *Mein Leben* (*My Life*), which Wagner wrote at the request of King Ludwig. Nietzsche delegated Lisbeth to find an illustration of a vulture for Wagner's heraldic crest, and when she asked her brother why Wagner chose a vulture rather than an eagle, he told her that Wagner meant to honor his beloved, natural father Ludwig Geyer (literally "vulture" in German). That Geyer—a dramatist, actor, and portrait painter—was of Jewish extraction was a widely assumed rumor known to Wagner and Nietzsche, while it was a fact that Cosima's grandmother, Marie Bethmann, came from a family of Jewish financiers. In the thrall of the Master, Nietzsche largely ignored obvious ironies and occasionally echoed the Wagners' anti-Semitic epithets.

For the sake of closeness to the Master and Cosima, Nietzsche overlooked much that was unpalatable, until both overstepped the line between friendship and his private life and artistic integrity. More and more Nietzsche sought time necessary for his writings beyond his teaching duties and he was becoming disenchanted with many of the new courtiers congregating in Bayreuth. The Wagners became irritated with Nietzsche's growing absence from Villa Wahnfried. During the Christmas days of 1874, Wagner tried the lure of manly *bonhomie,* with misfired humor, promising Professor Nietzsche better company at Bayreuth than with bachelors in Basel:

> . . . Among other things, in my life I have never found such male get-togethers as you have them at evenings in Basel. If all of you are hypochondriacs, then there is not much worth bothering with. It seems though that the young bachelors need women . . . but where to find them without stealing? But then again, one may steal if the need arises. I believe that you must marry, or compose an opera. One as well as the other will help you; but marriage, I consider the better thing for you.
>
> In the meantime, I can recommend a palliative for you. . . . You would spend the summer vacation with us.

> Oh God! Do marry a rich woman! Why did fate make Gersdorff a male!

Such "hale and hearty" provocations from Theseus-Wagner, the first in a line that was to be unendurable, struck a chill into Nietzsche's heart. After Wagner's 1874 Christmas letter, Nietzsche stayed away from Bayreuth for an entire year. Wagner had miscalculated the effect of his jocular bullying and impatiently directed his meanness, usually reserved for real or imagined enemies, toward his absent friend Nietzsche, and he abruptly broke the magic spell.

In other letters, Wagner dangled Cosima's solicitude and anticipations of his visits. But that too was beginning to pall when Cosima in her letters criticized his reading tastes and points of writing style. Nietzsche, who justifiably regarded himself as the best German prose stylist after Heine, took these lessons on taste and style with a smile, according to Lisbeth, and remarked that if the foreigner Cosima (daughter of the French Countess Marie d'Agoult and brought up in Paris) wished to improve upon German style, she ought to use her talent first of all to benefit the writings of Wagner. Lisbeth wanted the world to know after her brother's death that he never harbored any love-passion for Cosima who, though charming and masterful and of a good complexion, was too thin and tall and possessed too large a nose and mouth; above all, said Lisbeth, Cosima had neither the "gold-bright" laughter that could have provoked her brother's passion nor other qualities that, one might note, Elisabeth believed she herself owned. She did not wish to see her brother except though the veil of her idealizations, a virtuous figure of modesty and purity, rather than as a person who had to sublimate his drives. Yet Nietzsche's fantasy indeed transformed the real Cosima—a mother of five children, an energetic household manager, a religious and intellectual bigot, a faithful companion to the Master—into a suitable Ariadne for Dionysus. Likely, it was "abstinence," as Nietzsche noted aphoristically, that stimulates sensual inspiration.

Nietzsche's last act of homage to the Master, the monograph *Richard Wagner in Bayreuth*, was published in 1876 after a long delay occasioned by a deep split between the notes that Nietzsche made in preparation for the publication and what appeared in print. In the notes he took a hard look at Wagner's greatness and flaws, his "command-giving nature" and theatrical language, and his art as unsuited to social and workaday reality. "The music is not worth much, neither is the text and drama, the art of theatrics often is only rhetoric—but everything forms a great unity on an elevated level." It was devious of Nietzsche to disguise these judgements and heretical analyses so artfully in order to gain the compliments of the Wagners. Instinctively, however, Cosima in her diaries was slowly writing Nietzsche off as declining in his loyalty (meaning "usefulness") to the Master.

In this life-drama all were accomplished actors, all serving their own idiosyncrasies and needs. Toward the end of October 1876, the Wagners vacationed in Sorrento, whose breathtaking beauty allowed them to veil the horrendous financial problems of Bayreuth. Nietzsche and his new friends, Malwida von Meysenbug and Dr. Paul Rée, also stayed there. What transpired during the private walks and talks between Wagner and Nietzsche is not directly known. Lisbeth surmised that Wagner donned a pious mask, instead of honestly admitting capitulation to audience tastes; further, his life-denying and Catholic-romantic *Parsifal* stood in contrast to Nietzsche's life-affirming ideals. Actually, the Teutonic gods and heroes of Wagner and the pagan Greeks of Nietzsche never had much in common. But Nietzsche wished to preserve his friendship with the Wagners by making concessions and self-deludingly hoping for their acknowledgement of his stature as an independent philosopher equal to the Master. It became almost inevitable that the men would not meet again personally and that they would inflict serious wounds upon each other at a distance.

Within the next two years, the contest between different ideological positions hastened Wagner's rejection of Nietzsche as a friend. In January 1878, Wagner sent Nietzsche a handsomely bound copy of *Parsifal*, personally inscribed to "dear friend" Nietzsche but with a request that the book be forwarded to Nietzsche's colleague, the theologian Overbeck. In letters to confidantes, Nietzsche ridiculed the libretto as seemingly translated from a foreign tongue, as embodying the spirit of the Catholic

Counter-Reformation (a reactionary force, according to Nietzsche), employing hysterical heroines and actors with contorted throats, and as containing purely fantastic psychology—no flesh and too much blood of sacramental communion; but he did not retract his earlier admiration for the long, orchestral introduction to the music drama, rich with motifs. Ever since Nietzsche had left Bayreuth, claiming splitting headaches from performances of Wagner's music dramas and disillusionments with their contents, he had been working on materials brought together under the book title *Human, All Too Human*. After receiving *Parsifal*, he sent his own book manuscript to the Wagners, hoping for the blessings of the Master and the "intelligent favor" of Cosima. He felt like an "officer storming the barricades" with his new aphoristic approach, and he explained that he intended to publish the book pseudonymously in order to provoke sober, nonpartisan discussions. After a deafening silence from Bayreuth, Nietzsche edited the book once more to remove what Wagner might consider personally offensive. Nietzsche's publisher, however, thought that a bit of the scandal would not hurt sales and insisted on Nietzsche's name for the title page.

Even with pre-publication editing there was much to offend the Wagners in *Human, All Too Human: A Book for Free Spirits*. He took to task geniuses like Wagner, who retain religious incense in their music and art. He put a scalpel to the prejudices of his time, exemplified by the Wagners, and declared that the ostracized Jew is an essential "ingredient for the breeding of the most strong, European race" and "to whom one owes the noblest human (Christ), the purest philosopher (Spinoza), and the mightiest book." In sum, Nietzsche declared his intellectual emancipation from social and academic prejudices and gave notice of his intentions to revaluate continually the all-too-human, flabby thinking of his contemporaries.

Wagner idolaters then turned on Nietzsche, and the Master himself in the August and September issues of the house organ *Bayreuther Blätter* delivered a scathing attack upon Nietzsche (though unnamed), his philosophy, and the "rudderless and arrogant professordom." Nietzsche commented on Wagner's "human, all-too-human . . . bitter-evil and near-vengeful pages. . . ." He took Wagner's polemic in stride, giving the impression of feeling immense relief and reporting an upswing in his energies. Nietzsche's ego had gained maturity and free play. Lisbeth viewed the happenings with alarm and sent the Wagners an ameliorative letter; in return, she received a long, acerbic reply that enumerated her brother's flaws. Cosima had already branded Nietzsche a "traitor" and destroyed most of the letters he had addressed to her. For Nietzsche's part, he kept her old image alive in his interior fantasies. Though having experienced "the odd estrangement of many acquaintances and friends," he gained others more consonant with his new, purposeful directions. Among them were the motherly intellectual Malwida von Meysenbug, Paul Rée, and Heinrich Köselitz, a young musician who, as a surrogate for Wagner, was renamed Peter Gast or Maestro Pietro by Nietzsche, and became Nietzsche's life-long helper, part-time amanuensis, proofreader, and devoted—but never personally intimate—follower.

Nietzsche had met Rée in 1873 when the doctoral student, five years Nietzsche's junior, was working on his dissertation. Two years later he congratulated Rée on the publication of *Psychologische Beobachtungen* (*Psychological Observations*) and took pleasure in discussing with him the collection of maxims developed in the tradition of great European writers working in the aphoristic mode. Nietzsche already had incorporated aphoristic techniques in his writings as useful in pithy revaluations of given values, and he liked Dr. Rée's quick-witted deflations of pretensions that were his own targets also. "Long live Réealism," said Nietzsche, in view of such maxims as the following: "The philologist knows books as little as the paper does on which they are printed"; "Many a brain drowns in its own pedantry"; "The bookworm finds pleasure in study itself rather than in the objects of his studies"; "One combats newly emerging truths, partly because one envies their teacher and partly so as not to admit that one has been in error for a long time"; "The fact that every other person holds his opinion to be true, should make us suspicious of our own."

When Nietzsche in his *Human, All Too Human* inverts St. Luke's "he who humbles himself will be exalted" into "he who humbles himself wills to be exalted," we may think of Rée's maxims, "One humbles oneself because of the thought that one will be raised up," or "Martyrs prefer admiration to physical comfort." But already here, Nietzsche breaks new ground by talking of a "will to exaltedness" that later is developed into his idea of the will to power. Stimulating for Nietzsche as well was Rée's *Der Ursprung der moralischen Empfindungen* (*The Origin of Moral Sentiments*), published in 1877, which coincided with his own probings into human motivations and rationalizations for actions and behavior, as well as the origin and the changeability of morality in mankind's history. When Nietzsche complimented Rée in *Human, All Too Human*, the Bayreuthians ascribed Nietzsche's defection from the Master's cause and his new heresies to the contributive influence of Dr. Paul Rée, "a smooth, very cool Israelite" as Cosima declared with a finality that belied the indissoluble emotional, mutual, and continuing tangential contacts between the Wagners and Nietzsche.

Nietzsche's life moved in continual spirals of crises, prompted by conflicts between emotions and cold calculations. His longstanding resistance to philological teaching at Basel precipitated illnesses that in turn gained him periodic leaves from his duties. Speaking against his abandoning his post were the attending honors and security and the good will of many colleagues and students who at one point had wanted to organize a torchlight parade when he refused the solicitations of another university. His mother and sister panicked at the thought of his losing a creditable source of income. But he made the break and was aided by generous contributions to a short-term pension fund by university and private donors. Since he did not have continuous eight-year residence in Switzerland because of his service as a medical orderly with the Prussian army, he was stateless or, better still, on the way to becoming the cosmopolitan "good European" of the idealistic culture he envisioned as a necessity for the future. And so, his restless wanderings began; they were enclosed geographically within a large quadrangle from his mother's home in Naumburg, Germany, to the French coastal city of Nice, down to Italy's Sicilian city of Messina, and up to the Engadine highlands of Switzerland, with preference for sea or mountain locales.

Wherever Nietzsche journeyed, he stored staple items in his suitcase; emergency packages from Naumburg followed regularly. He needed little in addition to a flowing overcoat and shawl; perhaps another suit, underwear, writing paper, an extra set of spectacles that would complement the one riding on his nose when he scrawled away one inch from his paper, and a veritable medicinal arsenal consisting of tranquillizing chloral hydrate, veronal, various tinctures, and other medicaments. The string of doctors he had consulted for his eyes, stomach, and headaches were of minimal help, and he was right in asserting that "I am my own best doctor" and dietitian, because his ailments were preponderantly psychosomatic. As Lou Salomé notes from her association with Nietzsche and her reading of his works, he categorically took his sicknesses to be the means to knowledge. With variations, he held it to be a truism that sickness for a typically healthy person can be an energetic stimulus for life. Nietzsche's welcoming of such stimuli also show an astonishing capacity to bear, absorb, and conquer punishing illnesses and to transform them into lucid and impassioned thinking. Though mostly mild-mannered in conversation, he was transformed into a garrulous polemicist at the writing desk.

The catalogue of illnesses and their manifest symptoms are vast, if we scan Nietzsche's letters early on and through the retrospective generalizations he volunteered during his days in the asylum. The cardinal symptom most frequently mentioned is the recurrently attacking headache, then such equivalent components as abdominal pains, colic, vomiting, diarrhea, constipation, fevers, and associated reactions of blacking-out, tear-blurrings and flaming eye irritations, extreme fluctuations of mood, and neuralgia—"cerebral hurricanes" or neurological disturbances. These symptoms and attacks of frequent and long duration—meticulously recorded by Nietzsche—were invariably tied to turbulent emotions: sudden rages, depressions, elations. Migraine, mentioned in Nietzsche's catalogues, was a vaguely understood phenomenon in nineteenth century medicine, but in a modern landmark study, *Migraine: Understanding a Common Disorder* by Dr. Oliver W. Sacks, migraine is now identified as the locus from which radiate a variety of merging and overlapping syndromes. Through Dr. Sacks' clinical observation of the cycle of common migraine as a "paradoxical combination of inner violence and outer detachment," we gain a clearer perception of the cathartic and creative effects of Nietzsche's submission to and "conquests" of illnesses.

A dramatic variant of common migraine is "migraine aura" that enveloped Nietzsche's periodic states of intense terror, feelings of impending destruction, death fears, hysteria, and visions. Nietzsche solemnly revealed that "the *eternal recurrence idea*, the highest formulation of affirmation that can be achieved at all," belongs to his experience in the Swiss Upper-Engadine mountains, "at the beginning of August 1881 in Sils-Maria, 6,000 feet above sea level and ranging far above all things human (beyond man and time)." Nietzsche wrote, "That day I walked along the shore of Lake Silvaplana and through the forests, and came to a halt at a mighty, uprearing pyramidal rock not far from Surlei"—there a vision occurred. During the following harsh winter, and after sleepless nights caused by high-sounding seas, he overlooked the bay of Portofino, as if drawn by destiny, and felt the idea of the eternal recurrence coming to life in the figure of Zarathustra, "more accurately, *he overpowered me.*" It is true that Nietzsche had been absorbed in recent readings in the sciences touching on the indestructibility of matter and had retained his old acquaintance with the Greek philosopher Heraclitus' notion of the eternal flux that rhythmically causes the return of things to their original states. Those influences might explain his own aural experiences and his intuitive and mythopoetic sanctioning of a belief in recurrence, the terrifying "eternal hourglass of existence." With whispered awe and dreamy reminiscence he privately retold the experience later to Lou Salomé, and intimated a sense of Dionysian immortality.

The clue to Nietzsche's most creative moments—as he describes matters—is the state of depersonalization in which the "It" (*Es*) and not the author composes. "I am neither mind nor body," declared Nietzsche, "but a *tertium quid*"—another dimensional entity. That sense is particularly pervasive in *Zarathustra*. Deep tension, stress, and illness, Nietzsche saw as preconditions for the activity of the mind. This should not be misconstrued as a "flight into illness"—as Nietzsche's long, periodic bedridden spells and darkened chambers might suggest—but as a dangerous "experimental philosophy as I live it, even with the possibilities of the most thoroughgoing nihilism," for the sake of seeking knowledge.

Like fellow migraine sufferers, Nietzsche experienced anxiety during personal "anniversaries," and these often prompted claims in letters that he was at death's door. Certain dates, periods of the year, chiming of church bells, midnight, and other recurrent "triggers" caused migrainous reflexes. Many of these forcibly drew him back to childhood with the persistent trauma of his father's burial and Christmas and New Year's festivities. A cluster of such anniversary neuroses and his somatic reactions almost finished him in 1879. It was the anniversary of his father's death-year that coincided with his own age, and he sank to the lowest level of his vitality—"The happiness of my existence, and perhaps its uniqueness, lies in its fatefulness: To express it in the form of a riddle, as my own father I am already dead; as my own mother, I still live and grow old." ("Why I Am So Wise," *Ecce Homo*). It was also the anniversary of his post at the University of Basel, assumed in 1869 and which he left ten years later with feelings of guilt and relief. To cap things, he had to spend the Christmas and New Year's period with his mother in Naumburg: "the most sun-deprived winter of my life." In his childhood, winter celebrations had infused him with deep emotional and religious thrall, from which he strenuously departed subsequently; still, the disbeliever indulged obsessively in confrontations. But despite intermittent rages against the pious and maternal possessiveness of his mother, he was too ambivalently dependent upon her materially and emotionally to break the mannered rules of "Naumburg convention" and mutual exploitations; all too frequently then, her presence or impending visits made him ill. During that critical time, he recorded 118 days of heavy migrainal attacks. Here again, though, it should be noted that illness and recuperations—from 1879 into 1882—were followed by creativity: *The Wanderer and His Shadow* (completing *Human, All Too Human*); the 1881 publication of *Daybreak* (*Die Morgenröte*); and *The Gay Science* (*Die fröhliche Wissenschaft*, 1882)—

in which, despite his publisher's admonition that his scant reading-audience had enough of aphoristic writings, he joyously asserted autobiographical views and a "holy" coming to life.

The "Sanctus Januarius" section of *The Gay Science*—dated January 2, 1882, Genoa, and dedicated "to the New Year"—not only attempted to purge a phobia but also initiated an affirming "*amor fati,*" the love of one's fate: he spoke of hope and henceforth tasting "the sweetness of my life." That hope was going to be put to severe trial with the arrival of Lou Salomé and with repercussions as critical as those resulting from the abiding Wagner experience. When Nietzsche and Lou Salomé met in Rome in late May 1882, she knew little of his work and person, and Nietzsche knew even less about her. After a last meeting in October, many personal gaps had been bridged, but much also remained recessed and led to evasions and collisions.

Nietzsche's subsurface biography was moulded in the years of a suffocatingly pious upbringing and almost exclusively feminine surroundings. In contrast, the long schoolings from boyhood to maturity subjected him to disciplinarian and male environments. He was alternately attracted to and repelled by boisterous and adventuring students, but regularly chose intellectual companionships, some of which lasted long after. A veil of Victorian reticence is draped over the sex life of Nietzsche as a young man, and if it were not for a singular incident retold by his friend Paul Deussen, we would have scarcely anything that would permit us to speculate about Nietzsche's sexual imagination, one way or another.

One day, in February of 1865, Nietzsche travelled alone to Köln, let himself be guided by a porter to sites worth seeing, and then finally asked to be led to a restaurant. The porter however brought him to a house of ill-repute. "I saw myself suddenly surrounded," so Nietzsche told me the next day, "by a half dozen apparitions in spangles and costume-gauze, who gazed at me expectantly. Speechless, I stood stock-still for a moment. Then, instinctively, I quickly headed for a piano—as if it were the only soul-possessed being there— and struck several chords. These freed me from my petrifaction and I successfully made my way into the open air."

(Thomas Mann seized this anecdote—a mixture of disguised facts and improvisation—for his novel *Doktor Faustus* and had his hero return to the brothel a year later to be infected by syphilis.) Remarks by Nietzsche at the Basel asylum in 1889 to the effect that he was treated twice for syphilis in the late 1860s have been coupled mainly with this anecdote to adduce proof—entirely false—that Nietzsche's slow or sudden madness finds its roots here in disease. Almost every biographer has fallen into that chimerical snare. Clearly, Nietzsche did have furtive sexual encounters during his student days and incurred gonorrheal infections but never had been syphilitic, as he told an examining private physician, Dr. Otto Eiser, in 1877, and also admitted to having intercourse several times in the 1870s "in Italy, on medical advice." Nietzsche's madness has been willy-nilly saddled with syphilis. All the fragmentary medical records of examinations and diagnoses during Nietzsche's lifetime, and re-examined in our time, merit Erich F. Podach's conclusion that there is "no certain evidence of syphilitic infection nor any sure evidence of Nietzsche's 'paralysis.'" Perhaps, all this would not matter much, except that it casts clouds over Nietzsche's books and aspersions upon his ideas. Lou Salomé sufficiently discusses Nietzsche's will to health and illness in relationship to his work and throws considerable light upon the general question of genius and insanity and of Nietzsche's psychosomatic conditions—as well as his migraine reflective of traumas—as spurs to artistic creativity. That creativity was sustained up through the very last sentence of his work put into print.

Deussen retold Nietzsche's bordello story in a book of reminiscences, *Erinnerungen an Friedrich Nietzsche* (Leipzig: Brockhaus, 1901), intending to illustrate Nietzsche's manner of thinking and to assure posterity that "he never touched a woman," so to speak. He achieved precisely the opposite impression, although he added that one ought to remember Nietzsche never wanted to remain unmarried: women, in his view, should give themselves over to the service and care of man. "Already at Pforta," Deussen wrote, "Nietzsche used to say half in jest, 'for my own purposes, I will surely need to use up three women.'" Deussen would have been horrified to learn that the jest had latent seriousness when in the

Jena mental asylum Nietzsche boasted that 24 whores had visited him at night. The orientalist scholar Deussen was unable to read the psychological and fantasy content of the bordello story which is rendered dubious by the apparently unsolicited actions of a porter. The story proves Nietzsche neither a saint nor sinner. But the bordello figures vaguely appear again in his Dionysian poems; the moralizing attitude toward the "soulless" women suggests morbid fears of sexuality, and the soul-bearing piano represents the liberating triumph of music which was, of course, a main source of Nietzsche's emotional release.

Similar to the flight evidenced in the bordello fantasy were episodes that flared up in late spring of 1872, which can only be sketchily reconstructed due to purged correspondences. Rosalie Nielsen, a Scandinavian divorcée and roving European revolutionary, became a passionate admirer of Nietzsche after reading *The Birth of Tragedy*. She claims to have received a photograph from Nietzsche, which accented psychotic features of a sculptured face of Dionysus. Perhaps she fancied herself a bacchante but her disheveled appearance in a hotel at Freiburg-im-Breisgau prompted Nietzsche to evict her immediately, with the cry, "Monster, you have betrayed me!" When she persisted in her attentions, Nietzsche enlisted the help of his friend Overbeck in ridding himself of the "Nielsen ghost." Among her phrases in a parting letter, she told Nietzsche, "*Never* has anyone on earth so *understood me and so poorly judged me* as you did. Seldom or never has anyone made me so *happy* or caused me so much *pain*." When his Dionysian fantasy faced reality, Nietzsche retreated.

During most of his life, Nietzsche tacitly enlisted others—or did not discourage others—in seeking a wife for him; a few times, he took clumsy initiatives. Was all this a mask to satisfy conventionality? Partially. Could Nietzsche have revealed his inner personality and demons to another person? Hardly. He could only parade them in front of his private mirror because his inhibiting fears of women and innate reticence were too great. In his experience, women were "llamas" or other types of "*Tierchen*"— little creatures with possessive, predatory claws—or sphinxlike creatures that attracted and threatened like Cosima Wagner. The criteria he proposed kept shifting with his personal needs and circumstances as various candidates suggested themselves to him; only when he was not absolutely serious would he discuss them with his sister. Early on he wanted someone of doll-like qualities—cheerful, pretty, femininely charming, non-religious, and not possessed of too great an intellect, presumably to counter and tend to his moodiness or to narrow contacts to elemental levels, the kitchen, and other household and wifely cares.

As the bachelor circle around Nietzsche was slowly disbanding by 1876, with marriages and engagements, he wondered how long he could keep up the sporadic and unsatisfactory domestic arrangements with Lisbeth while his mother also was demanding her daughter's services. And so, along with the other social expectations already rife, Nietzsche was disposed to be venturesome when, in the company of the musician Hugo von Senger in Geneva, he was introduced to one of Senger's piano students. The dark-blonde, green-eyed, trim twenty-three-year-old Mathilde Trampedach was described as a girl who had stepped straight out of a portrait by Fra Filippo Lippi, and she enjoyed her conversations with "the famous man who despite the dim light carried a padded, green sunshade on his head." She further wrote with extreme pleasure about their literary conversations, and when Nietzsche said that he did not know Longfellow's poem "Excelsior," she volunteered to send him a German translation. She also spoke of feeling the probing gaze of Nietzsche's deep eyes. At a third meeting, Nietzsche improvised stormily for her on Beethoven's "Hymn to Joy," and the "festive harmonies dissolved in soft tones" on the piano. Several days later, Mathilde received a marriage proposal in the mail.

The letter asked that she gather all her "heart's courage" at the question: "Will you become my wife? I love you and I feel as if you already belong to me. . . . Do you not believe as I do that in a union each will become freer and better than in singleness? Well then, excelsior." Unknown to Nietzsche, Mathilde was in love with her teacher Senger, and later she became his wife; she could not say yes to Nietzsche. He buried his disappointment and never again in correspondence left himself open to rejection. Several days later in April, he wrote to Malwida von Meysenbug: "One of the highest motives I have discerned first through you is a mother love without the physical bond of mother and child; it is one of the most splendid revealments of *caritas*. Grant me your gift of some of that love . . . and regard me as the son who needs such a mother, oh so greatly needs!" Malwida responded graciously and also advised him to seek a "good but rich" wife (he was amused by the "but").

Malwida seemed not altogether clear about Nietzsche's marriage intentions but she and Paul Rée felt that they had a panacea for Nietzsche's intellectual loneliness; they were not worried about his social life because he had company whenever he chose it or could enjoy sociability through his abundant correspondence. Unfortunately, the first letter Rée wrote to Nietzsche about the young Russian, Lou von Salomé, has vanished, but his response to Rée was grotesquely jocular: "Greet this Russian for me, if that has any purpose: I lust for this species* of soul. Yes I shall now look forward to plunder, and with what I have in mind for the next ten years, I will need her. An entirely different chapter would be marriage—at the most, I could agree to a two-year marriage. . . ." (Genoa, March 21, 1882). Malwida also wrote to Nietzsche that the extraordinary girl was among the persons who helped her with her own book and could engage him in philosophical discussions of such mutual interest as practical idealism. Nietzsche briefly delayed a meeting but somewhat unconvincingly said that the unpleasant siroccos in Messina drove him north to Rome in late April. There with studied gallantry he greeted the strikingly handsome twenty-one-year-old Lou: "From which stars have we fallen to meet each other here?" Flustered, Lou told him that she had just arrived from Zurich. Indeed, Lou had intensively studied the humanities at the University, as did many of her friends who felt confined in the foreign enclave of the Russian metropolis of St. Petersburg and had ventured to Zurich. Her father was a general in the Russian army, and the family was of Baltic-German origins and had been of Huguenot persuasion. Lou was determined to establish her

---

*The German word "*Gattung*" refers to biological affinities, with echoes of "*Gatten*" that has conjugal meanings. Also, the boisterous two-year "wild" marriage suggestion caused trouble when Lou Salomé heard of it later.

social and intellectual independence and was rebounding from a sobering experience. For some time in St. Petersburg, she had enjoyed a maturing influence under the secular tutorship of the prominent clergyman Hendrik Gillot but tore herself away when he declared his love and the wish to abandon his family. Neither Nietzsche nor Lou Salomé knew of each other's emotional traumas: Nietzsche partially replayed the Mathilde Trampedach episode, while Lou soon found that behind the philosopher-teacher she sought stood a man with emotions, human all-too-human, like Gillot's. Their failure to acknowledge early enough incompatibilities of personal objectives led to unforeseen complications and a parting of ways; Nietzsche sought a true companion-disciple and Lou a distinguished teacher-friend as a step toward the realization of her intellectual ambitions. Possibly they did sense each other's feelings but shunted them aside in order to risk potentially dangerous as well as rich encounters. As we see things in her Nietzsche book, she had an opportunity to broach her ideas and discuss her writings with Nietzsche, who proved himself to be an incisive and unsparing critic, while he was able to unfold for her without fear—as never before—such privately tormenting ideas as that of the eternal recurrence.

What Lou Salomé has recounted in her Nietzsche book needs no repetition here; yet significant gaps, commissions and omissions—aware or unaware—all of which had consequences for their lives and future works, deserve a brief telling. Nietzsche on occasion had projected plans for a colony of intellects, like ancient Greek counterparts, of which he would be the centerpiece. These plans never came to be as his close friends married—events that roused him to open or repressed anger—and created a pattern (already previewed in the Tribschen paradise) in which he was to remain the third man out, an object of solicitude; he reluctantly made the best of such situations or later broke with them. Lou Salomé envisioned a communal life of the intellect, where she was to share the company of brilliant men—each living on either side of her chamber in an apartment containing a work-study filled with books and flowers; the acquisition of Nietzsche to complement Rée would constitute a Platonic triumph for her. Quite unaware of Rée's growing love for Lou, Nietzsche sought her for himself with a lightning-like campaign of gallantly worded letters and an effort to enlist her Mama who was chaperoning Lou in Rome. The strategies did not catch fire and he retreated to the possible alternative of communal living and study *à trois;* he launched inquiries for accommodations near a European university where he would explore the sciences for validation of his eternal recurrence idea. When Malwida saw the agitated Rée who wanted to flee from Rome after Lou turned aside *his* marriage proposal, she knew that trouble was brewing. And in two letters she reminded Lou of the apostolic role she was to set for women's emancipation, and prophetically warned that her idea of a neutral "threesome" would be destructive of friendships: "nature will not allow itself to be mocked." Malwida hinted that it would be best if Lou were to return to Russia with her mother or, failing that, to go to Wagner's Bayreuth with Nietzsche's sister for the first performance of *Parsifal* on July 26th; there they could meet and talk. Nietzsche had kept news about his new-found friend secret from his mother and sister for as long as possible,* but then he thought that Lisbeth could serve as chaperone for appearance's sake and disappear as he wished. Between the time that Lisbeth and Lou were to meet, the familiarity between Nietzsche and Lou deepened during short trips in the company of Rée and Lou's mother.

On May 5, at Lake Orta near Stresa, Lou and Nietzsche excused themselves from their party and hiked up Monte Sacro. What transpired between the two supremely self-centered persons is vaguely reflected in Nietzsche's telling Lou: "the most enchanting dream of my life, that I owe to you." Lou in her diaries professed not being able to remember if she went so far as to have kissed Nietzsche. And Rée humorously suggested that this would hardly have been possible because of the impediment posed by a bushy moustache. Descending from the mount of mystery, Nietzsche expressed his hope that through Lou, his "twin brain," he might find the person to help him toward his

---

*At the end of April 1882, he wrote to his sister about the young Lou von Salomé: "Anyway, she is plain [*unschön*] . . . but like all plain girls, she has cultivated her mind in order to be attractive."

goals. For Rée the episode confirmed his own aphorism that all humans are equal in vanity and selfishness.

As a follow-up to the "Monte Sacro" delirium, Nietzsche insisted on a rendezvous with Lou at Lucerne's Gletschergarten, a site preserved from the glacial ice-age, and specifically at the altar-like railing in front of the huge Lion Monument that commemorates the Swiss honor guards fallen during the French Revolution when the Tuileries were stormed. Not only was the lion a favorite Nietzschean symbol* but the inscription ". . . *fidei ac virtuti*" embodied a message for Lou. She claimed that Nietzsche again proposed to her but that she instead repeated what Rée had already told him, namely, of her momentary unreadiness for marriage and her idea of a threesome working-arrangement. The scene remained indelibly etched in Nietzsche's mind, and less than a decade later during his madness he made a drawing of the lion with the Swiss shield and cross and two embracing figures beneath. When Rée joined them at the Gletschergarten, Nietzsche hid his disappointment, or perhaps relief, and with a cheerful air had a photographer take a picture of Lou brandishing a lilac whip from a cart at whose handles Nietzsche and Rée were posed. Some biographers blame Lou for the photo that caused notoriety when it became public later, but Nietzsche reacted to it only with amusement. Lou and Rée had been unamused participants. A year later and with a disaffected retrospective view of the situation in 1882, Nietzsche put an in-

---

*For Nietzsche, the classical epithet for the lion as a blond beast of prey became a symbol for the barbarian or Dionysian instincts tamed by Christianity. The lion stood for the destroyer of conventional values— the master race or men of prey who imposed their will, through spiritual strength, upon wandering peoples in the past. Such animal vitality and even cruelty, he reasons, are raw materials for higher activities and the energies of the superior man: the animal in man must be released (a discharge or *Entladung*). Although Nietzsche expressly distinguished between the cultural effects of the so-called barbarians of old and the power-seeking and negative nationalism of 19th century Germany, later Nazi ideologues and nationalists misappropriated Nietzsche's metaphorical "blond beast" and "master race" for literal and what would have been, for him, nefarious purposes.

verted injunction into Zarathustra's mouth: "Are you going to women? Don't forget your whip!" During his lifetime, Nietzsche embarrassedly had to sidestep the implications of that peevish remark when it came up in conversations with women; but the echo of that shrill male-slogan still lingers.

Since Tribschen was in the vicinity of the garden, he persuaded Lou to accompany him to the paradise of old, where he revealed with deep emotion his abiding sense of loss of Wagner, so movingly described by Lou in her book.

Nietzsche kept spinning webs that he hoped would bring Lou closer to him. He arranged for Lou and her mother to stay at Basel with his old friend Overbeck and his wife, so that they could inform her more familiarly about himself; but at Basel, Lou's main hope was to converse with the famous Renaissance scholar Jacob Burckhardt. Nietzsche also sent Lou a book he had just published, *Human, All Too Human*. He prepared his trusted helper Gast for his new Platonic friend and his future plans by sending him Lou's poem *"An den Schmerz"* ("To Sorrow")*: "This poem

---

*   *An den Schmerz*

Wer kann dich fliehn, den du ergriffen hast,
Wenn du das dunkle Auge auf ihn richtest?
Ich will nicht fluchten, wenn du mich erfasst,
—Ich glaube nimmer, dass du nur vernichtest.
Ich weiss, durch jedes Leben musst du gehn
Und nichts bleibt unberührt von dir auf Erden,
Das Leben ohne dich—es wäre schön!
Und doch—du bist es wert, gelebt zu werden.
Gewiss, du bist nicht ein Gespenst der Nacht,
Du kommst, den Geist an seine Kraft zu mahnen,
Der Kampf ist's, der die Grössten gross gemacht,
—Der Kampf ums Ziel, auf unwegsamen Bahnen.
Und drum, kannst du mir nur für Glück und Lust
Das eine, Schmerz, die echte Grösse geben,
Dann komm und lass uns ringen, Brust and Brust,
Dann komm, und sei es auch um Tod und Leben.
Dann greife in des Herzens tiefsten Raum
Und wühle in dem Innersten des Lebens,
Nimm hin der Täuschung und des Glückes Traum,
Nimm, was nicht wert war unbegrenzten Strebens.

has such power over me that I have never been able to read it without shedding tears; it is like a voice for which I have waited since childhood . . . Lou is twenty years old, sharp-witted like an eagle, brave like a lion, though, finally, girlish. . . . In the Fall we will move to Vienna and live and work together; she is most astonishingly and precisely prepared for my ways of thinking." Not the amateur poem but his infatuation with its author prompted Nietzsche's enthusiasm. In this letter of July 13, he had already eliminated Paul Rée from the "threesome."

As planned, Nietzsche's sister and Lou went to Bayreuth in late July, where Wagner's *Parsifal* was to be performed. Slightly before, Nietzsche had carefully studied the *Parsifal* piano score with his sister, and quartered near Bayreuth just in case Wagner would personally request his presence; the summons—to which Nietzsche felt entitled—never came. In the tumult at Bayreuth, Lisbeth now was snubbed because of her brother's "defection"

Des Menschen letzter Sieger bleibst du nicht,
Ob er auch deinen Schlag die Brust entblösse,
Ob er im Tode auch zusammenbricht,—
—Du bist der Sockel für die Geistegrösse—.

To Sorrow

Who can escape when in your grip,/ when your dark eyes confront one?/ I do not wish to flee when you seize me,/ I never shall believe that you only destroy./ I know that you must course through everyone's life/ and nothing earthbound stays untouched by you,/ though life without you would be beautiful!/ And yet, it is worthwhile to experience you./ Indeed, you are not a night's phantom;/ you come to remind the spirit of its strength;/ it's the battle that has made the greatest persons great—/ on rugged roads toward the goal./ For that, and happiness and joy,/ give me only one thing: pain which lends true greatness./ So, come and let us wrestle breast to breast;/ do come, even if it means life or death./ Do come and dip into the heart's deepest interior/ and rummage through the depths of life./ Take away dream's illusion and joy;/ take away things not worth one's unlimited strivings./ You are not mankind's final conqueror./ Although we expose our breast to your blows/ and although we collapse in death,/ you are the pedestal for our soul's greatness.

from Wagner, and she watched with envy as Lou "coquettishly" gathered male attention; she left a week ahead of Lou. Amid the party-evenings at Wahnfried, Lou had the opportunity of long conversation with Cosima, through Malwida's personal introduction, and with Count Paul von Joukowsky, a Russian-German painter and scene designer, who belonged to the inner Wagner circle. Although tone-deaf to music, Lou could hardly be deaf to swirling gossip and terrible indiscretions; somehow these reached Nietzsche and inflicted a "deadly insult" beyond healing, as we shall see.

Through prearrangement, Lisbeth and Lou met again at the Jena home of acquaintances, Professor Heinrich Gelzer and his wife Clara. By this time, Lisbeth was almost clear out of her mind with fear of losing her brother Fritz, an innocent "sacrificial lamb," to the wiles of the passionate and intellectually gifted young Russian who possessed an "evil, egotistical and immoral character." An explosive incident ensued. According to Lisbeth, Lou released a flood of vituperations against Fritz: "He is a madman who does not know what he wants and is merely a crude egoist who had wanted to exploit her mental talents. . . . At any rate, Fritz would be crazy if he thought that she ought to sacrifice herself to his goals . . . or if he thought that fourteen days of communality would bring her into a 'wild marriage'—men's only aim, after all, as she knew from personal experience. . . ." Lisbeth responded that such may well be the case among Russians but that Lou did not know her pure-minded brother. Lou allegedly responded, "Who first besmirched the communality plan, with lowest intentions, who first agreed to an intellectual friendship when he could not possess me for any other purpose, and who first thought about a 'wild marriage' if not your brother? . . . Don't think that I have any designs upon your brother or that I am in love with him; I could sleep in the same room with him and not have any thoughts of arousal." When Lisbeth asked her to stop such uncouth talk, Lou supposedly shot back, "Pah, with Rée, I talk even more freely," and that it was he who told her about Fritz's "wild marriage" intention.* One may wonder then

---

*This episode is excerpted from a long letter to Clara Gelzer, which was written by Lisbeth between September 24 and October 2, 1882, because

why Lisbeth continued the trip with Lou to meet her brother the next day in Tautenburg? Because of the altercation, Lisbeth felt assured that Lou indeed had no marriage designs but only wanted to ride to fame on Fritz's coat-tails. The next day, she gave her brother a toned-down version of the quarrel; still, he remained "rabidly infatuated."

At Tautenburg, Lisbeth and Lou resided at a vicarage, while Nietzsche lived nearby, but Lisbeth was completely banned from their company. "During those three weeks," from August 7 on, Lou writes in her diary, "we positively talked ourselves to death, and in a remarkable way it suddenly happens that he is able to endure conversing for about ten hours daily . . . always we talk about work we have in common. . . . Curious that in our conversations we involuntarily descend into the depths and to those

---

she wanted to give a full account of the altercation that Clara had only partly overheard on August 7 at her house. Of interest also are her conventionality and antipathy for the aphoristically expressed ideas in her brother's non-philological writings: "My dearest Clara, Do not read my brother's books; they are too frightful for our hearts that strive higher than self-flattering egoism . . . they cannot be brought in tune with the earlier Nietzsche. Dear, dear Clara *tell no one* . . . Fritz has become different, he *is* just like his books . . . I have lost my ideal and am inconsolable. [Lou Salomé] is the *personified* philosophy of my brother—a rabid egoism, as well as complete immorality, that tears down everything in its path. . . . Lou always boasts of her evil nature (evil is supposedly a greater source of strength than the good), and so poor Fritz poses as evil as possible. . . . The poor fool only makes himself and his philosophy look ridiculous—and already he is being criticized for the superficiality of his aphorisms—but now a twenty-year-old girl is to represent him as a chief disciple!" Lisbeth complained about being mocked for her sacrifices, personally ridiculed by her brother, and, above all, being displaced by Lou. The sting of rejection struck deep. She also said that Lou had no money and needed to marry a rich man. This may have partially come from an argument concocted by Lou and Rée that she would lose her Russian subsistence if she married, an argument ostensibly designed to prove to Nietzsche that Lou could not entertain his marriage proposals. When mother Franziska was enlisted in Lisbeth's crusade, she thought mournfully that her son had only three choices—marriage to Lou, insanity, or suicide.

dizzying places, always choosing mountain-goat paths, and if anyone would have overheard us he could have thought two devils were talking. . . . Evenings, he would twice kiss my hand and begin to say something the rest of which would remain unspoken." This was an occasional stylistic habit in his letters and writings, as well. They walked through the pleasant countryside and laughed much, and Lou took great pleasure when the grimness vanished from his face and his eyes lit up brightly. It was as he had hoped: that through her he could become "human" again. Lou, he wrote to Gast, "is the most intelligent of all females." And yet he felt something stagey and giddy in his own enthusiastic tone; "Every five days there was a little 'tragedy theater-scene' . . . Lou and I are *all-too-similar*, 'blood related.'" Both had become "free spirits" or independent thinkers who rejected their given religion in favor of an independent quest for a "knowledge-God, a great goal under the impulse of the surrendering self." And yet, said Lou, "We are worlds apart in some hidden depth of our beings." Unlike herself, Nietzsche "will yet appear to us as the preacher of a new religion." Nietzsche's "heart lies in his brain . . . and he threw religion overboard when his heart no longer had any feeling for it and when he longed for a new, fulfilling goal in that vacuum." To Lou, however, disbelief was rational rather than emotional or instinctive. For Nietzsche, illness and pain were causative and passive conditions for his successive phases, explaining why he had to endure so much physically. She looked into Nietzsche's subjective abyss where Dionysianism resembled Christian mysticism which precisely at its high point of ecstasy returns in circular fashion "to a coarsely religious sensuality—a *false pathos* that abandons truth and the honesty of the emotions." "Is it this which estranges me from Nietzsche?" Very soon, it was. Lou also gained the impression that Nietzsche's willed psychological disorientation and experimentations with his identity and self were leading him to the brink of madness, while the donning of too many masks was an open invitation to chaos. She saw him as a man of powerful moods and caught in fluctuations between gaiety and morbidity; she was chilled by his prospects. Indeed, all these aspects of the man were to be found in his works—a conviction that became the spine of her Nietzsche book.

At Tautenburg, Lou kept a journal, many of whose entries she shared with Nietzsche, and by mail also with Rée, to keep discussions flowing. But such currents were broken when she felt that Nietzsche unsubtly kept putting Rée down; these divisive tactics offended Lou, especially his view of himself as a soldier-warrior: "Lou belongs to me." In correspondence with Malwida, however, he represented himself as a generous matchmaker and noted with mock chagrin that Rée was too much of a pessimist to think of marriage and progeny "increasing the count of unfortunates in this world." But unknown to him, Rée's letters to Lou became increasingly ardent and playfully intimate. He chafed at her absence: "My dearest, my Lou . . . my life's elixir . . . my little snail, it is a pity that I cannot always carry my little snail with me." Rée for his part had good cause to regret his letting charades get out of hand and possibly losing two friends. Before Tautenburg, he had warned Lou that Nietzsche was not as innocent as he seemed; Nietzsche had sworn him to secrecy when they were together several years earlier in Sorrento and it was obvious to Rée that his friend had entertained visits by a village girl. Nevertheless, Lou was undeterred from her aim of benefiting from Nietzsche's genius.

Retrospectively as idyllic and painful as Tribschen, Tautenburg ended on an ecstatic note for Nietzsche on August 25. As a parting gift, Lou had given him a poem, "Hymn to Life,"* written earlier but which Nietzsche mistakenly assumed to have been in his honor alone, and Nietzsche worked like a demon, as he said, to put it to music which he had carried with him also for some time.

---

*   *Lebensgebet*
    [an earlier version of *An den Schmerz*]
Gewiss, so liebt ein Freund den Freund,
Wie ich dich liebe, rätselvolles Leben.
Ob ich in dir gejauchzt, geweint,
Ob du mir Leid, ob du mir Lust gegeben:
Ich liebe dich mit deinem Glück und Harme,
Und wenn du mich vernichten musst,
Entreisse ich mich schmerzvoll deinem Arme,
Wie Freund sich reisst von Freundes Brust.

Nietzsche had ignored or mollified Lisbeth's anger, but it was to escalate into years of full-scale vendettas, punctuated by few periods of uneasy truce between them. At Naumburg, his mother had been incited by Lisbeth and angrily told him that he was "a disgrace to his father's grave." He promptly packed his bags and fled to Leipzig, busying himself at the University library. Lou and Rée also came to Leipzig during October, and Nietzsche joined them at concerts and the theater, with much conversation in between. Still harboring illusions about a threesome, Nietzsche sent housing inquiries to Paris and thought 1882 to be his "festive year." Yet he could not bridge the quiet estrangements that had set in; during late October, his friends left him forever, without plans for future meetings. As the Nietzsche biographer Curt Paul Janz so aptly described things: "Nietzsche was to suffer appallingly for months under the impact of this parting; the 'festive year' was over and heavy shadows fell over his moods, shadows which he was never again able to escape." Yet through the following years and up to his descent into madness, while family and friendship problems mushroomed, desperate surges of creativity produced a new work almost each year.

Mit ganzer Kraft umfass ich dich.
Lass deine Flamme meinen Geist entzünden;
Lass in der Glut des Kampfes mich
Die Rätsellösung deines Wesens finden,
Jahrtausende zu denken und zu leben,
Wirf deinen Inhalt voll hinein—
Hast du kein Glück mehr übrig mir zu geben,
Wohlan, noch hast du deine Pein.

Life Prayer

As certain as a friend loves a friend,/ I love you, riddle-filled life./ Whether I rejoiced or cried with you,/ or whether you gave me pain or pleasure,/ still, with all your joy and harm, I love you./ And if you must destroy me,/ I painfully withdraw from your arms,/ as a friend tears himself away from a friend's breast./ I embrace you with all my strength./ Let your flame ignite my spirit;/ let me find in the glow of battle/ the answer to the riddle of your essence/ and let me meditate and live thousands of years;/ throw all you have into the battle./ If no more is left of joy, well then, give me your anguish.

If Nietzsche had been able to resettle in Paris with his friends, his life after 1882 would have taken an entirely different turn. But when that escape route was cut off, he had to face other unresolved personal problems alone. Of deep embarrassment was information that somehow reached him after the Bayreuth festival and the *Parsifal* performance in July of 1882. But he only lifted the lid from his feelings after Wagner's heart attack and death in Venice on February 13, 1883. Eight days later, he struck some curious notes in a letter to Malwida von Meysenbug: "Wagner's death has put me in a terrible state . . . and yet this event, seen from a long-range perspective, I believe, is a relief for me. It was hard, terribly hard, for six years, to be an opponent of someone whom one has so venerated and loved, as I have loved Wagner; yes, and to have necessarily condemned oneself to silence. . . . Wagner has insulted me in a *deadly* fashion." But Nietzsche could not tell a lady the real nature of the insult, and he veered off toward his old complaint that Wagner had slowly regressed and sneaked back to Christendom, steps that affronted Nietzsche. Then he wrote something that seemed to be all out of proportion: "Had Wagner lived longer, oh what still would have transpired between us! I have terrible arrows upon my bow, and Wagner belongs to those persons who can be *killed with words.*" Not until April 21 does Nietzsche's "abscess" burst when he sends a letter to his dedicated Gast, with instructions to "burn the letter immediately." One passage reads, "Cosima has spoken of me as one does of a spy who has insinuated himself into the trust of others and then absconds when he has obtained what he wanted. Wagner is rich with evil ideas. But would you believe that these ideas are part of his correspondence (even with my doctors) in order to express his *conviction* that my changed way of thinking was the consequence of unnatural deviations, pointing to pederasty." With that, the aggrieved Nietzsche disguised Wagner's actual assertion in a note to Dr. Eiser "that Nietzsche, like other young men of great intellectual gifts, was debilitated by the effects of masturbation."

Salomé had seen at first hand just how emotionally indissoluble Nietzsche's ties were to Wagner, though no one guessed for some time about those with Cosima. The drafts of a letter which he sent to Cosima immediately after her husband's death show how he wrestled to express thoughts intended "wholly and alone for you . . . the most esteemed woman in my heart"; he also asserted that he served the highest of Wagner's hopes to which his own name would be linked forever. Indeed, during their heydays, Wagner had placed the "apostle" Nietzsche right after Cosima in line of personal importance. On the allegorical level, after reading Nietzsche's *The Birth of Tragedy*, Wagner characterized Cosima as the priestess of Apollo and himself as Apollo, while Nietzsche appeared in several of his dreams as a threatening force—surely as intuitive defensive reactions against a usurping would-be Dionysus-Nietzsche.

Nietzsche's ambiguous phrase about the "hallowed hour" in which Wagner died and his relief at the death of one who had inflicted a "mortal insult" brought hopes that "perhaps my thunderstorms will *now* come to an end"; yet, he failed to reckon with his sister Lisbeth. Her campaign against Salomé was still active, and just how far she went to gain sympathy for herself and enmity against Lou may be seen in one particular passage from a January 29, 1883 letter to Ida Overbeck, the wife of Nietzsche's old colleague: "I kept asking, horrified as I was, when I visited the Heinzes [Professor Max Heinze had been a colleague of Nietzsche in Basel]: 'Claire, how do you know what is being said about Fritz?' Claire refused to answer. What lovely things one seems to hear rumored: 'Fritz and Rée had brought with them from Italy a lover and cohabited with her in turn,' and that was one of the more terrible versions." So widespread were these vicious rumors that they have persisted into our own day. (They appear as "facts" in an Italian motion picture, *Al di là del bene e del male* (*Beyond Good and Evil*), 1984, by the director Liliana Cavani. For good measure, Cavani tossed into her lurid stew a scene that portrays Nietzsche's bordello visit in Cologne.) But on the scholarly side as well there are inexcusable canards as we find them, for instance, in a 1984 introduction to a new translation of *Human, All Too Human*, not the least of which is the gross fiction that "Lou Salomé joined Rée and Nietzsche to form the notorious, short-lived *ménage à trois*." There never was any such ménage.

After October 1882 Nietzsche was not again to meet either Lou or Rée, but he composed and discarded or sent several convoluted letters; to wit: "My dears, Lou and Rée! Don't be too disturbed over the outbreaks of my 'delusions of grandeur' or my 'wounded vanity'—and if, incidentally, I were to take my life during some bleak mood, not even that would be a cause for a great deal of mourning. But of what concern to you are my fantasizings! (Even my 'truths' have not been of interest to you.) Still, in your mutual talks I must appear as a headache sufferer and half-madman who has been completely disoriented by long solitude. . . . Friend Rée, beg Lou to forgive me everything. . . . One finds it harder to forgive friends than enemies. . . ." (a letter fragment, December 20, 1882). When angered by his sister's "revelations" of Lou's and Rée's so-called "perfidies," he lost control of himself and wrote in a castigating phrase that told more about himself than Lou, "Lou is a she-monkey with false breasts, a pseudo-girl." But on regaining equilibrium, he continued to give credit to her intelligence and her meaning for him as a "treasure trove" in his life. Years later he read her autobiographical novel, which protected by disguise real-life names, *Im Kampf um Gott* (1885; *A Struggle for God*), and was satisfied that he had taught her much at Tautenburg. As for Rée's books, he distanced himself from their contents. And he was right, in an intellectual sense, although he owed considerable intellectual and personal companionship to Rée.

Nietzsche had decided "*not* to live in Germany and *not* to be with relatives or family" in whose midst his near-fatal faintings and illness often crested, but he did pick up the broken threads of correspondences. Meanwhile, the personality of Nietzsche could be seen ever more starkly in his works that rendered his interpreted experiences. After the Lou episode particularly, we see him creating his own immortality through what he philosophically called the "Holy Writ," *Thus Spoke Zarathustra,* and the immaculate conception of "my son" and alter-ego, Zarathustra. But he could not divorce himself from his real family. A reconciliation with Lisbeth, the "magnificent little animal," brought on new wounds.

Against her brother's wishes, Lisbeth was about to marry Dr. Bernhard Förster, an adherent of Wagner and a notorious anti-Semite, and move to the forests of Paraguay to establish a "racially pure colony—a New Germany." She wished to avoid the fate of an "aging spinster" and escape their mother's little comedies and "clutch." In her letter of mid-May 1885, she told her brother that regretfully she could no longer serve him and she wished that he would find happiness with a wife, a surrogate for herself. Nietzsche caught the condescending implications and replied immediately with a biting edge that revealed old wounds and *his* perceptions of himself:

> I am much too proud as ever to believe that any person could love *me*, namely, this requires the precondition that a person knows *who I am*. Just as little do I believe that I will love anyone. That would require—wonder of wonders!—finding a person of my stature. Do not forget that I despise as much as I deeply pity such beings as Richard Wagner or A. Schopenhauer, and that I find the founder of Christianity superficial in comparison with myself; I have loved them all at a time when I had not understood what a human being is.
>
> It strikes me as one of those puzzles I have sometimes thought about—how it is possible that we are blood related? Whatever had occupied me, worried me, and elevated me has never brought me a co-knower and friend! It is a pity that there is no God, so that at least one knower would exist. —As long as I am healthy, I retain sufficient good humor in order to play my *role* and to hide from the world within that role, for instance as a Basel professor. Sadly enough, I have been very ill and would hate, unspeakably, the people I have come to know, myself included.
>
> My dear sister, let all this remain between ourselves—and you may promptly burn this letter. If I were not such a good example of a play-actor, I could not bear to live another hour.
>
> For people like myself, marriage does not fit into the picture: it could only be in the style of our Goethe [who chose to marry a non-literate seamstress]. I never think of being loved.
>
> When I have shown you great rage, it is because you forced me to relinquish the last human beings [Lou and Rée] with

whom I could speak without Tartuffery. Now—I am alone. With them, I had been able to converse without a mask about things which interested me. What they thought of me was quite immaterial to me.

Hide this letter from our mother and—. . . . do not be angry over this letter. There is more civility in it than if, as usual, I were to play a comedy.

In sum, Nietzsche verified what Salomé was to say about his role playing and masks; he revealed the vacuum in his life with the absence of Rée and Lou, his self-styling as a prodigal son with an incapacity for love or a desire to be loved—however much a rationalization it may have been for his natural and aggressive iconoclasm—and his progressive withdrawal from people. With a note of sadness, he plainly told her that people like Malwida (and herself, by implication) from whom his essence is hidden, have—despite the best of intentions—caused untold grief.

At this time, Rée and Lou were living in Berlin. Intellectually, Lou was restless and told her consort that she would continue to see an older man, Fred Carl Andreas, a brilliant and eccentric professor of Oriental philology and literatures, unless Rée were to object. Rée was hardly overjoyed by the new third party, yet he placed trust in Lou's eternal friendship. But at about the time she suddenly announced her engagement in November 1886, Rée sensed something tragic ahead and quietly moved out of her life. Rée had augmented his studies and became a physician; eventually he moved into a lodge he once shared with Lou in the Upper Engadine countryside and served the poor, with a selflessness that was long recollected. Whether it was suicide or an Alpine hiking accident that took his life in 1901 was never determined. Lou was deeply moved by his death, and her book on Nietzsche was to be for him: "with faithful remembrance, dedicated to one unnamed." No one throughout her long life was to be a comparable companion. The Salomé and Andreas situation sounds almost fictional. Desperate to gain her marriage consent, Andreas had plunged a knife into his chest, escaping death by a fraction. Lou agreed to a marriage but never to its sexual consummation nor to a giving up of her freedom to travel and to be wherever and with whomever she pleased. During their early years, he was exceptionally helpful in her preparations for her book on Ibsen's female stage-figures*—then both led separate careers.

Lou had not kept in touch with Nietzsche personally for many reasons: she wanted to stay clear of imbroglios with Lisbeth and further unpleasant incidents such as the ones Nietzsche created when he sent libelous letters to the Rée family. Protectively, Rée kept some of these letters from her. Actually, Lou was much too involved with her own life to pay attention to Nietzsche's, except to notify him of her engagement to Andreas; Nietzsche never replied. However, the association with Nietzsche brought something of the macabre to her imagination when we see that she induced Andreas to change his given first name to Friedrich.

* * *

IF ONE WERE TO MATCH Nietzsche's last days in Turin, which of course were unknown to Lou Salomé, with the last pages of her book, one finds chilling resemblances. She portrayed what she thought would ultimately be the consequence of Nietzsche's daring and perilous experimentation with "self" in his quest for knowledge: a laughing Dionysus-Zarathustra mask which he would no longer be able to remove. We are greeted, she wrote, "by a shattering double sound from his laughter, the laughter of a strayer—and the laughter of a conqueror." The French translator of the Salomé book takes the word *"Irrenden,"* as applied to Nietzsche, to be "one demented" (*le rictus d'un dément*), confusing it with the word *"Irren."* Salomé meant "strayer," one who failed to return from the realm of Dionysus, the Greek world of pagan antiquity that enticed Nietzsche away from the outer world.

Of the large cast of characters in the drama of Nietzsche's life, two women understood his personality intimately: his sister Elisabeth and Lou von Salomé. Elisabeth was disillusioned when she found that "Fritz" *is* "just like his books," but later, as the archivist of his works, she self-servingly refashioned that image

---

Henrik Ibsens Frauen-Gestalten (Jena: Diedrichs, 1892); *Ibsen's Heroines*, trans. S. Mandel (Redding Ridge, CT: Black Swan Books, 1985).

for public consumption. Salomé pursued an opposite aim: to fashion a truthful portrait of the man as it is to be found in his philosophizing. She was the only person allowed a look into his self-created hell, from which she recoiled, and then she delineated Nietzsche's lacerating search for knowledge primarily through his avowed intention of taking himself as the object of psychological experimentation. He interpreted the meaning of life in the light of his existential dilemmas and spoke about "philosophical systems" as forms which constitute one's *memoirs*. He voiced horror at the possibility of having his life and thinking viewed with "pity—itself a type of hell." Salomé respected that feeling and lent sympathy, understanding, and critical objectivity to her intellectual and personal portrait of Nietzsche.

In a diary entry of May 1913, Salomé once again reviewed her conversations with Nietzsche in 1882 at Tautenburg and recalled that at one point they had not dared to look at one another. For the first time in their lives they discussed openly such personal features as the female and male components in each other's psyche and the sado-masochism that attends probings into the self. Such perceptions lie at the heart of her book—not the status or stature of Nietzsche as a philosopher in the history of ideas. In view of her own experiences, she was intrigued with Nietzsche's discarding of inherited religious beliefs and the desperate search for new values to replace them. She was struck by his terror-induced vision of an eternal recurrence of life, the creative spirit and its courting of madness, the daring flight of ideas and its dangers, and the dynamics of ideas in the fashioning of one's life. From these perspectives, Salomé's book offers a guided view of the person and thinker, which is as valid and controversial today as it was in Salomé's time. It is a first-hand source of motifs in Nietzsche's thinking, but it also documents Nietzsche's exploration of the unknown self.

As great a *cachet* as Salomé's intimate association with Nietzsche is the arena of thought in her book; within it, two distinct kinds of thinking are pitted against one another. Salomé's discursive thinking has a logical and psychologically realistic grasp of human experience. She believes that only disaster can come of substituting an idolatrous version of one's self for the lost image

of God; further, she believes that the philosopher-creator envisioned by Nietzsche is an æsthetic fallacy and a creature of
religious mysticism. She implies that moral judgments lie not
beyond good and evil but are validated by the quality of human
sentiments and idealistic values. Nietzsche's quest for knowledge through an excess of intuition and instincts, she believed,
led to his self-wounding and an æsthetic philosophy that re-
creates the world only in one's own image. Much of Nietzsche's
manner of thinking, however, eluded Salomé's analytical
approach because his thinking was metaphorical and creatively
iconoclastic, breaking with conventional patterns and continually re-evaluating all values; it is a process that comes close to
being an end in itself. Nietzsche described himself as a *tertium
quid*, a disembodied third person or entity. Salomé viewed this
literally and, therefore, interpreted it as an aberration; but for
Nietzsche, the phrase is a metaphorical description of an induced
mental and psychic condition, a necessity for rising above inherited, conditioned, and acquired ideas.

Freedom through rationality was Salomé's aim. Nietzsche
gained his freedom through intuition and instinctual means.
These divergent ways of thinking lend an argumentative excite-
ment and tension to the reading of Lou Salomé's book on "the
philosopher of solitude."

Key to abbreviations of references to Nietzsche's works quoted in Lou Salomé's book:

- BT   *The Birth of Tragedy from the Spirit of Music (Die Geburt der Tragödie aus dem Geiste der Musik, 1872).*
- UM   *Untimely Meditations (Unzeitgemässe Betrachtungen, 1873–76).*
- OUDH   *Of the Use and Disadvantage of History (Vom Nutzen und Nachteil der Historie für das Leben, 1874).*
- DD   *Dithyrambs of Dionysus (Dionysos-Dithyramben, composed between 1883 and 1888).*
- HATH   *Human, All-Too-Human (Menschliches, Allzumenschliches, 1878).*
- WS   *The Wanderer and His Shadow (sequel to HATH; Der Wanderer und sein Schatten, 1880).*
- D   *Daybreak; The Dawn of Day (Morgenröte, 1881).*
- GS   *The Gay Science; The Joyful Wisdom (Die fröliche Wissenschaft, 1882).*
- Z   *Thus Spoke Zarathustra (Also sprach Zarathustra, parts I and II, 1883; part III, 1884; part IV, 1885).*
- BGE   *Beyond Good and Evil (Jenseits von Gut und Böse, 1886).*
- GM   *Genealogy of Morals (Zur Genealogie der Moral, 1887).*
- CW   *The Case of Wagner (Der Fall Wagner, 1888).*
- TI   *Twilight of the Idols (Götzen-Dämmerung, 1888/89).*

Reference notations will allow readers to find sources by title, sections, and headings in various English translations and in the most accessible German editions: Karl Schlechta, ed., *Friedrich Nietzsche*, 4 volumes (Munich: Carl Hanser, 1954–56); Giorgio Colli and Mazzino Montinari, eds. *Kritische Gesamtausgabe* (Berlin: De Gruyter, 1967); along with the ongoing volumes of letters to and from Nietzsche.

All quotations from Nietzsche have been newly rendered by the editor and translator of Salomé's *Nietzsche*. Omission marks in the Salomé text refer to deletion of some repetitious material; but the same marks in the Nietzsche quotes often are kept as Nietzsche's device for unspoken and rhetorical implications, while bracketed material in the letters represents restored lines.

Authors' works which have not been translated into English are given English working-titles.

SOURCES AND ACKNOWLEDGMENTS

The present translation takes as its text Lou Salomé, *Friedrich Nietzsche in seinen Werken* (Vienna: Carl Konegen, 1894 [with two photos of Nietzsche and three letter facsimiles]). Of the various reprints that differ only in the handling of photographs, the 1983 edition (Insel Verlag) also contains valuable editorial material by Thomas and Ernst Pfeiffer, especially helpful in locating Nietzsche quotes in German editions later than those used by Salomé.

Sources consulted and noted in my Introduction, the textual notes, and in the "Key to Abbreviations" are not repeated in the following selected bibliographical description. A guide still serviceable today, annotated with highly personal judgments, is found in Walter Kaufmann, *Nietzsche: Philosopher, Psychologist, Antichrist*, fourth edition (Princeton: Princeton University Press, 1974), pp. 483–510. Ongoing international research is reflected in *Nietzsche Studies*, a yearbook originating in 1972 and featuring articles, symposia, and book reviews.

In addition to letters from and to Nietzsche, biographical reconstructions rely largely on several main works. Lou Andreas-Salomé, *Lebensrückblick* (Zurich: M. Niehans, 1951; revised edition, Frankfurt: Insel Verlag, 1974), a diary of Salomé's life, including her encounter with Nietzsche. All of the books by Erich F. Podach contain material from archival and private sources previously unrevealed or expurgated: *Friedrich Nietzsches Werke des Zusammenbruchs* (Heidelberg: W. Rothe, 1930) [*The Madness of Nietzsche*]; *Gestalten um Nietzsche* (Weimar: E. Lichtenstein, 1931); *Der kranke Nietzsche, Briefe seiner Mutter an Franz Overbeck* (Vienna: Bermann-Fischer, 1937); *Friedrich Nietzsche und Lou Salomé* (Zurich: M. Niehans, 1937); *Ein Blick in Notizbücher Friedrich Nietzsches* (Heidelberg: W. Rothe, 1963). Ernst Pfeiffer, ed., *Friedrich Nietzsche, Paul Rée, Lou von Salomé, Dokumente ihrer Begegnung* (Frankfurt: Insel Verlag, 1970). C. A. Bernoulli, *Franz Overbeck und Friedrich Nietzsche, Eine Freundschaft*, 2 vols. (Jena: Diederichs, 1908). These significant memoirs take us into the circle of Nietzsche's friends but they also give evidence of unshared ideologies. Professor Overbeck, a scholar specializing in church history, was oblivious to the far-reaching implications of Nietzsche's ideas and

his recollection provides a sharp contrast to Salomé's view of the psychological shape of Nietzsche's thinking.

Other biographical studies varyingly interpret the Nietzsche and Salomé encounter and its aftermath: Charles Andler, *Nietzsche: Sa vie et sa pensée*, 6 vols. (Paris: Bossard, 1920–1931); W. H. Brann, *Nietzsche und die Frauen* (Leipzig: Meiner, 1931), a psychoanalytical approach that needs fuller attention; R. J. Hollingdale, *Nietzsche, the Man and his Philosophy* (Baton Rouge: Louisiana University Press, 1968), and *Nietzsche* (London: Routledge & Kegan Paul, 1973). Rudolph Binion, *Frau Lou: Nietzsche's Wayward Disciple* (Princeton: Princeton University Press, 1968). F. H. Peters, *My Sister, My Spouse* (New York: Norton, 1962) and *Zarathustra's Sister* (New York: Crown, 1977). Binion severely criticizes Salomé, while Peters tends to idealize her. Curt P. Janz, *Friedrich Nietzsche: Biographie*, 3 vols. (Munich: C. Hanser, 1979), an ambitious survey of Nietzsche's life and works, as well as secondary sources. Ronald Hayman, *Nietzsche, A Critical Life* (New York: Oxford University Press, 1980). Angela Livingstone, *Salomé: Her Life and Work* (Mt. Kisko, NY: Moyer Bell, 1984). The many idolizing biographical editions by Elisabeth Förster-Nietzsche of her brother's works must be used with caution.

Translations of Nietzsche's writings are prolific, but some of his earlier scholarly works have been neglected. Oscar Levy, ed. *The Complete Works of Friedrich Nietzsche*, 16 vols. (New York: Macmillan, 1901–11 [1964]); most translations in these volumes are by Thomas Common, A. M. Ludovici, and Helen Zimmern (who was personally acquainted with Nietzsche). These have mostly been superseded by modernized and sometimes more accurate versions by Walter Kaufmann, R. J. Hollingdale, H. L. Mencken, Francis Golffing, and Marion Faber, among others. Christopher Middleton, translator and editor, *Selected Letters of Friedrich Nietzsche* (Chicago: University of Chicago Press, 1969), presents an admirable collection for English readers and contains clarifying and connecting notes for biographical contexts. R. J. Hollingdale, translator of Nietzsche's *Dithyrambs of Dionysus* (Redding Ridge, CT: Black Swan Books, 1984), provides a much-needed translation and discussion of a group of poems that engage Salomé's attention in her *Friedrich Nietzsche in seinen Werken*.

In her Nietzsche book, Lou Salomé quotes from his Dionysian poem *"Zwischen Raubvögeln,"* whose verbal ambiguities can encourage different interpretations and translations. Mine stem from a discussion with Wolfram Groddeck during my stay in Basel, Switzerland. Professor Groddeck of the University of Basel graciously shared his insights, which will appear in book form, for which I am appreciative.

Richard Huett, an editor to whom many authors have cause to be grateful, commented rigorously on the original manuscript from his deep knowledge of Nietzsche's works. His queries prompted retranslations of passages in which Salomé's intricate but forceful thoughts had to be rendered with suitable clarity. His assistance went beyond the call of friendship, and my thanks are expressed with pleasure.

Lou Salomé's life and her deep, personal impact on Nietzsche, Rilke, Freud, and other great figures have been portrayed in several biographies, but translations have as yet not caught up with her prolific fiction and essayistic works. It is to the credit of John Walsh, publisher of Black Swan Books, that Salomé's major works of criticism are now finding their way into English. To Walsh, I owe encouragement for translating and editing the present and sole English edition of Salomé's *Nietzsche.* My Introduction accommodates his—and readers'—questions as to what ideological and biographical circumstances brought Lou Salomé and Nietzsche together, what drove them apart, and what was the response in the 1890s, and on, to her book. What was it that Nietzsche meant when he said to Zarathustra, in the section called "The Other Dancing Song," "I whispered something in her [Lou Salomé's] ear. . . . Nobody knows that"? Well, we do know much of what he told her. Lou Salomé's *Nietzsche* allows for such a reconstruction.

Frontispiece to 1894 Vienna edition

Nietzsche's sister

Mathilde Trampedach

Paul Rée

Peter Gast

Gletschergarten Monument

"Drawing by Friedrich Nietzsche (prepared in the Clinic for Nervous Disorders, Basel) drawn by my own hand."

Nietzsche and his mother (1891)

FRIEDRICH NIETZSCHE
The Man in His Works

With faithful memory,
dedicated to one unnamed (1894)

MOTTO — "Life is the return
of investment in life: A person
may preen himself ever so much
with his knowledge and flatter
himself as ever so objective; in
the final tally, he comes away
with nothing more than his own
biography."

—Friedrich Nietzsche
(*Human, All-Too-Human*, I, 513)

Nietzsche's letter to Lou von Salomé was probably written on September 16, 1882, and sent to Stibbe (the estate of the Rée family in Tutz, West Prussia) where she was vacationing with Paul Rée. The phrase "other paths" was typical of Nietzsche's affected and persistent overtures.—editor.

* "Request" ("*Bitte*"):
    I well know many a person's mind
    but know not where myself to find!
    My eyes are much too close to me—
    and I am not what I saw or see.
    I would have better served myself
    could I but take a distance from my pelt.
    Though not as distant as my foes,
    too far away there sit my friends.
    Yet between them and myself, in the middle,
    would you guess my wish and riddle?

A Letter from Nietzsche
(in place of a preface)

MY DEAR LOU, Your idea of reducing philosophical systems to the personal records of their originators is truly an idea arising from a "brother-sister brain." In Basel I myself taught the history of ancient philosophy in just *this* sense. I liked to tell my listeners that such-and-such "a system has been disproved and is dead, but the *person* behind the system cannot be disproved and that the person cannot be killed"—Plato, for instance.

. . . Professor Riedel here, president of the German Musical Association, meanwhile has become enthusiastic over my "heroic music." (I am referring to your [poem] "Prayer to Life"). He insists upon having it, and it is not impossible for him to ready it for his magnificent choir (called the Riedel Society, one of the best in Germany). That could indeed be one small path by which we would reach the afterworld *together*—without precluding other paths.

As for your "characterization" of me—as you put it—it is true, and so, I recall my little verses with the heading "Request"* in *The Gay Science* ("Joke, Cunning and Revenge," 25). Can you guess, my dear Lou, what I am requesting? . . .

Yesterday afternoon I was happy; the sky was blue, the air was mild and pure, I was in the Rosenthal, lured there by the music of [Bizet's] *Carmen*. There I sat for 3 hours and drank the second cognac this year in memory of the first cognac (which, ha! tasted too horrible) and I reflected in all innocence and with malice as to whether or not I had some predisposition for madness. Finally I told myself *no*. Then the *Carmen* music began, and for half an hour I was submerged in tears and felt the beating of my heart. But when you read this, you will at the end say *yes!* and make a note of it for your "characterization" of me.

Come to Leipzig right *soon! Why wait* until the 2nd of October! Adieu, my dear Lou! *Your* F. N.

I   NIETZSCHE'S ESSENCE

"MIHI IPSI SCRIPSI" is a recurrent cry in Nietzsche's letters after the completion of a work. And certainly, it must mean something when the premier stylist of his period says that "I have written for myself," for he has succeeded like no one else in finding the creative expression for each of his thoughts and their finest shadings. For those who know how to read Nietzsche's writings, it is also a deceptive phrase: it points to the reclusiveness of all his thoughts and the manifold, living husks that clothe them; it signifies that he basically thought and wrote for himself because he describes only himself and transposes his own self into thoughts.

If the task of the biographer is to explicate the thinker through his person, it applies in an unusual degree to Nietzsche because external intellectual work and a picture of his inner life coalesce completely. What he says in the "prefatory" letter about philosophers is pertinent to himself: one should test their systems against their personal actions. Later, he expressed the same concept: "Gradually, it has become clear to me that every great philosophy up to the present has been the personal confession of its author and a form of involuntary and unperceived memoir" (BGE, 6).

As mentioned in his letter, that was also the leading idea in my projected sketch or characterization of him, which I read and thoroughly discussed with himself in October 1882. In outline form, my work contained the first section of the present book and several selections from the second section; the content of the third section about Nietzsche's "system" had not yet come into being. During the course of years as Nietzsche's works rapidly grew, so did my Nietzsche "characterization," whose several aspects I treated in separate publications. My aim was to deal exclusively with the main trends of Nietzsche's unique intellectuality, from which alone his philosophy and its development could be understood. Toward this end I restricted myself to a selection of purely theoretical methods of observation as well as purely personal biography. Both should not be carried to extremes, if the basic lines of his essence be allowed to emerge. Readers wishing to discern the significance of Nietzsche as a theoretician (as perhaps the academic philosophers do) will turn away disappointed, without having penetrated to the core of Nietzsche. For the value of his thoughts does not lie in their originality of theory, nor does it lie in that which can be established or refuted dialectically. What is of value is the intimate force which speaks through one personality to another personality; "systems" can well be disproved, as Nietzsche said, but their originators cannot be "killed." Whoever wishes to proceed differently and view Nietzsche's exterior experiences in order to grasp the inner, would at best hold only an empty shell from which the spirit has escaped. One can say of Nietzsche that he actually *experienced* nothing:

> As far as life—the so-called "experience"—is concerned, who of us gives it enough serious attention? Or enough time? In such matters, I am afraid, we were not quite attentive nor, to be exact, was our heart in it—and not even our ear. ("Preface I," TGM)

All of Nietzsche's experience was so inwardly deep that it only manifested itself in conversation, person to person, and in the thoughts of his works. The sum of monologues that constitute the many volumes of his aphorisms is a single, great work of memoirs reflective of his intellectuality. I wish to attempt a picture of that here: the meaning of the thought-experience in Nietzsche's mental constitution—the confessions in his philosophy.

Although Nietzsche has been mentioned more frequently than any other thinker during recent years and many pens have been busy wooing adherents for him or polemicizing against him, he still remains virtually unknown with respect to his unique mentality. As the small, constant, dispersed group, who really knew how to read him, grew into a legion of followers when wider circles took him up, he was overtaken by the fate that threatens every aphorist. Several of his ideas were isolated from their context and turned into slogans and shorthand concepts at the service of contentious parties from which he was completely distant. His rapid fame is attributable to the sudden noise around his calm name, but the most incomparable, the best, the most unique he had to offer was blanketed over and remained un-noticed, pushing him into a deeper reclusiveness. Many, though, loudly celebrate him with naïve and uncritical faith; yet they remind one of his bitter saying: *The Disappointed One Speaks,* "I listened for response and heard only praise" (BGE, 99). Hardly any of them truly followed him by departing from others and their daily quarrels, or remaining alone in their own inner emo-tions; hardly anyone accompanied the solitary, secretive, un-canny and complex thinker who dared to carry immensities and who collapsed into overwhelming madness.

It seems therefore that he stands like a stranger and hermit in the midst of those who praise him most, as one who has strayed into their midst and from whose covered figure no one lifts the cloak. Yes, he stands there and the lamentation of his Zarathustra is on his lips:

> All of them talk about me as they sit around the fire during the evening, but no one thinks about me! That is the new silence about which I learn: their clamor about me spreads a cloak over my thoughts. ("Of Virtue that Makes Small," Z, III)

* * *

FRIEDRICH WILHELM NIETZSCHE was born on October 15, 1844, the sole surviving son of a German pastor at Röcken near Lützen from which he was transferred later to Naumburg. Nietzsche received his education at the Schulpforta boarding school nearby and then became a student of classical philology at the University of Bonn where the renowned philologist Friedrich Ritschl taught. He studied almost exclusively with him and came to know him well socially, following him in the fall of 1865 to Leipzig. During his final student days, there occurred the first personal contact with Richard Wagner; Nietzsche made his acquaintance in 1868 at the home of the composer's sister Ottilie (Frau Professor Brock-haus), after he had already familiarized himself with Wagner's works. Even before receiving his degree, the 24-year-old Nietz-sche was offered the chair vacated at the University of Basel, Switzerland, by the philologist Adolf Kiessling who went to the Johanneum in Hamburg. Nietzsche first was appointed Professor

Extraordinarius in 1869 and shortly thereafter became Professor of classical philology;[1] the University of Leipzig awarded him a doctorate, without his prior matriculation. Aside from his university duties, he assumed the senior level teaching of Greek at the Basel Pädagogium—a public school between gymnasium and university—along with other university professors like the historian of culture Jacob Burckhardt and the philologist Ernst Mahly.

Here he exerted great influence over his students; his rare talent for attaching young people to himself and for spurring them to personal growth came into full play. At that time, Burckhardt said that Basel never had a teacher like him. Burckhardt belonged to the intimate circle of Nietzsche's friends, as did the church-historian Franz Overbeck, and the Kant specialist Heinrich Romundt. With the last two, Nietzsche lived in a house that, after the publication of *Untimely Meditations*, was nicknamed "the poison hut"[2] by Basel society. Toward the end of his stay in Basel, Nietzsche lived for some time with his only sister Elizabeth, nearly his age; later she married Bernhard Förster, a friend during his youth,[3] and went with him to Paraguay. In 1870 Nietzsche took part in the Franco-Prussian war as a volunteer field-medic. Soon thereafter, the first threatening indications appeared of headaches which recurred periodically with pain and illness. If one is to believe Nietzsche's own assertions, his sufferings were of a hereditary nature, and to which his father succumbed. New Year's Day of 1876 his headaches and eye afflictions gave him so much trouble that he had to arrange for someone to assume his teaching duties at the Pädagogium. From then on, his condition worsened to the point where he was close to death: "I've avoided death's door several times, but was terribly tortured—and so, I live from day to day, and each day tells a story of sickness." With these words, in a letter to a friend,[4] Nietzsche described the sufferings he endured for about fifteen years.

He spent the winter of 1876-77 in Italy's Sorrento, but even the mild climate was in vain. There he was among visiting company. From Rome came his friend of many years Malwide von Meysenbug (author of the well-known *Memoirs of an Idealist* [*Memoiren einer Idealistin*] and a follower of Richard Wagner); from West Prussia arrived Dr. Paul Rée, with whom he had already shared a friendship and common goals. The small communal household was joined by a young man (and former student of Nietzsche) from Basel, named Albert Brenner, who soon died of lung sickness. When the stay in the south did not ameliorate his pains, Nietzsche gave up his teaching at the Pädagogium in 1878 and a year later his professorship. After that he led only a reclusive existence, partly in Italy—mostly in Genoa—partly in the Swiss mountains, namely in the small Engadine village of Sils-Maria not far from the Maloja passes.

The external course of his life therefore appears closed and at the same time ended, while his life as a thinker actually begins. . . . And yet, we shall have to return with greater detail to the turns of fate and experiences briefly sketched here as we concern ourselves with the various periods of his intellectual development. In the main, his life and works fall into three overlapping periods, each encompassing a decade.

Nietzsche's teaching activities lasted ten years, 1869-79, in Basel. His philological effectiveness coincides completely with the decade of his Wagner discipleship and the publication of those works influenced by the metaphysics of Schopenhauer; they lasted from 1868 until 1878 when he sent Wagner his first original and positive work, *Human, All-Too-Human*, signaling a new philosophical turn.

From the beginning of the seventies, he formed a relationship with Paul Rée that was to end in November, 1882, coincident with the completion of his *The Gay Science*, the last of those works that Nietzsche grounded in positivism.

In the fall of 1882, Nietzsche decided to disengage himself from all writing activity. During that time of deepest silence, he wished to test the proper direction of a philosophy turned toward the mystical and then to emerge as its proclaimer in 1892. That aim he did not carry out, for precisely in the eighties an almost unbroken productivity unfolded and then ceased before the date he set for himself: in 1889 the overwhelming outbreaks of headaches set the limit for all further intellectual work.

The time between resigning his Basel professorship and the cessation generally of all mental activity again encompassed a decade, 1879–89. After that the seriously ill Nietzsche lived with his mother in Naumburg, after having been temporarily committed to Professor Binswanger's asylum in Jena.

The companion photographs in this book show Nietzsche in the midst of his last ten years of suffering.[5] And certainly, it was during this time that his physiognomy, his entire exterior, appeared to be formed most characteristically. It was a time in which the total expression of his being was already permeated by his deeply emotional inner life and even was significant in what he held back and hid. I may say that this hidden element, the intimation of a taciturn solitude, was the first, strong impression through which Nietzsche's appearance fascinated one. To the superficial observer, his appearance showed nothing remarkable. Nietzsche was of middle height, dressed modestly but with evident care, of tranquil demeanor, and with plain, brown hair combed back; he could easily have been overlooked. The fine and highly expressive lines of his mouth were almost completely covered by a great, bushy, combed moustache. His laughter was quiet and he had a noiseless manner of speaking, carefully and thoughtfully bending his shoulders slightly. One could only with difficulty imagine his figure amid a crowd; he gave the impression of standing aside, alone. His hands were incomparably hands were not revealing!)" (BGE, 288). He attributed a similar attention. He believed that his hands revealed his inner spirit and aptly commented on this: "There are people who unavoidably possess an intellect; it matters not how they may twist and turn and hold their hands in front of their revealing eyes (. . . as if hands were not revealing!)" (BGE, 288) He attributed a similar significance to his unusually small and finely modelled ears of which he said that they were the authentic "ears for things outrageous" ("Prologue", 9, Z).

And in truth, his eyes spoke with involuntary revealment. Though half-blind, they did not possess any spying or flinching quality nor did they impose themselves undesirably upon others, as does the vision of the near-sighted. Above all, his eyes appeared like guardians and protectors of his treasures—silent secrets—not to be glimpsed by the uninvited. His defective eyesight gave his features a completely unique kind of magic in that they only reflected whatever coursed through his inner being rather than reflecting changing, outer impressions. These eyes looked into the interior and, at the same time, looked far beyond immediate objects into the distance: better put, the interior was like a distance. Basically, his probings as a thinker were nothing less than intensive probings into the human psyche for its undiscovered world and for "its still unfinished possibilities" (BGE, 45) which he restlessly formed and reshaped. When he relinquished himself to the spell of a dialogue that excited him, there appeared sometimes a gripping illumination that could just as rapidly disappear in his eyes. But, in a dark mood, his loneliness would speak gloomily, and almost threateningly, from his eyes as from uncanny depths, depths in which he always remained alone and which he could share with no one. At times, these depths gripped him with horror, and in these his mind finally drowned.

Nietzsche's behavior gave a similar impression of reclusivity and secretiveness. Usually he displayed great courtesy, almost feminine mildness, and an even-tempered geniality. He took pleasure in stylish conventions and thought highly of them. Moreover there was an enjoyment in his costuming, as mantle and mask covered a rarely exposed interior. I remember that when I first spoke with Nietzsche during a day in the Spring of 1882 in St. Peter's in Rome, his studied, elegant posture surprised and deceived me. But not for long was one deceived by this recluse who wore his mask so awkwardly, like someone who has come out of the wilderness and mountains and who is dressed conventionally. Very soon a question surfaces, which he formulated in these words: "Whenever a person permits something to become visible, one can ask: 'what does it hide? From what does it wish to divert someone's gaze? What preconception should it arouse? And further: to what extreme does the subtlety of this disguise go? And, does he misperceive himself in all that?'" (D, 523).

This trend of thought only represented the obverse of the loneliness through which Nietzsche's inner life must be understood—a steadily growing self-isolation and preoccupation with himself.

In proportion to the escalation of this trend, everything which is objective reality becomes appearance—only a deceptive veil which the isolated depth weaves about itself in order to become a temporary surface intelligible to human eyes. "People who think deeply feel themselves to be comedians in their relationship with others because they first have to simulate a surface in order to be understood" (HATH, II, 232). Yes, one can even consider Nietzsche's thoughts—insofar as they are theoretical expressions—to be part of this surface, behind which silently and profoundly lie inner experiences that have given rise to them. They resemble a skin "which reveals something but *conceals* even more" (BGE, 32), because, he says, "one either hides one's opinions or one hides behind them" (HATH, II, 338). He finds a lovely designation for himself when he talks in this sense about those "hidden under the cloaks of light" (BGE, 44), referring to those who cloak themselves in the clarity of their ideas.

In every period of his intellectual development, we therefore find a characterizing masquerade in some form or fashion: "Everyone who is deep loves the mask . . . every profound spirit needs a mask; moreover, around every deep spirit there continually grows a mask" (BGE, 40). "Wanderer, who are you? . . . Rest here . . . recuperate? What will serve your recuperation? . . . 'My recuperation? My recuperation? Oh, you inquisitive one, what are you saying! But, give me only, I beg . . .' What? What? Say it!—'One more mask! A second mask . . .'" (BGE, 278).

And it is emphatically clear to us that to the degree to which his self-immolation and moody withdrawal becomes more exclusive, the significance of his periodic masquerade also becomes deeper, so that the true being retreats ever more imperceptibly from his forms of expression and appearance. Already in "The Wanderer and His Shadow" (HATH, 175), he points to "mediocrity as mask." "Mediocrity is the happiest mask which the reflective person can wear, because the great mass or mediocre do not think of it as a mask. And yet he assumes that mask for their sake, in order not to provoke them and not seldom out of a sense of pity and goodness." He exchanges this harmless mask for a gruesome one, which hides something even more gruesome beneath it: "occasionally folly itself is the mask for an unfortunate unholy all-too-knowing knowledge" (BGE, 270); and finally it becomes a deceiving photo of godly laughter which aims to transform pain into beauty. And so, during his final philosophical mysticism, Nietzsche slowly sank into a last loneliness into whose silence we can no longer follow him. Only his idea-masks remain, like symbols and emblems, open to interpretation, while for us he has already become what he once signed himself as in a letter to a friend: "The one eternally lost" (July 8, 1881 in Sils-Maria).

During all of Nietzsche's transformations, that inner aloneness and reclusiveness remains the unchanging frame from which his picture looks at us. However he may have costumed himself, he always carried with him "the wastelands and the holy, inviolable perimeter, wherever he went" ("The Wanderer and His Shadow," HATH, II, 337). And with that, it expresses only his need for a correspondence between the outer present and his lonely inwardness, as he wrote to his friend Rée, on October 31, 1880, from Italy: "As a recipe, as well as a natural passion, it appears to me ever more clearly that solitude, namely a total one, as well as a condition in which we can create our best, must be constructed with much readiness for sacrifice."

The compelling reason for making his inner isolation into an exterior one, as completely as possible, was first offered him by his physical suffering. This suffering drove him from people. And even the relationships with individual friends were possible only with long interruptions, while dialogues were rare.

Suffering and loneliness then are the two great lines of fate in Nietzsche's biography, which become ever more pronounced the nearer one comes to the end. And they bear the strange double-face of an *exteriorly fated life* and at the same time a purely psychically determined, *willed inner necessity*. Also his psychic suffering, no less than his reclusiveness and isolation, reflected and symbolized something of the vast inward depth. He joined his suffering to other outer providential acts, so that suffering became like a personified companion and earnest friend *intended* for him. At one time when he expressed sympathy for someone's loss, he wrote, "I am overcome constantly by misery to hear that you are suffering, that you miss something, that you have lost someone; to me, though, suffering and doing-without are *natural* and not, as with you, unnecessary and unreasonable elements of existence" (to Rée, end of August 1881, from Sils-Maria).

Related to this are the individual aphorisms, strewn throughout his works, about the *value of suffering for the gain of knowledge*.

He describes the influence of mood upon a person who is ill and the influence of recovery upon one's thinking; he accompanies the subtlest transitions of such moods upward into intellectuality. A regularly recurrent decline into sickness, as he experienced it, always demarcated one period of his life from another, and consequently defined one period from a preceding one. This "double existence" gives to experiences and consciousness a dual mode of being. All things then become new, even to the mind—"*neuschmeckend*" or "new tasting," as he called it tellingly—and to one's eyes the most common and everyday assumes a new cast. Everything absorbs something from the freshness and dew of a morning's beautiful dawn because one morning has separated it from the preceding night. And so, every recuperation becomes his own rebirth and with it all of life around him—and as always, the pain is "entwined in the victory."[6]

If Nietzsche himself already interprets the nature of his physical suffering as being reflected to a certain extent in his thoughts and works, so it emerges even more noticeably if one observes his creativity and its development as totally unified. Here we do not see the gradual transformation of intellectual life that everyone experiences who ripens into his natural maturity, nor the changing phases of growth; instead, we see a sudden turn and change, an almost rhythmic up and down of mental conditions which, in the final analysis, seem to stem from nothing else than *falling ill because of thoughts and recuperating through thoughts*.

Only through the innermost need of his entire nature, and only through the most torturing demand for healing, do new insights open up to him. But no sooner is he captured by them and been refreshed, assimilating them into his own strength, than he is immediately gripped again by something like a fever or restlessly surging overflow of inner energy that ultimately turns its sting against him: he is the cause of his self-induced illness. "Excess of strength is the only proof of strength" ("Preface," TI), says Nietzsche. With this "excess," his strength does itself injury, rages and exhausts itself in passionate conflicts, and irritates itself into becoming those tortures and emotional shocks through which his mind wishes to become fertile. "Is there a predisposition to the severe, the horrific, evil, and the problematics of existence that stems from a sense of well-being, from overflowing health, from excess itself? . . . And here is a question for psychiatrists: Are there perhaps neuroses of *health*?" ("Attempt at a Self-Criticism," BT, 4).

Nietzsche makes a proud assertion: "Whatever does not destroy me, makes me stronger" ("Maxims and Arrows," TI, 8). With these words he flagellated himself, not to the point of destruction or death but to a fever-pitch and a self-wounding he deemed necessary. This seeking of pain courses through the entire history of Nietzsche's development and is its essential intellectual and spiritual source. As he appropriately notes, "Spirit *is* that life which itself cuts into life: with its own suffering it increases its own knowledge. Did you know that? . . . You only know the spark of the spirit but you do not see it as the anvil, nor see the gruesomeness of its hammer" ("On the Famous Wise Men," Z, II). "That tension of the soul during misfortune . . . its shuddering when looking at great devastation, its inventiveness and courage in carrying burdens, enduring, interpreting, exploiting misfortune; and, whatever has been given to the soul—depth, mystery, mask, spiritedness, trickery, and greatness—has it not been bestowed through suffering and through the discipline of great suffering?" (BGE, 225).

And so, two things stand out emphatically: the close connection between the life of the mind and the life of the soul—the dependence of his intellect upon the needs and excitations of his interior being. And then the unique feature, that this close relatedness must always yield anew to suffering; the light of knowledge requires the high glow of the soul, each time. . . . Here, as in the letter quoted, suffering is *natural* and necessary to Nietzsche's existence.

Just as Nietzsche's bodily suffering was the provocation for his outer isolation, so his psychic suffering was one of the profoundest sources that should be searched for his sharply honed individualism and for the strict emphasis upon the "solitary" as a recluse, in Nietzsche's special sense. The story of the "solitary," most certainly, is a story of suffering and is not to be compared with the common type of individualism; its essence is rather less than "self-sufficiency," its essence is more like "self-toleration." If one observes the pain-wracked ups and downs of his intellectual explorations, one also reads a story of as many self-transformations that harbor the long, painful and heroic struggle with himself. Nietzsche boldly inscribed the following over his philosophy: "This thinker needs no one to refute him, he does it well himself!" ("The Wanderer and his Shadow," HATH, II, 249).

His extraordinary capacity to adapt himself always to the most difficult self-conquest and to feel at home in every new insight seems to serve the purpose of delineating the newly-won and to render it so movingly: I come! Abandon your hut and join me! demanded the spirit, and with a stubborn hand he made himself homeless. Anew he seeks the dark, adventure, and the desert, and a lament is upon his lips: "I must continue to raise my feet, these tired and wounded feet; and because I must wander, I often look back grimly at the most beautiful thing that could not hold me—*because* it could not hold me! (GS, 309). As soon as he felt comfortable with a particular point of view, his own prophetic saying takes over: "Whoever has reached his ideal transcends it precisely at that point" (BGE, 73).

Changes of opinion and urges to wander are deeply embedded in the heart of Nietzsche's philosophy; they are categorically decisive for the manner of his acquisition of knowledge. Not in vain does he call himself a "wrestler who has too often wrestled himself to the ground, who has too often braked his own strength, and who has wounded and hampered himself through victory over himself" ("From the Heights," BGE, 5).

Through the heroism of his willingness to relinquish his own convictions, his urge inward assumes straightaway a position of *remaining true to his convictions.* For that reason, he says, "Convictions are more dangerous enemies of truth than lies" (HATH, I, 483). He notes, "We would not allow ourselves to be put to the torch for our opinions because we are not so sure of them or perhaps because we may be allowed to have and change our opinions" ("The Wanderer and His Shadow," HATH, 333). These dispositions he expresses handsomely: "Never keep silent or hold back what may be thought against your thoughts! Solemnly promise yourself that! It belongs to the obligatory honesty of thinking. Also, every day you must campaign against yourself. Victory and a conquered field-trench are no longer your concern, but truth is; be not worried about your defeat either" (D, 370). For that reason, these thoughts are entitled, "To what extent the thinker loves his enemy." But this love of the enemy springs from the dark intuition that within the enemy may be hidden a future companion and that new victories await only the submissive person. Nietzsche intuits that the unavoidable requisite of all creativity for him lies in the constant and painful process of self-transformation. "It is the *mind* which saves us from burning up or becoming charred. . . . Saved from fire, we march from opinion to opinion, driven by the intellect . . . like noble *traitors* to everything" (HATH, I, 637). . . . "We *must* become traitors, practice faithlessness, and always relinquish our ideals" (HATH, I, 629). At the same time, the recluse must divide himself into a multiplicity of thinkers. His urge for self-laceration was only a form of his drive for survival: only by plunging into pain did he escape his sufferings. "Only in my heel am I invulnerable! And only where there are graves are there resurrections! Thus spoke Zarathustra" ("The Tomb Song," Z, II). "Life once also confided to me this secret: 'Behold,' it said, 'I am that which must always overcome itself'" ("On Self-Overcoming," Z, II).

Through that drive to overcome himself, he developed—more than he wished to perceive—into a "Don Juan of knowledge," who is pictured as follows: "He has spirit, and finds titillation, intrigue, and pleasure in hunting for knowledge in realms reaching toward the highest and most distant stars—until nothing more remains to be hunted than what is *injurious* to knowledge. And so, he finally lusts after the ultimate experience of hell, which *seduces* him. Perhaps, like all that is finally understood, this too is disillusioning! And then he would have to remain nailed to his disillusionment for all eternity and become a visitor turned into stone, yearning for a supper of knowledge, which will no longer be offered him! Indeed, the entire world of objects does not have any food to appease this hungry one" (D, 327).

There was nothing that Nietzsche thought about more often and deeply than the riddle of his own existence, and there is nothing that can be more instructive about his works than precisely this: basically all of his existence riddles were synonymous with knowledge riddles. The more profoundly he understood himself, the more uninhibitedly his entire philosophy became a vast reflection of his self-portrait, and all the more naïvely he attributed it to a likeness as such. Among philosophers, some abstractly systematize their own concepts into a generalized world order; in that fashion, Nietzsche abstracts and generalizes his idea of soul into a world soul. But drawing a picture of Nietzsche at this point does not require tracing his collective theories back to his biography, as in subsequent parts of this book. A certain understanding of that link is already possible here where Nietzsche is observed simply in regard to his intellectual bent. Its riches are too diverse to justify putting them into definite categories; each of his individual talents and intellectual drives possessed liveliness and a will to dominance, leading necessarily to an unremitting and unpacifiable competition among all his talents. Within Nietzsche various talents lived in constant disquiet, jostling and tyrannizing each other: he was a musician with great gifts, a thinker with independent directions, a genius of religious speculation, and a born poet. Through this diversity, Nietzsche himself tried to explain the uniqueness of his intellectual individuality and he engaged in thorough-going conversations on that subject.

He made distinctions between two main groups of human characters: those in whom different impulses and drives exist in mutual harmony, effecting a healthy unity, and others in whom impulses and drives hamper and attack each other. The first group, he compared with the condition of a herd-like humanity during prehistoric times of pre-social and non-hierarchical organization, when each person possessed individuality and a sense of power only in association with the mass of the herd; that is analogous to the modern person in whom the various drives become the sum total of a unified personality. In contrast, the inner natures of the other group—like warring people—to a certain extent dissolve personality into a vast sum of high-handed personalized drives, resulting in a multiplicity of inner personalities. This condition can be overcome only when a higher outside-power creates a stronger authority which will exert dominance over all; that is analogous to a law-imposing hierarchical state to which all wills are subsumed. Whereas the subordination of the individual person and his inclinations—or the merging of the individual into the whole—is quite instinctive with the first group mentioned, that kind of subordination within the other group can only come about with the taming of high-handed personalized drives and the structuring of their relationships. As Nietzsche said, "To *have to fight* the instincts—that is the formula of decadence: as long as life is *ascending,* happiness is the equivalence of instinct" ("The Problem of Socrates," TI, 11). In this fashion Nietzsche makes a distinction between decadent and innate aristocratic natures.

Here one sees the source of Nietzsche's view about the possibility that *self-assertion becomes a unity through the suffering of each internal impulse and drive.* Here is the original significance, locked within a tight bud, of Nietzsche's later teachings on decadence: a constant enduring and wounding may yield the greatest possessions and creativity. In brief, here he saw revealed the significance of *heroism as an ideal.* His own painful sense of incompleteness hurled him toward the ideal and its tyranny: "Our deficiencies lie in our eyes with which we view the ideal" (HATH, II, 86).

"What makes one heroic? Going out to meet, at one and the same time, one's highest suffering and one's highest hope" (GS, 268), says Nietzsche. I would like to add to that three of the aphorisms he once put into writing for me [August 1882 in Tautenburg] and which accentuate his meanings:

> The opposite of the heroic ideal is the ideal of the harmonious development of all—a handsome, as well as a very welcome, contrast! But it is only an ideal for fundamentally good people (Goethe, for instance).*

---

*Incidentally, here Nietzsche interprets Goethe quite differently from what he wrote years later in *Twilight of the Idols.* Here he still sees in Goethe the diametrically opposite of his own unharmonious nature;

Further,

> Heroism is the cast of mind of a person who strives toward a goal which regards him with utter indifference. Heroism is the well-intentioned will toward absolute self-destruction.

And,

> People who strive for greatness are usually evil; it is the only way they can tolerate themselves.

The word "evil" like the word "good" here is not to be taken as a commonplace judgment but as a description of a fact; as such it always designates for Nietzsche the "warfare" within a human being, something he later calls the "anarchy of instincts." This picturing was part of a determined development of ideas until it broadened during his last period of creativity into a portrayal of human culture. The passwords are the following: "inner warfare" equals decadence; "victory" equals self-destruction of mankind to make possible the creation of a superior mankind. Originally, however, he was concerned with a portrait of his own psyche.

He makes a distinction between the harmonious or unified natural disposition and the heroic or multi-split natural inclinations as the two types of humans: the *action-oriented* and those who are *cognitive*. In other words, he describes a type opposed to his manner of being, while the other typifies his own.

Nietzsche sees the *active* personality as undivided and unconflicted, as opposed to the person of instinct and aristocratic being. If the former follows his natural development, he must become more self-confident and purposeful, and his compressed strength must discharge itself in healthy actions. The potential obstructions by the outer world pose simultaneously a stimulus and a challenge, for nothing is more natural to him than a healthy combativeness directed outward, regardless of the scope of his intellect.

The *cognitive* individual is completely different. Instead of seeking to yoke his drives, he gives them all possible free rein; the

---

later he saw in Goethe a deep affinity of spirit—an unharmonious person who recreated himself into harmonious shape through planning and dedication.

broader the fields they explore with all their senses, the more they serve the individual's purpose—a drive for knowledge. *"Life is a means to knowledge."* And he calls out to his companions, "We want to become the subjects of our own experiments, our own guinea pigs!" (GS, 324, 319).[7] And so, he willingly relinquishes personal unity—the more polyphonic the subject, the more it pleases him:

> Sharp and mild, coarse and fine,
> Friendly and strange, dirty and clean,
> Am fool's and wise man's stand-in,
> All this I am, and want to mean—
> Dove as well as snake and swine.
>
> ("Joke, Cunning, and Revenge," GS, 11)

As persons of knowledge and inquisitive to a fault, we must be grateful "to the god, devil, sheep, and worm within us . . . we have anterior and posterior souls, whose ultimate intentions no one can fathom easily, and we have foregrounds and backgrounds to whose limits no feet can wander . . . we are the born, sworn, and jealous friends of *solitude* . . ." (BGE, 44). A perceptive person has a "soul which contains the longest depth-reaching ladder . . . a capacious soul that can stray within itself, roam, and swerve . . . that takes flight from itself and then overtakes itself in the widest circle; the wisest soul which is sweet-talked by foolishness . . . which loves itself best and in which all things have their ebb and flood . . ." ("Of Old and New Tablets," Z, III, 19).

The subtle intellect fears being misled by a soul of this kind and becoming "a centipede which has a thousand antennas" (BGE, 205) and is always ready to run away from itself and to ensconce itself in a foreign being. But, "When a person has found himself, one must then also understand how to *lose* oneself from time to time, and then to rediscover oneself—if one is a thinker" (The Wanderer and His Shadow, HATH, 306). It is detrimental for him to be bound always to himself. The same idea is expressed in the following verses:

> . . . I find it odious to lead myself!
> Like creatures of the forest and the sea,
> I love, at length, to lose self and identity

In a blessed wilderness, to crouch brooding,
And from a distance, eventually, enticing
Myself homeward—to seduce myself to myself.

("Joke, Cunning, and Revenge," GS, 33)

These verses are entitled "The Solitary" and speak of the missions and battles of an outsider against the exterior world. The more combative that attitude is the more it mitigates the inner life, relative to preoccupations with the victories and defeats and conquests within his own drives. The inner life seeks, above all, a protective cover against the loud and lacerating events in the life outside. Valid for this philosopher is his self-description as "a person who constantly experiences, sees, hears, suspects, hopes, and dreams extraordinary things, and who is struck by *his* own thoughts as if they were the lightning strokes of events intended for him" (BGE, 292).

With all that, the combative relationship of his inner drives is not lifted but instead it is heightened: "But whoever may wish to look at the fundamental drives of man, with the notion of discovering to what extent they may have instinctively played the game of *inspiring* genii (or demons and goblins), he will find-
. . . that each drive would readily and eagerly represent itself as the alpha and omega of existence and the rightful lord over all the other drives. Every drive lusts for dominance and *as such* attempts to philosophize." And precisely that subjective [moral] recognition by the philosopher is "decisive evidence of *who he is,* namely, in what ranking order the innermost drives of his nature are related to one another" (BGE, 6). . . .

And yet, through the recognition of the inner warfare, a transformation is achieved which provides a new and releasing meaning: that recognition gives all drives a common goal, a direction toward conquering the self-same thing. With that, the tendency toward splintered activity and the tyranny of willfulness is broken. Although the drives still retain firmly their "subject multiplicity," they submit like servants and tools to a higher power . . . so that within self-discipline an heroic ideal arises and points toward greatness. The danger of anarchy thus has been displaced by a secure and "communal structure of drives and affects" (BGE, 12).

I recall something that Nietzsche told me which very appropriately expresses the joy that the seeker of knowledge takes in the vast breadth and depth of his nature; from it springs the desire to regard his life henceforth as "an experiment of the seeker of knowledge" (GS, 324). He said, "I resemble an old, weather-proof fortress which contains many hidden cellars and deeper hiding places; in my dark journeys, I have not yet crawled down into my subterranean chambers. Don't they form the foundation for everything? Should I not climb up from my depths to all the surfaces of the earth? After every journey, should one not return to oneself?"

In the aphorism called "The sigh of the searcher for knowledge," one finds the same sentiment: "Woe, my greed! Selflessness does not live in this soul. Instead there is a self greedy for everything and which would like nothing better than to possess more eyes to see with and more hands so as to retrieve the entire past, without losing a single thing that it could possibly clutch! Oh, to transcend the flame of my greed! Oh, that I could only be reborn in hundreds of beings!" (GS, 249).

In this fashion, one's capacious, convoluted, unharmonic, and "incongruous" nature becomes a tremendous advantage: "If we would wish and dare to construct an architecture corresponding to the nature of our soul we would have to take the labyrinth as a model!" (D, 169); yet, it need not be a labyrinth in which the soul would lose itself but one out of whose confusion the soul can penetrate to knowledge. "To give birth to a dancing star, one must first have chaos within" ("Prologue," Z, 5). Zarathustra's phrase is as true of the one born to the light and life of a star as it is true of its living genius and own transformation. That was described by Nietzsche with the title "A light kind of shadow": "right next to the nightside of persons, almost invariably there is a soul of light, as if it was fastened to them. She is, so to speak, the negative shadow cast by them" ("The Wanderer and His Shadow," HATH, II, 258).

. . . Nietzsche's conception of "knowledge" varied with his different intellectual periods, and accordingly there is at all times a disarrangement of the "inner hierarchy of drives," as Nietzsche phrased it, the conflict within this richly endowed genius. One can say that from the changing pictures of shifting drives, one can piece together the essential story of Nietzsche's development until his last period of work, when his entire inner life was mirrored in philosophical theories and when the dark or the light souls became for him the representatives of the human or the superior human.

Despite the changes mentioned, the process itself was constant: "If one has character, one also has one's typical experience, which always recurs" (BGE, 70), said Nietzsche. This then is *his* typical experience, which always recurs, through which he rears himself up and transcends himself, and through which he overreaches and finally perishes.

And so, with certainty, he *had* to perish. The very same process which repeatedly shielded him from permanently healing and transcending himself also hid the pathological aspect of that kind of intellectual progression. At first glance, none of this is quite noticeable. One might rather think that within a strength of will that knew how to heal the self, there would at least have to be as much health as in a tranquil and harmoniously unfolding strength. In fact, a far greater healthiness would be required, which immunizes itself against fevers and wounds and remains assertive, and which is capable of transforming sickness and conflictedness into a *stimulant* for life and the acquisition of knowledge, as well as transforming hurts into a spur and clairvoyance for its purposes: in sum, that healthiness advantageously *embraces* combative conflictedness and sickness. That was the way in which Nietzsche wished to have his history of suffering interpreted—especially during his sickliest moments—namely, as a story of *recovery*. At any rate, his powerful nature was capable of self-healing and pulling things together, in the midst of pain and contradictions; healing was prompted by strivings for the ideals of knowledge. But after recovery was achieved, his nature inexorably again required suffering and battles, fever and wounds. That nature which had healed itself then called up its opponents; it turned against itself and boiled over into new conditions of illness. Above every goal of knowledge and the joy of being healed stood the recurrent inscription, "Who has achieved his ideal, at the same time surpasses it," because "one's surpassing bliss becomes one's burden" ("Joke, Cunning, and Revenge," GS, 47), while Zarathustra "feels wounded by his happiness" ("The Child with the Mirror," Z, II). "We are only in *our* bliss when we are in the greatest *danger*" (BGE, 224). "Inviting pain: Ruthlessness of thinking is frequently the sign of an unquiet inner cast of mind which wishes to be anæsthetized" (HATH, XI, 581).

Here then, health is not something overtowering which converts the pathological into an incidental instrument for its own purposes; instead, health and pathology represent indeed a unique split of the self and a mutuality within one and the same intellectual life. . . . The mysterious interconnection between the healthy and the pathological in Nietzsche brings us to the essential Nietzsche problem.

As the many separate drives group themselves into two opposites of being—one dominates and the other serves—it becomes possible for a person not only to identify with *another* mode but also to identify with and experience a higher mode. In that he sacrifices a part of himself, he has come close to *religious exaltation*. By daring to bring about the heroic ideal of exposing and relinquishing the self, he causes an eruption that brings about a religious mood.

Of all his great intellectual dispositions, none is bound more profoundly and unremittingly to his whole intellectual being than his religious genius. In no other time or period of culture could that have prepared the son of a pastor to develop into a thinker. Under the influences of his time, however, his religious bent of mind thrust him toward the acquisition of knowledge . . . but, he fell back upon himself, instead of an outer life force! And so, he achieved precisely the opposite of his goal: not a higher unity of his own being but its innermost division, not the fusion of all stirrings and drives (into an *individuum*) but a split and divided self (a *dividuum*).[8] And yet, health was gained by means of sickness; true worship by means of illusion; and, self-assertion and uplifting by means of self-wounding.

All of Nietzsche's knowledge arose from a powerful religious mood and was insolubly knotted: self-sacrifice and apotheosis, the cruelty of one's own destruction and the lust for self-deification, sorrowful ailing and triumphal recovery, incandescent intoxication and cool consciousness. One senses here the close entwining of mutual contradictions; one senses the overflowing and voluntary plunge of over-stimulated and tensed energies into chaos, darkness, and terror, and then an ascending urge toward the light and the most tender moments—the urges of a will "that frees him from the distress of fullness and overfullness and from the affliction of the contradictions compressed within him" ("Attempts at a Self-Criticism," BT, 5)—a chaos that wants to give birth to a god, and must give birth to one.

"In man *creature* and *creator* are united: in man reside not only matter, fragments, superfluity, clay, excrement, folly, and chaos but also a creator, sculptor, a hammer-hardness, a spectator-divinity and a seventh day of rest" (BGE, 225). And here it is evident that relentless suffering and self-deification are mutually dependent—evermore each gives rise to its own opposite. Nietzsche has found this expressed in the Vedic story of King Viçvamitra, "who after a thousand years of self-imposed martyrdom won such a feeling of power and self-confidence that he undertook to build a *new heaven*. . . . Everyone who has ever and anywhere built a 'new heaven' first had to find the power to do so in his *own hell*" (GM, III, 10).

There is another passage in which Nietzsche recalls the legend of King Viçvamitra; it follows closely upon the depiction of that power-hungry sufferer who has chosen himself as the worthiest object of lustful rape: "The triumph of the ascetic over himself marks the final tragedy of the drive toward excellence. His eye turns inward, as it were, and beholds a person split into a sufferer as well as an observer; further, it only searches the outer world for wood that will serve as the person's flaming pyre. Here is the tragic spectacle of self-consuming immolation. . . ." This passage contains a description of all asceticism of the past and its motives, and it concludes with this observation: ". . . truly, has then the circle of the ascetic's striving for excellence reached a dead-end and completion? Could this circle not be run through once again from the beginning, as the ascetic holds on to his basic disposition and the pitying god to his own?" (D, II, 113).

In *Human, All-Too-Human,* Nietzsche comments further on ascetic ideals and motives: "There is such a thing as *defiance directed against oneself* and to whose most sublimated expressions belong several forms of asceticism. Certain people, namely, have so great a need to put into practice their power and urge to dominate that they . . . finally and ruinously resort to tyrannizing certain parts of their own being. . . . This fragmentation of one's self, this ridiculing of one's own nature and the despising of self division *(spernere se sperni)*—of which religion has made so much—all are a high degree of vanity. . . . A human being takes genuine pleasure in ravaging himself with these exaggerated objectives and afterwards deifies the tyranny-fostering elements in his soul" (I, 137). And, "actually he only cares about the discharging of his emotions; to ease his tensions, he seizes the spears of his enemies and buries them in his breast" (I, 138). And finally, ". . . with self-contempt and cruelty, he scourges his self-deification and takes pleasure in the wild uproar of his longings; . . . he knows how to string a trip-wire for his extreme emotion, the will to dominate, so that he falls into the deepest abasement, until his maddened soul is torn from its moorings by the contrast between domination and abasement. . . . At bottom, here is a strange kind of yearning, one in which perhaps all others are knotted. Novalis, among authorities on the question of holiness through experience and instinct, once told the whole secret: 'It is strange enough that in time the association of lust, religion, and cruelty did not alert people to its intimate ties and their common tendency'" (I, 142).

In fact, a genuine Nietzsche study would require the psychology of religion that would spotlight the meaning of his being, his suffering, and his self-induced bliss. His entire development, as it were, derived from his loss of belief and therefore from his emotions that attend the death of God. These tremendous emotions reverberate in his writings up to the final work, the fourth part of *Thus Spoke Zarathustra*[9] that was composed on the threshold of madness. *The possibility of finding some substitutions for the lost God by means of the most varied forms of self-idolization* constituted the story of his mind, his works, and his illness. In regard to the quest to fill the void of a God-relation, we find Nietzsche's verses about the human condition as it is fulfilled in God's creation of mankind:

The pious responds:
"God loves us, for it is *us* he has created!"
"Man has created God!" reply you subtle ones.
And should not one love what one has fashioned?
Therefore, should man reject his own creations?
That logic limps—it has the devil's hoof imprinted.

("Joke, Cunning, and Revenge," GS, 38)

Nietzsche's story involves the "continuing effect of a religious drive within the thinker," which remains powerful even after the God to whom he had related was smashed. There was an afterglow: "The sun has already set but the heaven of our life glows and shines as if reflected from something we no longer see" (HATH, I, 223). Along with that, one hears the emotional cry of "the madman": "'Where has God gone?' he exclaimed, 'I will tell you! *We have killed him*—you and I. All of us are his murderers! . . . Do we not yet hear the noise of the gravediggers who are burying God? Do we not as yet smell anything of the divine decay?—even the gods decay! God is dead! God stays dead! And we have killed him! How do we, the murderers of all murderers, console ourselves? The holiest and mightiest that the world has owned until now has bled to death under our knives: who will wipe that blood away from us? With what waters can we cleanse ourselves? . . . *Is not the magnitude of this act too great for us to bear? Are we not compelled to become gods ourselves, if only to seem worthy of this act?* There never was a greater deed, and whoever is born after us will—because of it—belong to a higher history than all of history until now'" (GS, 125).

Through the words of Zarathustra during Nietzsche's last creative period, he provided himself with an answer to his outbreak of torture and yearning: *"All gods are dead: now we want the superior man to live!"* ("Of the Gift-Giving Virtue," Z, I).[10] And with these words, Nietzsche expressed the inner substance of his philosophy.

In its tortured quest, the yearning for God becomes a drive for God-creation, and that of necessity had to express itself in self-deification. With precise vision, Nietzsche perceived within religious phenomena a tremendous drama of personal will and demand for self-induced bliss. In all religious phenomena resides a kernel of individualism and a "sublime egoism" which streams freely and naïvely toward a presumed exterior life- or God-force; but, in the case of the "knowing" Nietzsche, egoism circled back to himself as object. And so he matched his rational atheism with a bold conclusion: "*If* there were gods, how could I tolerate not being one! *Hence,* there are no gods" ("Upon the Blessed Isles," Z, II). Other Zarathustra sayings link up with that: "And worship will still reside in your vanity!" In them are expressed the extreme dangers of inner splits and multiplications that hover over the "solitary" and the "individualist": "One is ever much too much about me. . . . Always one times one—in the long run—makes two."

Nietzsche's preoccupation with and attitude toward this "two-ness" and his resistance or yielding to the idea, all determine his road to knowledge and wisdom, as well as the uniqueness of his different intellectual periods, until his "two-ness" finally became a vision and hallucination and a living reality, clouding his spirit and choking his reason. He could no longer defend himself against himself: this was the Dionysian drama that could be entitled *The Soul's Fate* ("Preface," GM, 7) as it unfolded within Nietzsche. The loneliness of the interior life, from which the mind wishes to find an exit, is nowhere deeper and more painful than at the end. One could say that the strongest wall in this fateful self-immurement was a dazzling, godly halo . . . a mirage which obliterated and hid boundaries from him. Every passage outward always led back to the depth of his self, which ultimately had to become God and world and heaven and hell; every passage took him farther into his final depth and his decline.

These main lines of Nietzsche's uniqueness contain the reasons for his craftiness and exaltation, as did his philosophical work, lending it greatness, significance, and pungent seasoning. That seasoning will be sharply evident not only to young and healthy persons who have untried tastebuds, but also to those who are sheltered by tranquil faith and who have never experienced the terrible and fiery battles of a religiously inclined free-spirit. But that has made Nietzsche, in so great a measure, the philosopher of our time. His person typifies the underlying inner dynamics of our time: "the anarchy within instincts" of creative and religious forces that so energetically desire satiety that they cannot be content with the crumbs that fall from the table of modern knowledge. . . . The great and moving feature in Nietzsche's philosophy is an insatiable and passionate demand. That comes to the fore in every new turn of expression: a series of tremendous attempts to solve this problem of modern tragedy, to solve the riddle of the Sphinx and hurl it into the abyss.

And so, we must direct our attention to the human being and not the theorist in order to find our way in Nietzsche's works. In that sense, our contemplation will not gain a new theoretical world picture but the picture of a human soul in all its greatness and sickliness. At first, it would seem that Nietzsche's philosophical implications during his changes would be weakened by the inner process that occurs every time. On the contrary, his meanings deepen and sharpen because the changing outlooks always cross over into the essence of things. Not only are the exterior outlines of a particular theory changed every time but the entire mood, atmosphere, illumination change as well. We hear ideas clash, see worlds sink, and new worlds emerge. The essential originality of Nietzsche's mind is manifested through the medium of his nature which attracts everything toward itself and its most intimate needs but which also yields and entirely gives itself over to everything. Thus, inner experiences and consequences that stem from his worlds of ideas open up to him; reason can only graze those worlds, it cannot exhaust them or become creative.

As for theories, Nietzsche frequently leans upon foreign models and masters, but the ripest point of their creativity becomes the spur for his own.[11] The slightest touch felt by his mind sufficed to give rein to a fullness of inner life—a life of ideas. He once said, "There are two kinds of genius: above all, one which begets and another which will gladly allow itself to become fertile and will give birth" (BGE, 248). Undoubtedly, he belonged to the latter. In Nietzsche's spiritual nature was something—in heightened dimension—that was feminine.* But, his genius is such that the source of his initial stimulation is almost immaterial. Putting matters into perspective, we notice several seeding kernels that made his ground fertile. If we enter into his philosophy, we are in a rustling forest of shade-giving trees and are surrounded by the luxurious vegetation of a superbly wild nature. His superiority consisted of being fertile ground for each seedling, a capacity he himself recognized as a sign of true genius: "the new, thriving cultivated field with its primeval, fresh, and unexpended strength" ("The Wanderer and His Shadow," sequel to HATH, 118).

---

*Sometimes when Nietzsche was particularly aware of this, he was inclined to regard feminine genius as the essential genius. "Animals think differently than men do about females; they consider the female as the productive being. . . . Pregnancy has made females milder, more patient, more fearful, more joyfully submissive; and just so does spiritual pregnancy produce the character of the contemplative types akin to the feminine character: they are the male mothers" (GS, 72).

II NIETZSCHE'S TRANSITIONS

". . . Ever someone different and yet
always the same!"

"THE SNAKE which cannot shed its skin will perish. It is the same with minds which are prevented from changing their opinions: they cease to function as minds" (D, 573).

* * *

THE FIRST CHANGE during Nietzsche's mental life came after a battle that goes far back to the dawn of his childhood, or no later than his early days as a boy.

It is his break with institutional Christian belief. In his works one seldom finds this separation mentioned. And yet, it can be regarded as the beginning of his changes because it already casts a light upon the uniqueness of his development. His remarks about this situation, which I discussed very thoroughly with him, concerned themselves mainly with the reasons that brought on the rupture. By far, most people who are inclined toward religion and are prompted first by intellectual motives to pull themselves free from their religious conceptions do so through painful struggles. In rarer instances, the first alienation comes from emotional sources in life and is a painless process; here, the person's rationality dismembers only what has already died and is a corpse. In Nietzsche's case there was a strange convergence of both possibilities: neither were there only intellectual reasons that originally freed him from acquired concepts nor did the old belief cease to match the needs of his emotions. Instead, Nietzsche repeatedly emphasized that the Christianity which imbued the pastor-home of his parents suited his inner being—smooth and soft, like a healthy skin—and compliance with all its commandments was as easy to follow as his own inclinations. This, so to speak, inherent "talent" for the whole of religion, Nietzsche thought to be one of the reasons for the sympathy which serious Christians accorded him, even though he was already separated from them by a deep gulf.

The dark instinct, which for the first time drove him from routines of thought that had become precious to him, awoke within him precisely when the warm feeling of home comfort enveloped his being. In order to come into his own powerfully, his spirit craved spiritual conflicts, pains, and upheavals; he craved a new mood, induced by the break with tranquillity, because his creativity depended upon inner emotions and exaltation. Here, for the first time in Nietzsche's life, appears the self-imposed suffering in his "decadent nature." "In times of peace, the militant person attacks himself" (BGE, 76) and seeks the exile of a strange world of thoughts in which he becomes an eternal wanderer destined to have no respite and quiet. Within Nietzsche's restlessness, from now on, lived an insatiable longing for a return to Paradise while, at the same time, his intellectual development forced him to distance himself from it ever farther.

Speaking to Nietzsche about the changes that already lay behind him, I elicited from him remarks he made half in jest: "Yes, things take their course and continue to develop, but where to? When everything has taken its course—where does one run to then? When all possible combinations have been exhausted, what follows then? How would one then not arrive again in belief? Perhaps in a *Catholic* belief?" And from the background hiding place of these assertions emerged the added, serious words: *"In any case, the circle could be more plausible than a standing still."*

Indeed, the hallmark of Nietzsche's entire manner of thinking is a never-ceasing motion of returning into himself. However, the possibility of combinations is not endless; in fact, it is quite limited in that the forward-driving and self-wounding impulse which gives his thoughts no respite springs from the inner uniqueness of his personality. Although his thoughts seem to roam widely, they still are bound to the same intellectual processes that ever subjugate his thoughts to dominant necessities. We shall see to what extent Nietzsche's philosophy forms a circle and how toward the end the *man* again nears the *youth* through several of his most intimate and concealed thought-experiences. Relevant to the ways of his philosophy are the words, "There, behold a stream that through its many windings returns to its source!"

("Of Virtue that Makes Small," Z, III, 1). It is no coincidence that during his last period of creativity, Nietzsche arrived at his mystical teaching of the eternal recurrence: the picture of a *circle— eternal change in an eternal recurrence*—stands like a wondrous symbol and mysterious cypher over the entrance to his works.

At a boyish age, Nietzsche wrote what he called his first "juvenile attempt at literary play," an essay "about the origin of evil" ("Preface," GM, 3) in which he made God "quite properly, the *father* of evil." Conversationally, he also mentioned that this essay was proof of having given himself over to philosophical ruminations at a time when he was under the academic discipline of philology at Schulpforta.

If we follow Nietzsche from his early school years into the long period of his philological activities, we recognize quite clearly even here how his development from the beginning on takes its course superficially under the influence of a certain kind of compulsion. Although the strict philological schooling did contain such compulsion for the young firebrand, his richly creative strengths remained empty. Orientation came especially from his teacher, Professor Ritschl. Precisely here, the main pedagogical thrust was directed toward formal and outer relations in dealing with problems and methods, while the inner meanings of the written works took a back seat. Nietzsche's uniqueness later was marked by his taking problems almost exclusively from the inner world and subordinating logic to the psychological.

And yet even here under strict discipline and on barren ground, his spirit ripened early and accomplished much of distinction. A series of excellent philological studies designated his path from his student years until his professorship at Basel[12]. . . . For a time then, the cool strength of philological research was a unifying element for his splintered drives, while much that slumbered within him were shackling elements.

The pain caused by the strong talents that lay neglected while he pursued academic studies became no less than a deep suffering. It was the impulse for music, however, that he was not able to reject, and often he listened to tones at a time he wanted to listen to thoughts. Like resounding laments, these accompanied him through the years until his head pains made every pursuit of music impossible.

But no matter how great the contrast between the realms of specialized philology and later his philosophy, there was no lack of mediating features that led from one phase to the next. Although Ritschl's orientation sharpened the contrast, it also allowed Nietzsche's determined intellectuality to enlarge and hone itself productively. Within his intellectuality resided a drive for a certain formal and artistic rounding-out and virtuoso treatment of scholarly questions by intense delimitation and concentration upon a specific point. Nietzsche needed to bring each task to an artistic close, cast off what he had created, relegate it to the past, and then go on. Such a transition to other problems is natural for the philologist, as characterized by Nietzsche's saying, "A problem which has been solved ceases to concern us" (BGE, 80). But there are sharply divergent reasons for the transition to new problems and thoughts as found in philosophers' methods, including Nietzsche's.

The philologist tangentially and temporarily draws on the inner person only as required by the solution of a problem. For Nietzsche, on the other hand, the concern with a problem means above all, *insight:* to allow himself to be shaken to his depths, to be overwhelmed. To be convinced about the truth of a matter, meant for him "to be thrown in a heap," as he said. He took up a thought or idea as one takes up something fateful, and which enthralled his entire person: more than thinking an idea through, he lived it with passion and with such measureless abandon that it exhausted him. And, like something fated and which has played itself out, the ripened thought fell away from him. Only when sobriety ensued after each excitation did he allow his hard-won knowledge to work upon him in a purely intellectual way; only then did he pursue that knowledge with a calm and probing rationality. His notable drive for change in pursuing ideas in the realm of philosophical knowledge was conditioned by the tremendous drive for new emotions of a spiritual sort; and so, complete clarity was always only the companion of surfeit and exhaustion.

But even when he was exhausted, his *problems* never left him. The found solution, therefore, was for Nietzsche a signal, each time, for a *conversion;* only in this way could a problem be gripped and a solution be attempted anew. With genuine passion, and in a rearguard fashion, he inquired into what had driven him to the problem. Since "a problem which has been solved ceases to concern us," Nietzsche basically did not want to know about the ultimate solution of a problem. And that word which brought an ostensible and completely satisfying elucidation of a problem through successful thought, at the same time signified for him the tragedy of his life: he did not wish the problems under inquiry ever to cease to concern him; he continually wanted them to cause inner turmoil. To a certain extent, then, he resented the solutions that robbed him of his problems, and thus he threw himself upon solutions, each time, with the complete subtlety and oversubtlety of his skepticism and gloatingly forced them to yield up his problems again. He was happy with the damage inflicted upon himself and with his own sufferings! With certain justification, therefore, one can say this from the outset: The dynamics which gripped Nietzsche's thought, the perspectives of his passionate spirit, and what it was that would make a new turn and change impossible, all must ultimately remain *unexplainable* for him; he must oppose the force of all attempts at a solution, oppose the force that frayed his mind with deadly riddles—riddles that also crucified. When his inner upheavals had become stronger than his forced strength of mind, no escape or avoidance was possible. Then of necessity, the ending lost itself in darkness, pain, and mystery: like a tempestuous sea, the obsession of thought stimulated by emotions engulfed him.

If one follows Nietzsche's zig-zag path until the end, one comes close to that point at which he stood, in horror of a final elucidation and solution—and from which he unequivocally plunged into the eternal riddle of mysticism.

Nietzsche's intellectual talent distinguished itself further through two qualities, which were as useful for the philologist as for the later philosopher. The first was his talent for subtleties, his ingenuity in dealing with things so fine that they needed a tender and sure hand if they were not to be obliterated or disfigured. It is the same talent which, in my opinion, caused him to be more *keen* than *great* as a psychologist, or put another way, he was at his best in grasping and shaping subtleties. Highly appropriate in that regard is the expression he once used, "the filigree of things" (CW, 1), to indicate how things present themselves to the knower.

Nietzsche habitually searched out the hidden and the secretive, drawing them into the open. With empathy and intuition, he instinctively filled the gaps left by science. That characterized the greater part of Nietzsche's ingenuity . . . and broadened into an organic view which united details. In the service of disciplined philological critiques, he practiced that talent in order to draw conscientiously from old and neglected texts, but in these endeavors he was already prompted to go beyond purely acadcmic studies.* How this occurred is illustrated by his most significant philological work, his study *Contributions toward a Source Study and Criticism of Laertius Diogenes* (*Beiträge zur Quellenkunde und Kritik des Laertius Diogenes*, 1870).

Nietzsche's preoccupation with this work became the occasion for his pursuit of the lives of the ancient Greek philosophers and their connection with the total life of the Greeks. In his later works he discussed that point (HATH, 261). One sees how he presided over the ruins and gaps of the transmitted material and how he may have brooded over the means for recapturing the old figures, ecstatically wandering "amidst creations of the mightiest and purest types." He looks into the dawn of those days "as into a sculptor's workshop of such types." And with surprise, the question occurs to him, "What if Plato had remained free from the magical charm of Socrates; would he perhaps have found a higher type of philosophic man?" All that, however, is to be taken for more than a mere transition from the philologist to the philosopher. What revealed itself in his longing for creative thoughts while he was practicing dry scholarship also bares his high ambition. For good reasons Nietzsche did not enter philosophy by way of abstract academic specializations; he pursued studies toward a deeper conception of the philosophic life and its innermost meaning. And if we wish to designate the goal intended

---

*He read well, as he once noted, for "reading *well* means to read slowly, deeply, and cautiously with hind- and forethought, with doors left open, and with tender eyes and fingers" ("Preface," D, 5).

by the peregrinations and battles of his insatiable spirit, we may not find a more appropriate phrase than his longing to discover "a new, and hitherto undiscovered possibility for the philosophical life" (HATH, 261).

And so, the work on Laertius Diogenes, a purely philological study, is like a small, half-hidden gate in a wall, which leads right into the series of his later works that resemble a spacious structure. . . . Nietzsche's Greek studies showed him the entire panorama of Greek culture, and those pictures of ancient Hellenism uncovered a submerged art and religion from which he eagerly drank a "fresh, full life." He then placed his philological expertise in the service of cultural history, aesthetics and philosophical history, and he conquered their formalism.

Then the meaning of philology changed and deepened for him into something "which was neither a Muse nor a Grace but a messenger of the gods; and just as the Muses descended upon the dull and tormented Boëotian peasant, so philology comes into a world full of gloomy colors and pictures, a world filled with the deepest incurable pains, and philology speaks to people consolingly about the luminous god-figures in a blue and distant, happy fairyland."

These were among the concluding words of Nietzsche's inaugural address, *Homer and Classical Philology,* given at the University of Basel and printed in 1869 for a circle of friends only. Two years later, also privately printed, appeared another short work with the same intellectual orientation, *Socrates and Greek Tragedy,* which was incorporated with only minor changes in the connection of ideas into Nietzsche's greater and first ambitious philosophical work, *The Birth of Tragedy from the Spirit of Music,** published in 1872. Both works are solidly grounded in philology,

---

*At its appearance, this book provoked the liveliest displeasure of the philological "guild." The author had dared not only to include in his exposition the teachings of the frowned-upon philosopher Schopenhauer but also the artistic views of the equally maligned "musician of the future," Richard Wagner. A young philosophical hothead, Ulrich von Wilamowitz-Moellendorff, one of the outstanding representatives of classical philology in Germany, in an unpleasant and taste-

while he shaped his investigations into cultural philosophy; they contributed to his reputation among philological specialists. Yet, his investigations into the arts and history were to lead him from philology into a closed world-view of a specific philosophy. It was the world-view of Richard Wagner, joined to an artistic involvement with Schopenhauer's metaphysics. When we open Nietzsche's pages, we find ourselves in the thrall of Wagner, Master of Bayreuth.

Through him, Nietzsche first integrated philological and philosophical realism. That fusion lent truth to the words which ended his Basel lecture, *Homer and Classical Philology*, inverting a maxim by Seneca: *"philosophia facta est quae philologia fuit"* ["philosophy has become what philology was"]. "With that I mean to say," Nietzsche noted, "that all philological activities should be enveloped and hedged in by a philosophical world-

less fashion made himself the mouthpiece of the "guild's" one-sidedness. Without doing any justice to the uniqueness of Nietzsche's book, he attacked it violently from a narrow philological viewpoint in a pamphlet called *The Future Philology! A Response to Nietzsche's "The Birth of Tragedy,"* Berlin, 1872. In an open letter to Nietzsche (published June 23, 1872 in the *Norddeutschen Allgemeinen Zeitung*), Wagner rose to his defense, as did Erwin Rohde, already at that time a strong authority on Greek antiquity. In the well-written polemic [aided by ammunition given him privately by Nietzsche] called *Afterphilology* [a pun: "anus philology"] Rohde took up the position on the opponent's ground and rejected his accusations, whereupon von Wilamowitz responded with a replica *Future Philology! Second Act, A Reply to Attempts at Rescuing Friedrich Nietzsche's "The Birth of Tragedy,"* Berlin, 1873.

(These pitched theatrical polemics tarnished everyone's reputation. Nietzsche playfully hid behind Rohde, instead of confronting the challenge squarely, and completely alienated his admired benefactor, Professor Ritschl. Rohde who allowed himself to be coaxed into the rebuttals by his friendship with Nietzsche, suffered academic setbacks. Wagner was roundly ridiculed for his layman's pretentiousness. And Wilamowitz, whose own "star" first rose with his polemics against Nietzsche, retained traumatic memories of this episode throughout his long and distinguished academic career. Nietzsche's book made its major contribution by stimulating far-ranging reinterpretations of the ancient Greek spirit and civilization—editor.)

view in which all solitary and individual things are discarded, so that only the totally unified remains.

The spell that made Nietzsche a disciple of Wagner for years is explainable particularly by the fact that Wagner, in the context of Germanic life, wished to turn into reality the ideal of an art-culture which Nietzsche perceived in the context of Greek culture. Schopenhauer's metaphysics in the main contributed nothing more than a heightening of this ideal into the mystical and unfathomably meaningful, like an accent placed upon the *metaphysical interpretation* of all experience through art and the knowledge of art. One experiences this accent most clearly when one compares *Socrates and Greek Tragedy* with its elaborated version in *The Birth of Tragedy from the Spirit of Music*.

In that book Nietzsche aims to relate the developments of all the arts back to the operation of two diametrically opposed "artistic drives of nature," which he attributed to two Greek gods of the arts, namely, the Dionysian and the Apollonian. The Dionysian he took to be the orgiastic element as it is lived in blissful raptures, in the mixture of pain and lust, of joy and horror, and in the self-obliterating drunkenness of Dionysian festivals. In them the conventional barriers and boundaries of existence are broken, so that the individual seems to melt into the totality of nature again. The principle of individuation is broken and "the road to the Mothers of Being[13] and to the innermost core lies open." We are brought closer to the essence of this drive, through the physiological appearance of intoxication. Music is its corresponding art. In contrast stands a sculptor's form-shaping drive which is embodied in Apollo, the god of all artistic power in the plastic arts. United in him are measured demarcation, freedom from wild impulses, and the wisdom of tranquillity. He must be viewed as the noble expression of "the apotheosis of the *principii individuationis*," "whose law of individuality—that is, the imperative retention of its boundaries—constitutes the *measure* of man in the Hellenic sense" (BT, 4). The power of the drive symbolized by Apollo reveals itself physiologically in the beautiful illusion of the world of dreams. His art is that of the sculptor's.

In the reconciliation and union of these initially conflicting drives, Nietzsche perceived the origin and essence of Attic tragedy and thought; they were Dionysian and Apollonian drives, as personified by the two gods of the arts. Further, Attic tragedy developed from the dithyrambic chorus that celebrates the god's suffering, and which originally consisted only of the chorus. It was an art-form that magically transformed the singers through excitation, so that they felt themselves to be satyrs or servants of the god Dionysus; and, as such, they beheld their lord and master. The chorus reached a state of Apollonian completion when it gave birth to its vision. Attic drama became fulfilled when "the Apollonian element rendered perceptible to the viewers' senses the Dionysian insights and mode of operation." And "the choral parts that interlace the tragedy, in a sense, form the womb of the drama proper" (BT, 8); they are its Dionysian element, while the dialogue is the essential Apollonian component. Through the dialogues in the scenes, the heroes speak as the representations of the original tragic hero, personified by Dionysus; they are the apparent masks behind which divinity is present.

We shall see at the end of our book in what odd fashion Nietzsche ultimately comes back to these ideas, although he tried to represent various phases of his development and ideological peregrinations as if they had not been central expressions of his mind but, in a sense, only the arbitrary and adopted masks, "Dionysian illusions," behind which his Dionysian self had eternally remained the same, with a sort of divine reflectiveness. At the end of our book, we will understand the causes of this self-delusion.

The significance which Nietzsche attached to the Dionysian is characteristic of his entire mentality: as a philologist and with his interpretation of Dionysian culture, he sought a new entrance to the world of the ancients; as a philosopher, he made this interpretation the basis for his first unified view of the world; and, beyond all of his later peregrinations, that view still surfaces during his last creative phase. During that phase, however, it was transformed because its connection with the metaphysics of Schopenhauer and Wagner had been sundered; yet it kept itself intact because even then his own, hidden spiritual inclinations sought expression; transformed, it appeared in images and symbols during his last, most lonely and inward experience. Above all, Nietzsche, during his Dionysian intoxication, sensed something homogeneous in his own nature—a mysterious unity of being in woe and bliss, self-wounding and self-deification—a life of the emotions heightened into excess, in which all things become mutually dependent and swallow each other up. That, as we note, always recurs in Nietzsche.

The sharpest contrast between the Dionysian and the art-culture born from it is formed by the intellectual direction of persons inclined to theory or alienated from intuition, and baptized in the name of Socrates. In *The Birth of Tragedy*, Nietzsche attempts to portray in broad strokes the intellectual directions of philosophy and science through the centuries up to our own time. With Socrates, whose teachings of rationality turned against the original Hellenic instincts in order to tame them, "Greek taste turns around in favor of dialectics," and then began that triumphal march of the theoretical which attempted to discover the fundaments of being in order to correct them through rationality. Kant's critique first put an end to this optimism, in that he pointed to the limits of knowledge through reason. And as Nietzsche wittily remarked later, philosophy was reduced to "a theory of knowledge, in fact no more than a timid 'periodism' and a doctrine of forbearance, a philosophy that never even crosses the threshold and embarrassingly *denies* itself the right of entrance" (BGE, 204). And with those assertions, Nietzsche managed to create room for the regeneration of philosophy through Schopenhauer, who finally opened up an entrance to the unexplored self and its refashioning through intuitive knowledge.[14]

During 1873–76, Nietzsche published *Untimely Meditations*, a collective title for what represented the spirit and sense of his preceding work; they comprise four short pieces, intended as an effective "counter to the times, and thus *for* its time and, it is hoped, for the benefit of future times." The first is entitled *David Strauss: The Confessor and the Writer* and consisted of a devastating critique of a popular and widely celebrated book by Strauss, *The Old and the New Faith (Der Alte und der Neue Glaube)*, 1872, and an attack on the one-sided intellectualism[15] of our modern education. Of lasting interest is the second and highly valuable work which Nietzsche called *Of the Use and Disadvantage of History for Life* whose main thoughts recur in his last works in a modified but no less clear way than in his earlier conception of the Dionysian. The word "history"[16] refers to the life of the mind in a general sense, in contrast to the instinctual life: recognition of the past, as well as knowledge of what has transpired, in contrast to the full life-force of the present and future becoming. The work dealt with the question of how is knowledge to be subordinated to life? Nietzsche sharpens his point with the following sentence: "Only insofar as history serves life, will we serve it." But it is of service to him only as long as the most important spiritual function in humans remains intact relative to the dismembering and burdening influences of intellectuality: "the *plastic strength* of a human being, a nation, a culture . . . I mean that strength which promotes growth outward in a unique way, which can reshape and absorb the past and the foreign, and which can heal wounds, replace the lost, and reproduce broken forms" (UM, II, 1). Otherwise, we will be afflicted by a chaos of strange riches that flow toward us, which we are incapable of dominating or assimilating, and whose multiplicity will therefore dangerously threaten the integrity and the organic constitution of our personality. In that case we would become the passive arena in which seesaw battles ensue, so that the most diverse thoughts, moods, and value judgments incessantly threaten each other; we suffer under the victories of the one as well as the defeats of the others, without being able to become their master.

Here, for the first time, we find reference to Nietzsche's much-discussed concept of *decadence,* which plays a great role in his later works. Not without justification does this first portrayal of the danger of decadence warn us about Nietzsche's own state of mind as we have described it. Already here, we can recognize clearly its spiritual origin: it is a secret anguish that prompts his passionate spirit to endure the constant crush of knowledge[17] and stream of ideas. All of his thinking had a forceful impact upon his inner life, so that the fullness of the inward and contending experiences threatened to burst the circumscribed boundaries of his personality. He said, "It should also not be concealed that experiences which stimulated certain painful feelings stemmed mostly from myself and only serve as a comparison with the feelings of others"* ("Preface," UM, II). What he found to be taking place within himself signaled a generalized danger that threatened his own time; and this escalated itself later into a deadly threat posed against all of mankind, a notion that called upon him to become mankind's redeemer and savior.

The consequence, however, of this situation is a peculiar double meaning which courses through the entire work, becoming immediately evident to the knowledgeable Nietzsche reader: since that element of the reigning "spirit of the times" which called up his serious reflections was something essentially different from his own spiritual problem, he turned against two dissimilar things, without discriminating between them. First he inveighed against the deterioration of a full, rich spiritual life because of the chilling and laming influence of a one-sided education of mental faculties: "Modern man, in the last instance, drags around with him an enormous amount of indigestible wisdom-stones that on occasion rumble around in one's belly, as in the fairy tale" (UM, II, 4). "Inwardly there resides then a feeling akin to that of a snake which has swallowed a squirrel and placidly lies in the sun, avoiding all except the most necessary motion. . . . Everyone who passes by has the single wish that this kind of 'education' not perish through indigestibility" (UM, II, 4). Second, Nietzsche turned against the suffocating effects of intellectuality upon the psychic life. As well, he turned against the elicited contention of disparate and wild power-drives.

The difference may be compared with a spiritual denseness or spiritual madness. In Nietzsche the most abstract thoughts habitually could reverse themselves into the power of moods which could carry him off with immediate and unpredictable force.

The portrait of our age as drawn by Nietzsche had to be a mixture of these diametrically opposed affects of the intellect; and, in regard to the chaotic unchaining of his spiritual life, two

---

*Compare Nietzsche's comment, "What I have said against the 'historical sickness,' that I said as one who slowly and laboriously learned to recuperate from it" ("Preface," HATH, II, 1).

different causative elements also merged. The question concerns not only purely intellectual influences or dangers posed to the practical mind by instinctive demands but also concerns the inherited and ingrained influences of times past, which long ago stemmed from an intellectual source but which now live within us in the form of drives and subjective feelings.

The self-contained personality is threatened by exterior dangers as well as those carried within since birth, namely, that "instinctive contrariness" which is the inheritance of all the late-born, for the late-born are half-castes.

The conquest of the disadvantage that "history"—learned or experienced—can bring, lies in turning to the "unhistorical." By "unhistorical"[18] Nietzsche refers to a return to unconsciousness or the will to not-knowing [a selective discarding or retention of historical facts] or limiting one's horizon; without boundaries there is no life. "Every living thing can only become healthy, strong, and fruitful within a limited horizon. . . . The unhistoric is similar to an enveloping atmosphere in which life as such is created . . . in an excess of historical facts, man ceases to be" (OUDH, 1, 2).

. . . History can be viewed from three perspectives,[19] without falling into any direction exclusively. *Monumentalistic* history focuses on the great figures of the past and relates to their work and will: they become inspirational predecessors and companions. Through the spirit of *antiquarian* history, one wanders over the landscape of the past as if it were the ground of an earlier life—as one would re-enter the state of one's own childhood in which everything, even the smallest detail, appears valuable and significant: "one understands the wall, the domed entrance, the town council's ordinances, the folk festivals that are like the pictures in the diary of one's youth, and one again finds oneself in all these—with one's strength, diligence, pleasures, judgments, stupidities, and bad habits. Here, one can live and live freely, one says to oneself, because we are tenacious and cannot be broken overnight. And so, with this 'we' one surveys the ephemeral and wondrous individual life and feels himself to be the spirit of the household, the family, and the city" (OUDH, 3). *Critical* history looks at the past judgmentally, with the objective of undermining the past in order to construct a future. And for that purpose one needs extra strength because even greater than the danger of becoming a mere enthusiast or collector of facts is the possibility of remaining a naysayer. "It is always a dangerous process that also endangers life: . . . Since we are the products of earlier generations . . . it is not possible to free ourselves completely from that chain. . . . At best, we confront inherited and ingrained nature and our knowledge . . . we plant new habits and a new instinct—a second nature—so that our first and inherited nature withers away. It is an attempt, as it were, to construe *a posteriori* a past from which one would have liked to originate instead of the one from which one did descend. But here and there, one does gain a victory" (OUDH, 3).

One can apply the three ways of looking at history to Nietzsche's own development, in the sense that the beginnings of the philologist are linked to the *antiquarian* view which is followed by the *monumentalistic* that prompted him to become a disciple at the feet of the masters, and finally his later positivistic phase that can be described as a *critical* view of history. However, when Nietzsche conquered even the critical view, all three views melt into one, as we find it expressed in the pointed paradox of his formulation: The historical is subordinate to the individual life whose constant requirement is the unhistorical. A strong, individual nature is equally historical and unhistorical and therefore an inheritor of all the past, fruitful because it lords over the past and enormously fills the life of the present. Such an inheritor thus becomes the first harbinger of a new culture, and as a bearer of the past he becomes a shaper of the future. . . . He is one of the great "untimely ones" who stand out in their own time as strangers, although the present gathers its greatest strength through them.

Here lies the first spur to the thoughts of Nietzsche's last creative phase: the solitary genius of mankind, who alone is capable of interpreting the totality of the past from the vantage point of the present and therefore also of deciding the future as a totality with its goal and significance—even into the far reaches of all eternity.

On the face of it, the roots of this view reach down into Nietzsche's philological realm, which led him to avail himself knowingly of the culture of antiquity. Knowledge and existence were always one in his intellectual makeup; and so, for Nietzsche to be a classical philologist meant to be a Greek as well. Certainly, this must have increased the instinctual and torturesome contradictoriness which pointed up for him the contrast between the modern and the ancient; at the same time here were the means to come to terms with the present through the past and to build a future. . . .

Discussions dedicated to two such "untimely ones"—that is, ones out of their time and of the past and future—are found in Nietzsche's *Untimely Meditations:* "Schopenhauer as Educator" and "Richard Wagner in Bayreuth." In these overflowing and statuesque portrayals of genius, it is particularly clear to what extent the attempted culture of these untimely ones peaked in a cult of genius. Through such geniuses mankind not only finds its educators but also its leaders, prophets, and ultimate goals. The representation of the single, noble solitary, for whose sake alone the remaining "mass products of nature" exist is one of Schopenhauer's thematic ideas which Nietzsche never relinquished. Something within his inner spirit thirsted insatiably for the escalation of the egoistic ideal of the self, as well as the dark side of the human lot, and for the "solitary" and "heroic." During his middle period, he ostensibly departed from the earlier representation of genius because it had lost something of its metaphysical background that would allow the great "solitary" to rise to superior human significance, like a figure out of a higher and truer world. But his thoughts about the cult of genius harbored what was to be continued at the end of his development, namely, as figurations in the grip of inspired madness. As a substitute for metaphysical interpretations, Nietzsche was to develop the positive life-value of genius that ranged far above Schopenhauer's conception.

As long as the cult of genius, so to speak, remained metaphysical within human development, it stretched like a chain of which individual links were of equal value. They were not regarded as essential parts of the developing line of humanity; they "do not continue a process but live timeless and simultaneously," they form "a type of bridge over the barren stream of *becoming*. . . . A giant calls out to another one through the desolate connecting rooms of time, undisturbed by the malicious, noisy dwarfs who crawl away, as highly intellectual conversations continue" (OUDH, 9). Since mindless dwarfism determines the whole development of history and its events, as well as its laws, one thing is certain: "The goal of mankind cannot lie in its ends but only *in its highest types*."

But since the highest types only bring to the surface what rests in human depths, its metaphysical soil, so they distinguish themselves from the mass of mankind mainly by displaying a divine nakedness. The man of the mass, however, wears thousands of layers that cover his true being, the world, and all of life's surfaces which in spots harden and become impenetrable. If a great thinker despises people, he despises their laziness which, according to Schopenhauer, makes them into the likes of the factory-produced. . . . The person who does not wish to belong to the mass needs only cease being smug with respect to himself. A loving upbringing and solicitude are the results of this attitude, which puts everyone on an equal footing because it honors the metaphysical kernel within the husk; this view, however, is far distant from Nietzsche's later assertions about slavery and tyranny.

Were this metaphysical background to be destroyed, as it was in Nietzsche's later philosophy, the supra-sensual being would dissolve in the unending *becoming* of reality and the solitary might raise himself above the mass only through a difference in characteristics that matches the greatest difference in rank: in that he represents the quintessence of this process of becoming, he embraces it possibly in its entirety, while the man of the mass can only experience it fragmentarily. This solitary one *as* a solitary person would be capable, as it were, of giving meaning to the long development called history; he would not himself be created, like the Schopenhauerian man, out of supra-sensual stuff, but for all that he would be a creator through and through and be able to replace for the world that significance of things in which the metaphysicians believe. Instead of many equals in rank . . . there is only the great solitary in Nietzsche's late philosophy, who represents himself as the peak of everything. As the culmination of historical development and as the highest example of the genre, he is most lonely but also hard and domineering toward those below him, giving them a defined hierarchical order. . . . It can readily be understood why with Nietzsche the cult of genius first grew into something monstrous in order to persuasively counter the Schopenhauerian.

The following represent four ideas rife during Nietzsche's first philosophical phase, which continued to engage him in constantly changing guise and view until the end: the Dionysian, decadence, the untimely,[20] and the cult of genius. Wherever we find Nietzsche or his ideas, the other is invariably present, and to the degree that he injects himself ever more personally into his philosophy, he fashions ideas ever more characteristically. If one observes his ideas in their process of change and variegations, they appear almost immense and all too complicated. If however one tries to peel from them their constant features and what remains despite changes, one is astonished by the simplicity and steadfastness of the problems. "Ever someone different and yet always the same!" was an observation Nietzsche could make about himself.

The Wagner-Schopenhauer views of the world gained such deep meaning for Nietzsche that later, after all his battles, he again approached their basic views but from a completely different intellectual direction. That shows the affinity between their world-view and one which slumbered within him. Elevated from the philological to the philosophical realm, Nietzsche, doubtless, felt like a prisoner from whom the chains had dropped. . . . His artistic instinct luxuriated in the revelations of Wagnerian music; his strong predisposition for religious and moralistic exaltations thrived in the metaphysical interpretation of that art and its uplifting potentials; his comprehensive and thorough knowledge, mirrored in his conceptions of Greek culture, served the new world-view well. Just as in Wagner's person the genius of art and the "releasing redeemer" had become reality, so the role of the knower and scientific mediator fell to Nietzsche; for that reason, he saw his mission to be that of the philosopher. But hard-won knowledge only triggered the full unfolding of his artistic and religious mode. . . . What he sought in the lives of the ancient philosophers became a reality: thinking as experience, knowledge as a co-worker and co-creator of a new culture. Every spiritual fiber had to work together in thinking: he demanded the total human being. Nietzsche expresses his sense of release when he exclaims, "Oh! There is magic in these battles because whoever views them must also participate!" (BT, 15).

And while his individual manner of thinking roamed more freely, that phase in Nietzsche's life also stood for those deepest—near-feminine—inner needs for personal adoration, for being looked-up to, for fullest gratification—which later and painfully had to find gratification through his self. Of the Wagner-Schopenhauer philosophies and the felicitous happinesses which resulted, the most valuable was his personal relationship with Wagner and his enthusiastic regard for him. Nietzsche's enthusiasm was enflamed by a personality different from his own but in whom, at the same time, he thought his own essential ideals to be embodied. All this suffused Nietzsche's writings with something of a healthy glow, if not with naïveté which was pointedly different from his later idiosyncratic works. It is as if Nietzsche first understood and ferreted out his own self through the picture of his master, Wagner, and his philosopher-teacher, Schopenhauer. For with instinctive modesty he rejected at that time the self-conscious art of making himself the "object and experiment of the knowledge-seeker," that art which later made him so great and so deathly ill. "How is a person to know himself? He is an encapsulated subject; and if the hare has seven skins, a human being has seven times seventy skins that he might peel away and still not be able to say, 'Here is the real *you*,' without further encasement." "With that comes a torturesome and dangerous beginning of self-excavation and a forcible descent into the next layer of his being: How easy it was to injure himself to the point that no doctor could heal him" ("Schopenhauer as Educator," 1). And for that reason, he tells the young generation which desires insights into the self, "What has your soul attracted, what has it dominated and, at the same time, made happy? Imagine a series of such venerated objects and perhaps they will reveal to you a law, the fundamental law of your true self. Compare these objects and see how they form a stepladder upon which you have climbed up to yourself; your true being does not lie deeply hidden within you but rages far above you . . ." (1).

With a frankness he lost later during the time of his most painful self-analysis, he bares the motives that prompted his discipleship from the beginning and his fervent searching, at the same time, for a sophisticated "guide and taskmaster." "Let me stay a while, in my discussion, with something I imagined so frequently and urgently as nothing else during my youth. While I roamed to my heart's content in my wishes, I thought that fate had removed from me the terrible effort and obligation to educate myself; and so, at the right time, I found a philosopher who was an educator, a true philosopher whom one could obey without hesitation because one could trust him more than oneself ("Schopenhauer as Educator," 2). It is interesting to note how, for that purpose, Nietzsche attempts to find the ideal person behind Schopenhauer* the thinker, and how in contact with Wagner he proceeds from a deep affinity in their mutual natures. In fact, there is a surprising correspondence, as described by Nietzsche, between the natural and mental dispositions of Wagner and the "many-sidedness" of his own, noted in the first section of this book. And so, Nietzsche says in "Richard Wagner in Bayreuth," "Each of his drives surges into the infinite, all are joyous gifts for existence and wish to tear themselves loose and seek their own gratification; the greater their fullness, the greater was the tumult and so much greater was the clash when they converged" (3).

With the appearance of "mental and moral" manliness, in Wagner's life, his "multiplicity" merged and, at the same time, caused a "split within." "In a terrible fashion, his nature seemed reduced to two drives or spheres. At bottom, a gusting will stirred with a sudden streaming out from hollows and ravines and

---

*Compare "Schopenhauer as Educator," 2: "I sensed having found in that educator and philosopher one for whom I have searched for a long time, albeit only in books, and that was a great deficiency. All the more then did I strain to penetrate the book and visualize the living person whose great testament I was reading and who promised to make heirs only of those who aspired to be more than readers, namely, to become his sons and pupils."

toward the light, demanding power. . . . The whole of the stream plunged into one valley and then bored into the darkest ravines; during the night when this semi-subterranean upheaval occurred, a star appeared high over Wagner . . . " (2). We gaze into the *other* sphere of Wagner. "It is his own primal knowledge which Wagner experiences in himself, and he venerates it as if it were a religious secret. The knowledge and experience are wondrous because each sphere of his being remains true to the other: the creative, innocent, and lighter sphere and the dark, untamed and tyrannical sphere" (3).

"In the mutual containment of both these deep powers and in the yielding of one to the other lay the necessary condition through which he could retain his wholeness and self" (3).

Toward the end of that Wagner piece (9), Nietzsche also sought to understand Wagner's music by way of its uniqueness and personal affinity; the genius of Wagner became a kind of mirroring of Nietzsche's own spirit:

> . . . his music submits itself with a certain grimness to the determined way of the drama, unremitting like fate, while the fiery soul of his art for once craves a roaming about without reins in freedom and in the wilderness.
>
> Above all the awesome individuals and the conflicts of their passions, above all the maelstrom of contrasts, there hovers . . . a mighty symphonic rationality which constantly asserts a harmony throughout all contentiousness.
>
> At no time is Wagner more himself than at the time that difficulties multiply and when he can rule with the imperious desire of a lawgiver, when he can tame recalcitrant masses through simple rhythms, and when he can assert his will over a confusing multiplicity of demands and wishes.

But precisely this similarity of their natures led Nietzsche ultimately to develop his own intellect, pursuing lonely paths; it was only a matter of time before he had to tear himself away from Wagner. As soon as Nietzsche had reached a high point in this phase, the first step of his unavoidable descent was already clearly foretold. It appears later as a complete reversal of facts when he remarked in his injudicious book *The Case of Wagner*, "My greatest experience was a *recovery*. Wagner belongs only to my sicknesses" ("Preface"). One can say, on the contrary, that only long after Nietzsche's break with Wagner did his development turn into sickness, and in a sense his Wagner period belonged to his conquered health. Still, one should not ignore the truth in his assertion that he had not yet achieved his own high point, no matter how healthy and happy he had been during the Wagner phase.

That state of health he could only have maintained at the cost of foregoing greatness. Above all, to be transformed from disciple to master, he would have needed to enter his self. Since, however, his nature compulsively sought discipleship in a religious sense, there remained one possibility, namely, to unite disciple and master within himself, even though it meant suffering and even though it meant perishing through the merging of both. Of his way to greatness, Zarathustra's assertion is appropriate, "Peaks and abyss—those are not joined as one!"

Nietzsche's break with Wagner has received the most diverse interpretations. Some have thought that it was prompted by idealistic motives, an irresistible quest for truth, and also as something human, all-too-human.[21] In reality both converged in the same sense as they did during Nietzsche's very first transformation when he turned away from religious faith. It was precisely because he enjoyed peacefulness and an intellectual home in Wagner's world-view which seemed to fit smoothly and softly like "a healthy skin," that that "skin" —in Zarathustra— prompted an itch to strip it away; seemingly, his "overjoy became his hardship" and allowed him to "be wounded by his happiness." In a brief passage headed "Speculation on the Origin of the Free Spirit," Nietzsche charts origins and directions born from an all-too-strong bliss and world-view: "Just as in equatorial regions glaciers grow when the sun burns them with a greater glow than ever before, so a strong and spreading free-spiritedness may also be proof that somewhere the glow of feeling has grown extraordinarily" (HATH, 232).

Only through his self-willed and sought-out pain did his spirit grow the combative, tough armor with which he went into battle against his old ideals. Undoubtedly, he found it a release from a last dependence by doing without the elevated and the beautiful. And yet, this emancipation represented an act of renunciation; he suffered the consequences of such self-inflicted wounds.

The break was final and for Wagner it was completely unexpected. With his creation of *Parsifal,* Wagner reached Catholicizing tendencies, while Nietzsche's intellectual development took a sudden turn toward the positivistic philosophy of the English and the French. The break between Nietzsche and Wagner not only meant a separation of minds; it tore apart as well a relationship in which both had stood as close as only son to father, as brother to brother. Neither could forget the break. As late as the Fall of 1882, a half year before Wagner's death, an attempt was made during the Bayreuth festivals, when *Parsifal* premiered, to mention Nietzsche to the Master. At that time, Nietzsche was staying in the vicinity, in the Thüringian village of Tautenburg, near Dornburg, and his old friend Fraülein von Meysenbug thought unjustifiably that he and Wagner could be brought together for a reconciliation. The attempt failed, as Wagner left the room in great agitation and forbade anyone to mention Nietzsche's name ever again in his presence. From about that time originated the following letter in which Nietzsche eloquently describes his own position in the break with Wagner:

And now, my dear friend, till now all is well, and on Saturday eight days hence we will see each other.

Perhaps you did not receive my last letter? I wrote it on a Sunday 14 days ago. I would think that a pity; in it, I described for you a *very happy moment:* many good things came to me with a rush, and the "bestest" of these things was your letter of assent!

[However: If there is good mutual trust, it does not matter *even* if letters are lost.][22]

I have thought about you often and have shared so many different things that have been elevating, touching, and gay, even to the point of having lived with my esteemed woman friend. You cannot know *how* novel and strange that seems to an old hermit like myself! How often this has made me laugh at myself!

With regard to Bayreuth, I am satisfied not to *have to* be there; and yet, if I could be near you in quite ghostly fashion and whisper this-and-that in your ear, even the music of *Parsifal* should be tolerable to me (otherwise it is intolerable). I would like you to read beforehand my little essay "Richard Wagner in Bayreuth"; friend [Paul] Rée certainly has a copy. In regard to this man and his art, I have lived through a great deal—it was a very long PASSION—I can find no other word for it. The renunciation, finally made necessary by my rediscovery of myself, belongs to the hardest and most melancholy moments of my fate. The last words Wagner wrote to me appear in a handsome presentation copy of *Parsifal:* "To my dear friend Friedrich Nietzsche. Richard Wagner, Senior Church Councillor."[23] Exactly at the same time he received from me my book *Human, All-Too-Human*— and with that everything became sky *blue* [that is, "very clear"], but it also brought everything to an end.

How often have I experienced in many possible ways just *this*: "Everything is clear, but also everything is at an end!"

And how happy I am, my beloved friend Lou, to be able to think now about the two of us, "Everything is on the verge of beginning and yet *everything is clear!*" Trust me! Let us trust one another!

With very best wishes for your trip.

Your friend
Nietzsche

Tautenburg near Dornburg (Thüringen)[24]

When I read this brief description, he reappears to me in recollection of a joint trip from Italy through Switzerland when we visited the estate of Tribschen[25] near Lucerne, a locale where he had spent unforgettable times with Wagner. For a long, long while, he sat silent on the banks of the lake and was deeply immersed in heavy memories; then, while drawing in the moist sand with his cane, he softly spoke of those times past. And when he looked up, he cried.

Nietzsche's heaviest physical suffering had coincided with his inner and outer self-release from the influences of Wagner and the philosophy of Schopenhauer. Physically and mentally those storms and pains brought him close to bodily and spiritual death. His illness had broken out during the years of heightened productivity, stimulated by much too far-ranging and irritable preoccupation with scientific examinations of philosophical problems, the stifling mores of the time, the art of Wagner, and with music itself. It is surely not coincidental that even the last fateful outbreak of headaches at the end of the eighties also followed upon a period of tremendous spiritual creativity and productivity. When he felt himself to be most ready and healthy amid the fullness of his powers, he was constantly able to cope with illness; and times of involuntary leisure and rest always brought with them recuperation which held catastrophe at bay.

Seen purely from a physical point of view, this process mirrored something of that strange pathological feature of the "overhealth" of his spiritual life against whose high point sickness would surge and overflow. Out of this flooding he would constantly emerge to health because of the tenacious strength of his tremendous nature.[26]

As long as he was able to contain the pains and feel an inner energy, suffering could not yet dent his indestructibility and self-assertiveness. And so, he wrote in a letter from Basel, on May 12, 1878, in a tone of confident mischief, "Health vacillates and is dangerous—but, I almost said, 'of what concern is my health to me?'"

One hears the bitter lament: "Nothing seems to help me anymore; pains were too excruciating. . . . Always it is said: Endure! Endure! Oh, one can have one's fill of patience. We need to have more patience for patience!" There were indications of an anticipated stepping-down from his professorship at Basel: "I cannot deny that I find myself in the position of being tortured like an animal or of being in an antechamber of hell. *Apparently* that would cease with the giving up of my academic activity, or even *possibly* all activities. . . ." [April 23, 1879, to Paul Rée].

During the same time he had written in a quiet tone of submission, from Geneva: "Things are not at all well with me, but I am an old bearer of suffering and will continue to drag along my burden—but not for much longer, I hope!"

Soon thereafter, in May of 1879, he resigned his professorship, and forever was enveloped by loneliness. The rejection of teaching activities was difficult for him, though basically it was a rejection of further strict academic work. As he wrote to Rée, he considered himself a "sick person who regrettably was seven-eighths blind and unable to read any longer without headaches, and then only for quarter-hour stretches." He would have been prevented from thoroughly researched formulations of his ideas. The lectures he had given at the University and Pädagogium in Basel showed the sweeping scope of his studies.

At that time, at any rate, he still had limited himself to studies of Hellenism and, from the standpoint of philosophy, remained fettered to a metaphysical system. But his later emancipation from the compulsion of this system would have worked all the more favorably under other conditions of health. The cultural picture he elicited from Greek life, which he generalized into a profound view of the world and of human life through the eyes of a metaphysician, would have broadened eventually, with further humanistic research, into a total picture of the development of mankind's history. With the finesse of empathy and an artistic power for reconstructing, he was destined precisely for great historical-philosophical accomplishments. But his urge toward productivity would have been hampered by losing himself too greatly in subjectivity. Often he had felt that the more winged, urgent and passionate one's thoughts, the more comprehensive and severe must be the matter and form by which one is dominated and bound. Up to the last, for that reason, we always find in his works strenuous and fruitless attempts to broaden his horizons and to base his thinking on scientific grounds. There is something of the hopeless beating of the wings of an eagle about all this. His illness *necessitated* taking himself as the material of his thought, as well as the submission of his self to a philosophical world-picture and the spinning out of it from his own inner being. If all this were otherwise, perhaps he would not have been able to accomplish things so individualistic and unique. And yet, one cannot help but look back with deep regret upon this turning point in Nietzsche's fate and that uncanny *compulsion* toward self-isolation. One cannot escape the feeling that the greatness reserved for him passed him by.

At that point, Nietzsche's night began. One after another, here vanished his acquired ideals, his health, his working strength, his circle of influence—everything which had brought brightness, glow and warmth into his life. It was a cataclysmic collapse, and it was like being buried under its ruins. Then began his *dark times* ("The Wanderer and His Shadow," HATH, II, 191).

The works which followed, unlike the preceding ones, did not originate from a goal-oriented fullness within him; rather they tell us how he slowly groped his way forward with painful, combative, and finally victorious motion toward an obscure goal in his night.

"As I went forward alone," he confessed many years later in *Human, All-Too-Human* (II, "Preface," 3), "I shuddered; not long afterwards I became ill, more than ill, namely, tired out by the relentless disappointment with everything that remains for us moderns to be enthusiastic about. . . ." But, he does not lament as he fights his way through the ruins. He is correct about the charm of those writings when he says "that here speaks a sufferer and renouncer, as if he were *not* a sufferer and renouncer" (5).

And he always creates anew and discovers things anew. He descends far below the world of ruins, boring, undermining, and rummaging among its last foundations, searching out with eyes that are accustomed to the night, the hidden treasures of the inner earth. Like another Trophonius[27] who cunningly slips in and out of the earth, he can give an explanation of the outer world and interpret its riddles from the depths of the world below. And so, we see him as a *"subterranean man* at work, digging and excavating, moving forward cautiously and with gentle relentlessness, without betraying much of the consequences of his long renunciation of light and air." And with that comes an intimate question with which he looks back upon years past, and which enlightens our examination of his future development: "Does it not seem as if . . . perhaps he *wants* his own protracted darkness, the unintelligible, the hidden, and the riddles because he knows what lies at the end of them: His own tomorrow, his own salvation, and perhaps his own glowing *break of day?*" (D, "Preface," 1).

58

[In a letter of July 3, 1882 to Lou Salomé, Nietzsche writes:]

My dear friend,

Now the sky above me is bright! At noon yesterday, I felt as if it was my birthday: *You*[28] sent your consent, the loveliest present that anyone could have given me now. My sister sent cherries, Teubner sent the first three printed pages of proofs for *The Gay Science;* and, along with all that, I have just finished the very last part of that manuscript and thus the work of six years (1876–82), my entire "free-wheeling thinking" [*"Freigeisterei"*—loosely, "wild and unpedantic critical speculations"]. Oh, what years! What tortures of all sorts, what isolation and weariness toward life! And equally poised against death *and* life, I brewed my medicine, concocted of my thoughts with their small stripe of *unclouded sky* above. Oh, dear friend, whenever I think about all that, I am moved and touched and do not know how it did *succeed:* I am filled with self-compassion and a feeling of victory. For it *is* a victory, a complete one, because even my health has reappeared, though I know not from where, and everyone tells me that I look younger than ever before. Heaven preserve me from doing foolish things! But, from now on, in matters upon which *you* will advise me, I shall be WELL advised and need not be afraid.

In regard to *winter,* I have been thinking *seriously and exclusively* about Vienna. The winter plans of my sister are quite independent of mine, and I have *no* second thoughts about that. The south of Europe is far removed from my mind now. No longer do I wish to be alone, and I wish to learn again how to become a human being. Ah, in *this* workaday goal, I have yet to learn practically everything!

Accept my thanks, dear friend! *Everything,* as you have said, will be well.

All the best to our Rée!

Yours entirely,

F. N.

Tautenburg near Dornburg (Thüringen)

With these feelings of self-compassion and self-admiration,

Nietzsche looked back upon a period of intellectual activity. As for what lay ahead, we already sense the wounds he will incur in formulating a new view of the world, only to fall into the sickness out of which he will create his renewed health. His originality then expresses itself less in theories and insights than in the strength with which he tore himself loose from old ideals in order to understand them. He did not, like others, attain a heightened independence and spiritual activity through intellectual development that leaves one indifferent and cold towards abandoned and unripe ideas. His forceful indignation against earlier thought was *accompanied*—and not *determined*—by intellectual reasons. When he began changing his ideas, we always note that Nietzsche takes up new ideas as he finds them, with a certain uncritical dependence. The new theories, as such, form only a temporary "foreground philosophy" (BGE, 289)—a favorite Nietzschean phrase—while conflicts play themselves out decisively within the hidden inner background.

The more he is entwined with the old, the more forceful is his leap into the new; the change represents a complete uprooting from familiar soil. The greater the effort, the deeper is the inner meaning of the change. In a certain sense, one can say that the seeming inner dependence with which Nietzsche temporarily yields to a foreign mode of thought, straightaway harbors an heroic kind of independence. While he is tempted by the most precious ideas, he submits defenselessly to that circle of thoughts toward which he feels himself a stranger and secretly an antagonist. He captures that process in these lovely words: "A victory and a conquered fortress are no longer your concern; your concern is truth—but also your defeat is no longer your concern" ("To what extent the thinker loves his enemy," D, 370).

If one is to do justice to Nietzsche's unmediated changes of attitudes and understand the origins of his first positivistic work, one must take into account a work which sprang surprisingly and unexpectedly from his spirit. After his enthusiastic work "Richard Wagner in Bayreuth" (1876, a part of *Untimely Meditations*), there originated in the Winter of 1876–77 the first of his collections of aphorisms, *Human, All-Too-Human: A Book for Free Spirits*. The book was dedicated to the memorial celebration of

Voltaire, who died on May 30, 1778; it contained an appendix entitled "Mixed Opinions and Sayings." Of all the books he wrote during this phase, none fits more accurately his description of them: "My writings *only* speak of my conquests. I am within them and they include all things inimical to me. . . . Lonely at that point . . . I took sides against myself and stood up for anything which pained me and made life difficult" ("Preface," HATH). That work mirrored his condition so starkly that two completely different components seemed to be at work: on the one hand, we see the fledgling positivist Nietzsche whose newly derived theories as yet contain almost nothing of his own . . . and on the other hand, there is Nietzsche the campaigner and endurer who determinedly wrestled himself loose from old ideas and an old self . . . in order to come into his own through originality. That explains the passionate and ruthless attacks against Wagner and his views. No one is less capable of rendering balanced judgment than one who has completed a conversion of convictions, a conversion not for purely intellectual reasons but through the "human, all-too-human" depth of his nature. There is no thought which we toss so far and so violently away from us as one which has injured and moved us, and has caused wounds disguised by our pride: Hate is the reverberating echo of our unforgettable love.

Quite typical of Nietzsche's sudden and inner change is the fact that this time, as well, it proceeded from *a personal relationship*. Just as the most bitter sting in the break with an old ideal was the shattering of a friendship, so a new ideal took its place through a new type of knowledge embodied in a new friendship. The more painful the loneliness into which he was cast by the breakup of the Wagner friendship, the more intimate became Nietzsche's relationship to Paul Rée: "For a deep-dyed solitary, 'a friend' becomes a more precious thought than it is for sociable persons."[29]

If Nietzsche's relation to Wagner consisted of a discipleship, his friendship with Rée formed more of an intellectual companionship, despite the fact that Rée could only periodically leave his homestead in West Prussia to meet with Nietzsche at different locales. On November 19, 1877, for instance, when he lived in

Basel, still amid a companionable circle, Nietzsche complained of Rée's long absence caused by his friend's illness:

May I hear from you soon, my friend, that the evil spirits of illness have fled; then there would be nothing more for me to wish for your birthday, except that you remain what you are and that you continue to be for *me* what you were during the last year. . . . I must indeed tell you that in my entire life I have not had as much pleasure as through your friendship during this year, not to speak of what I have learned from you. When I hear of your studies, my mouth waters with anticipation of your company; we have been created for an understanding of one another, like good neighbors to whom it occurs simultaneously to visit and are halfway to the border of their property. Perhaps it is more in your power than in mine to overcome the great spatial distance . . . may I hope for that during the coming year? I myself feel too fragile in that respect and am immodest in my request for a good personal conversation about things human, and not an epistolary conversation for which I become more unfit. . . .

The more Nietzsche's bodily ills forced him into solitude, the more he had to distance himself from all people in order to endure these ills. But, all the more, he yearned for friends who would turn his loneliness into a "twosomeness": "Ten times a day, I wish to be at your side, with you" (letter to Rée from Basel, December 1878). "I always tie the spirit of my future to yours" (letter to Rée from Geneva, May 1879). "I have had to relinquish many wishes but never *the wish for a life together* with you in my 'Epicurean garden!'"[30] (letter to Rée from Naumburg, end of October 1879).

The violent pains and attacks suffered by Nietzsche awoke in him thoughts of death, and these gave his longings for each reunion a particularly deep meaning. "How much pleasure you have given me, my dear and extraordinarily dear friend!" he would exclaim after one such meeting. "And so, I have seen you once again, and found you just as my heart has preserved you in my memory. Those six days were like a steady, pleasant intoxicant. I must admit that I dare not hope for another meeting, the upheaval in my health is too deep; it is torture to keep holding on. Of what use to me are self-conquest and patience! Yes, during the times in Sorrento, I still had hopes, but those have vanished. So, I prize having had you here, my dearly beloved friend" (letter to Rée from Naumburg, end of January 1880).

During those years, both friends reached coincident views through studies that had much in common. Rée sent Nietzsche most of the books he needed and he read to Nietzsche, who was afflicted with eye troubles; he was in constant, lively communication with Nietzsche, either through letters or personal exchanges of ideas. After a somewhat lengthy separation, Nietzsche wrote:

My dear friend! Within me, much is prepared for our reunion, should that happy event still be permitted me. A box of books also sits ready for that moment. The box is labeled "Réealia," and there are many good things in it about which you will be happy. Could you send me an instructive book, of English origin[31] if possible, but translated into German and with good, large type?—As one who is seven-eighths blind, I live without books, but I would gladly take the forbidden fruit from your hand.—Long live *conscience,*[32] for now it will have a history; you, my friend, have become a historian! May your path be one of good fortune and well-being. From the closeness of my heart

Your
Friedrich Nietzsche

With variations, he continued to write to his friend Rée in that fashion: "With all the good things you are preparing, my table too is set and I have a lively appetite for *Réealism,* as you know!"

Through *Réealism* to begin with, Nietzsche took up philosophical realism and buried the old idealism. When Rée's first small work, *Psychological Observations* (*Psychologische Beobachtungen*), appeared anonymously in 1875, written in the spirit and style of La Rochefoucauld, Nietzsche not only valued but overvalued the book, as a surviving letter to Rée tells us. Rée's favorite authors then also became Nietzsche's: the French aphorists—La Rochefoucauld, La Bruyère, Vauvenargues, Chamfort—extraordinarily influenced Nietzsche's style and thinking. Along with Rée, he preferred Pascal and Voltaire among the French philosophers, and Stendhal and Merimée among the novelists.

Of unequalled and deeper significance, however, for Nietzsche was Rée's second work, *The Origin of Moral Sentiments* (*Der Ursprung der moralischen Empfindungen*, 1877);[33] for a time and in a certain sense, it shaped Nietzsche's positivistic philosophy. With all this, Nietzsche was led to the English positivists with whom Rée had cast his lot and for whom Nietzsche developed a preference over similar works in German. The main attraction exerted by positivism lay for Nietzsche in the answers to one essential question treated in Rée's book, namely, the question about the origin of the moral phenomenon.

This, for Rée, was coupled with the question about the root causes of sanctions for altruistic sentiments; his investigations were mainly directed toward the ethical systems of previous metaphysics. Because Wagner's and Schopenhauer's ethics were grounded in altruism and its metaphysical and sentimental value, Nietzsche had to find the most appropriate counter-weapons in Rée's book in order to combat his former beliefs. The subject of *The Origin of Moral Sentiments* actually became Nietzsche's object of investigation. . . . Nietzsche's philosophizing turned toward an analysis and history of human prejudices and errors, and the metaphysician became a psychologist and historian who planted his feet on the firm ground of positivism. He closely joined the English school of positivism, which attributed the origin of moral value judgments and phenomena to the *utility, convention, and forgetting* of the original causes of use. Without elaborating upon his theories, it will be sufficient to point out the directions from which he derived them.

Let us compare passages, such as the following, from Nietzsche's *Human, All-Too-Human:* "The history of moral sentiments . . . ran its course through the following main phases. At first, one called each single action good or bad only in terms of its useful or injurious effect, without any consideration whatever for the motive behind the action. Soon, however, one forgot the origin of these distinctions and surmised that the qualities of 'good' or 'bad' reside within the action itself, without taking into account the consequence of an action" (39). "How much less moralistic would the world appear without such forgetfulness! A poet could say that God has placed 'forgetfulness' as a temple guardian upon the threshold of human dignity" (92). This is how the so-called morality of action came to be: "*now* it is complacent habit, inheritance, and drill, while *originally* it was useful and more for the gain of honor" (II, 26). Further, "The meaning of forgetfulness in the morality of sentiments: The same actions which were intended originally for a communal *usefulness* within an earlier society, later were performed with different motives by different societies out of fear or veneration for those who demanded or recommended the actions, or out of habit because one had seen certain things done since childhood, or out of a sense of well-being because they brought pleasure and general approval, or out of vanity because they were praised. Such actions that had lost the attributions of usefulness were then called *moral* actions." "The content of our conscience is everything which has been unquestioningly and regularly demanded of us" (II, 52), so that whatever has been transmitted to us . . . becomes the sum of firmly stamped concepts of duties as sanctioned by religion. "Custom represents the experience of earlier generations as to what they deemed useful and injurious; yet *the feeling for custom* (morality) applies not to those experiences as such but to the age, the sanctity, and the rigidity of custom" (D, 19).

The entire book is suffused with what the title indicates characteristically: the annihilating effect of ideas, the ruthless baring of the "all-too-human," or what up until then had been called holy, eternal, and suprahuman. In order to see how Nietzsche turned against himself severely and exaggeratedly, it will repay our effort to pursue his reversal of values, relative to his earlier philosophical phase and consonant with the meaning of the terms Dionysian, decadence, the untimely, and the cult of genius.

In *Human, All-Too-Human*, the figure of the earlier maligned Socrates took the place of Dionysus; Socrates became the patron and temple guardian of the new sanctuary of truth. "If everything goes well, the time will come when people will wish to foster reason and morality and prefer to take in hand the legacy of Socrates rather than the Bible, as well as adopt Montaigne and Horace as guides to the understanding of Socrates' imperishable mode of moderation. The most diverse roads of philosophical living lead back to Socrates. Basically, these represent different modes of living and temperament determined by reason and habit, all of which are pointed toward a joy of life and of one's self . . ." ("The Wanderer and His Shadow," 86). The victory of Socratic reason and wise dispassion, the victory over the Dionysian, with its heightened emotion and self-obliterating intoxication, all peak in the observation that "the scientific man is the further development of the artistic man" (HATH, 226), who signifies dependence upon intoxication rather than reason, "for, in himself, the artist is a regressive [childlike] being" (159). "For Greece, therefore, the rise of the Socratic spirit meant an enormous step forward. To borrow forms from foreign sources, rather than creating them, and to reshape them into the most pleasing appearance was Greek practice: imitation for the purpose of artistic illusion rather than utility . . . organizing, beautifying, and leveling continued from Homer to the sophists of the third and fourth centuries. These forms had an air of superficiality, pompousness, and inspired gestures, and were attractive to emotional souls hungering for hollow illusions and sounds. All the more, one can now see the greatness of those exceptional Greeks who quested for knowledge. Whoever recounts their stories also recounts the heroic story of the human spirit!" (HATH, II, 221; *see also* D, 544, where Nietzsche contrasts the modern to the ancient reception of Plato's dialogues; the ancients rejoiced "over the new invention of *rational* thinking").

The origin of all manners of feeling and judgments needs to be exposed to those who regard the life of the emotions as the highest form of life. "Feelings are nothing final or anything fixed from any originating point on. Behind feelings stand judgments and evaluations which we have inherited in the form of feelings (inclinations, aversions). Inspiration which stems from a feeling is the grandchild of a judgment—and often a false judgment!—and, in any case, it is not your child! To trust one's feelings would mean obeying one's grandparents and their grandparents more than the gods who are in *us:* our reason and our experience" (D, 35).

The "noble enthusiasts," who attempt to prevent the subordination of feeling to rationality, mislead one into *"blasphemy against the intellect"* (D, 543). "To these wild inebriates, mankind owes much that is wicked. . . . For all that, those enthusiasts seek to implant with all their might a belief in intoxication as if that were a life within living—a terrible thought! Just as savages are quickly corrupted and ruined by 'fire water,' so it is with mankind . . . which has been slowly and thoroughly corrupted by the intoxicating feelings produced by spiritual fire water" (D, 50). "They do not consider that *knowledge* of even the ugliest reality is beautiful. . . . The happiness of the possessor of knowledge increases the beauty of the world. . . . Two such basically different people as Plato and Aristotle agreed upon the sources of the *highest happiness* . . . namely, in the search for knowledge, in the activity of a well-practiced *mind* that inquires and invents (and not somehow in 'intuition' . . . and also *not in visions* . . . and also *not* in practical creations . . .)" (D, 550).

Nietzsche, at the same time, chopped down the conventional adulations of the cult of genius[34] rife until his time: "Pity the cheap fame of 'the genius'! How quickly his throne has been erected and worship of him has become the custom! One always kneels before *power*—like the old habituation of slaves; and yet, the degree of worthiness of that worship should be assessed decisively only to the degree of rationality in that power" (D, 548). The time has come, says Nietzsche, for disciplined and humble spirits to take a closer look at "the over-evaluation" of the artistic personalities; they "do not stand in the vanguard of enlightenment and progressive civilization" (146, 147). Ostensibly, the genius does fight for "the higher dignity and meaning of man," although he "considers the continuance of his art of creation as more important than scientific devotion to truth no matter in what modest form it appears" (HATH, 146).

If one examines so-called "inspiration," it becomes evident that a work of art is not so much a marvel that stems from creative fantasy as it is the result as well of a "strength of judgment" which creates a work of art through clear vision, organization, and selection. "As we can see now in the notebooks of Beethoven, he composed the most magnificent melodies and has interpreted them, so to speak, through varied starts. . . . His artistic improvisation is strongly subjected to earnest, exquisite and arduous artistic thoughts" (HATH, 155). Therefore, genius is much more *learnable* than most have assumed: "Don't talk to me about being gifted, or of inborn talent! We can name great men of all sorts who were not very talented. But they *became* great and became 'geniuses' . . . they had the earnestness of craftsmen who built parts from the ground up first before attempting to shape a grand design; they allowed themselves sufficient time for that because they took more pleasure in perfecting small and incidental things instead of aiming for a dazzling effect of the whole design" (163).

Nietzsche's urge to explain and to reduce one's admiration for genius was directed against the Wagner phenomenon but became just as intense in the other direction during his last creative period when he extolled the impulse of genius—his own—and glorified it to the utmost. In *Human, All-Too-Human*, he still thought of every great phenomenon as something fatal because it aimed to "crush many weaker forces and seeds," whereas it is only just and desirable that not only the great individual have life but that the "weaker and more tender individuals also enjoy light and air" (158). "The prejudice in favor of greatness: People significantly overvalue the great and prominent . . . who arouse too much attention; but a much less demanding culture also is necessary in order to allow oneself to be captivated by the great ones" (260).

Nietzsche cannot find enough words to flay the high-handedness of those who wish to exclude themselves from public concerns: "It is sheer fantasy to imagine that one is a mile in advance and that all of mankind will follow *our* road. . . . One should not so readily speak in favor of arrogant solitude" (375). For this fantasy rests mostly upon our illusions about the motives of our actions and inactions; the true thinker knows that such a strong emphasis upon the difference in rank among humans is unjustified and that the human element itself in its noblest and highest impulses still remains "human, all-too-human." With the strength of this insight he is able to think things through and raise himself a step above his own insufficient being: "May not a time come when courageous thinking will be so natural that it soars haughtily *above* humans and things; when the sage, the most courageous thinker, will acutely view his self and all of existence lying below him?" (D, 551).

And so, the wise person is inclined to test human actions in terms of their all-too-humanness: "One will rarely err if one attributes extreme actions to vanity, mediocre actions to the habitual, and petty actions to fear" (HATH, 74). The significance of vanity as a leading motive in human actions is continually emphasized and brought up (a subject to which Rée devoted a special chapter in his second book). "Whoever denies one's vanity, usually possesses it in so brutal a form that he closes his eyes to it in order not to be forced to despise himself" (HATH, II, 38). "How poor would be the human spirit without vanity!" (79). Vanity is "the human thing-in-itself" (II, 46).[35] "The worst plague could not injure mankind more than the possible disappearance one day of vanity" ("The Wanderer and His Shadow," 285). Even what we have accustomed ourselves to view as of highest inner worth—feeling of strength and consciousness of power—is in the main only an effort of vanity to flow out and exert itself. Man wishes to count for more than he can actually justify in terms of his strength. "Early on, he notices that it is not what he is but for what he counts that will lift him up or cast him down: Here is the origin of vanity" (WS, 181). By describing "Vanity as being of great usefulness," Nietzsche puts the powerful on the same level as the idlers, the cunning, or the clever, who hide their fears and defenselessness behind counterfeited appearances. The views hammered home here are in the sharpest contrast to his later views about slave and master mentalities, as well as in contrast to his views about the earliest historical societies. (*See also* the aphorism "Vanity as the residual drive of unsocial conditions," WS, 31). Vanity dwindles to the degree that the superior man becomes conscious of the sameness or similarity of all human motives and recognizes himself in the "all-too-humanness" of his drives that are common to all.

The one truly valid difference between people lies exclusively in the art and degree of their intellectual wealth; *ennobling* of people means nothing more, after all, than gaining *insight* into them. Even that which is designated as "evil," from a moral point of view, shows itself mostly necessitated by spiritual poverty and coarsening. "Many actions are called evil and are foolish only because the degree of intelligence of their proponents was exceedingly low" (HATH, 107). The inability to estimate correctly injury or anguish caused to others, allows the so-called criminal, one retarded in mental development, to appear particularly gruesome and heartless. . . . The more advanced, however, a person may be, the more refined and milder—yes, even thinned-out, so to say—becomes the raw power-instinct of the original passions from which even now stem the actions of the retarded: "Good actions are sublimated evil ones; evil actions are coarsened and stupefied good ones. . . . The degree of judgmental capacity decides as to where someone allows . . . himself to be drawn. . . . Yes, in a certain sense, all actions are foolish because the highest degree of human intelligence . . . will surely be surpassed: and then . . . the first experiment will be made to see if mankind can *transform itself from a moral into a wise mankind*" (107). Its tell-tale sign will appear in humans when "the instinct of violence becomes weaker and justice in all matters becomes stronger" (HATH, 452) and there is a cessation of violence and slavery. Enviable are those in whom a mild, compassionate, and loving sense have become ingrained through generations: "The descent from good ancestors constitutes a genuine nobility of birth; a single break in that chain, one evil ancestor for instance, nullifies any nobility of birth. Anyone who speaks of his own nobility should be asked: Among your ancestors, do you have any who were rapacious, possessively greedy, devious, malicious, or cruel? If in all good conscience and recollection he can answer that question with a 'No,' then one ought to court his friendship" (456). "The best way to begin every day well is to ask, upon awakening, if it would not be possible during the coming day to give pleasure to at least *one* human being. If this were to become a substitute for religious conventionality of prayer, fellow humans would enjoy a great advantage through such a change" (589). And such extolling of tender and compassionate impulses comes at the expense not only of brutal coarseness; it also replaces the soulful passions of religious or artistic intoxication, and it tolls from a lovely formulation not indebted to any religion: "There is not enough love and goodness in this world to permit us to give up any of that to idolatrous figments of our imagination" (129).*

Later we will see the strong direction Nietzsche's philosophizing takes against these concepts of moral pity and the weakening of instinctual life; he will extol only that superior human who harbors within himself the entire fullness of passionate drives and instincts—in brief, the "evil" person. Up until that time, however, human worth was unthinkable outside of goodness and selflessness because only these represented the conquest of an animalistic past.

And so, one ought to call the wise person good not because he is of a friendly nature in contrast to the unwise but because . . . [he seeks knowledge about so-called good and evil, virtue and sin, without tormenting conceptions] so that "the savageness of his disposition had been soothed" (56). "Moderation in conduct comes about through a full decisiveness of thinking and investigating—that is to say, through a free-wheeling spirit—and becomes an inherent quality of character: moderation weakens covetousness" (464). "With that, boredom rapidly disappears . . . as does an excessive excitability of temperament. The wise person moves among people like a botanist among plants, and perceives himself as a phenomenon—a perception which greatly stimulates his discerning instinct" (254). All human greatness is based upon a refinement of the instinctive and a shedding of the animalistic; negatively expressed, he can be thought of as "no longer an animal." As a "dialectical and reasonable being," he also is "a superior animal" (40) in that "gradually a new habit—which conceives of not-loving, not-hating, and of overlooking—can take root" (107).

At that time however, Nietzsche thought that any notion of the superior man [*Über-Mensch*] as a being with positive, new, and higher qualities was a perfect fantasy and its invention the strongest proof of human vanity. "There must be more ingenious creatures than humans if only to taste fully the humor of man's belief that he is the purpose for which the universe has been

---

*This possession of "love and goodness as the most healing herbs and powers in human contact" (48) is worth far more than great and individual self-sacrificing which is much praised . . . (49).

created and of man's serious and contented belief in his world-mission" (WS, 14). "In former times, one ascribed the sense of grandeur in man to his godly origin: this path has now become closed because at its portal stands the ape, amid other horrible animals, and apprehendingly bares his teeth as if to say, 'no farther in this direction!' And so, one now tries an opposite direction, a path which mankind takes to prove its grandeur. . . . Alas, that too is in vain! . . . However high mankind's development may be—and perhaps it will ultimately even sink deeper than at its very beginning!—there is for mankind as little chance for transition to a higher order as there is for the ant and the earwig to ascend to godhead and eternity at the end of their earthly journey. One's 'becoming' drags around with it one's 'having been': why should they be any exception to this eternal theatrical play? . . . Away with such sentimentalities!" (D, 49).

If a person were able to face life squarely, "he would have to despair of life's value; were it possible for him to sense and grasp the entire consciousness of mankind in himself, he would collapse with a curse upon existence because mankind has altogether *no* goals; consequently, man cannot . . . find consolation or security in that situation but only his despair" (HATH, 33). "The first principle of the new life," therefore, decrees that "one should order one's life according to certainty and the provable" (WS, 310). One should again become "a good neighbor of the nearest things" (WS, 16), and instead of luxuriating in the "untimeliness" of the most distant past and future, one should embody the highest thoughts born of contemporary knowledge. Instead of fantasy-goals, "the recognition of truth as the sole overriding goal" (D, 45) ought to be before one's eyes. "On, toward the light—let your last thrust, an exultation in knowledge, be your last outcry" (HATH, 292).

It is possible that this sort of commanding intellectualism will spoil one's capacity for life and happiness, so that in a certain sense it is a "symptom of decadence"; but here, the concept of decadence gains nobility. "Perhaps mankind will even perish of this passion for knowledge! . . . Are not love and death brother and sister. . . . All of us would prefer the fall of mankind to a decline in knowledge!" (D, 429). Such "a tragic ending for knowledge" (D, 45) would be justified because no sacrifice would be too great: *"Fiat veritas, pereat vita!"* (UM, II, 4). This phrase summed up at the time Nietzsche's ideal of knowledge; it is a thought against which he had inveighed bitterly shortly before and which he was to condemn again a short time later. These changes are quintessential to Nietzsche's teachings during each of his phases. The *desire to live* at any cost—even at the cost of the knowledge of life—is his "new teaching" which he later posed against the exhausted feeling that emerged as the insight into the worthlessness of all creation: "In the midst of one's mental and living maturity, a person is overwhelmed by the feeling that one's father committed a wrong in begetting him" (HATH, 386), for "every belief about the value and dignity of life is based upon unsound thinking" (33).

If one pursues Nietzsche's thoughts in the groups of works discussed, one can discern the inner compulsion that sharpened them into brusque conclusions, always through self-conquests. But as a consequence of such contrasts demanded by the mode of his inner needs and demands, the knowledge of truth became his ideal; it assumed for him the epitome of an overpowering element distinct from himself. His compulsive submission fostered an enthusiastic—and near religious—attitude and made possible a religiously motivated self-division that allowed him objectively to view his own being, stirrings, and drives as if these belonged to another creature. At the same time that he sacrificed himself to truth and the power of an ideal, he attained a release of emotions of a religious kind. This effected a much more intensive glow within him than would have been the case had he contented himself with a placid pacification of his inner wishes and inclinations. During this period then, paradoxically enough, his battle against rapture and his glorification of the unemotional appear simply as attempts at inducing rapture by ravaging himself.

With that, he completed his change in an extreme way. One can even say that the energy he mustered, a loud and ruthless affirmation to counter his new mode of thinking, merely represented a violent act of negation through which he sought to subjugate his own nature and its deepest needs. The "unprejudiced coldness and tranquillity of knowledge," his ideal during this intellectual period, signified for him a kind of sublime self-torture, and he endured it only by thinking resolutely of his suffering as "one of those illnesses requiring ice-packs" (HATH, 38) which are salutary—"the pungent coldness is as good a stimulant as great heat."

Nietzsche's concurrence with Rée's intellectual direction is nowhere more completely clear than in the fledgling work *Human, All-Too-Human;* it appeared at a time when he suffered under the break with Wagner and his metaphysics. And his exaggerated intellectuality suited itself in many ways to the personal characteristics of Rée. And so, he formulated an ideal image to serve as a guideline: the superiority of the thinker over other persons and the rejection of all values which stem from the emotions. Unconditional and unreserved devotion to scientific investigation lent his philosophy a unique stamp and he regarded like-minded practitioners as higher types of knowledge-seeking persons.

Through the need to embody in human form purely scientific thoughts derived from positivism, he entangled himself in creating a portrait of a specific personality very much his opposite, and he even tortured himself to sharpen the features of that portrait. An escalation of Nietzsche's self-denial always required voluntary pains, explained here as well through the seeming contradiction that in order to save his independence from the hypnotic circle of Wagner and metaphysics, he had to put himself again under a foreign spell that would seek to remove his sense of self. Yet neither in terms of his philosophical direction nor in his personal relationship was there reason for this; the causes went much deeper. They alone drove him into a close alliance with someone new and his ideas; at the same time, they also drove him away from collaborative thinking (HATH, 180). In that sense he was able to write to his friend Rée when he sent him *Human All-Too-Human:* "It belongs to you . . . to the others it is sent as a gift!" And Nietzsche immediately added: "All my friends are now of one opinion that my book was written by you and originated with you: Therefore, I congratulate you on your new paternity! Long live Réealism!" [Nietzsche to Rée, April 24, 1878.]

A strange kind of complement was formed between both friends, a contact far different from that which had once existed between Nietzsche and Wagner. For Wagner, the genius of art, Nietzsche had to be the thinker and knowing, scientific mediator of the new art-culture. Now, on the contrary, Rée was the theoretician and Nietzsche complemented him in the sense that he drew up practical consequences for theories and sought to determine their inner meanings for life and culture. And so, where one of them stopped short, the other began. As to the question of values, the intellectual modes of these friends differed. Rée was a thinker who with a brusque one-sidedness . . . departed completely from Nietzsche's artistic, philosophical, and religious wealth of spirit. Of the two, however, he was of keener mind. With amazement and interest, he saw his strong and clean-spun threads of thought come unraveled in the magical hands of Nietzsche and transformed into living and freshly blossoming vines. It is characteristic of Nietzsche's work that even his misperceptions and errors contain a largeness of suggestion that heightens their general meaning, even though their scientific worth is diminished. By way of contrast, one may note that Rée's works contain more flaws than errors. The last sentence of Rée's foreword to his *The Origin of Moral Sentiments* expresses the contrast most clearly: "In this work there are gaps, but gaps are better than stopgaps!" Nietzsche's brilliant intellectual range, however, exposes new views precisely in areas for which logic has no key and is forced to put up with the gaps in knowledge.

Thought and sentiments were fused in Nietzsche's total inner life, while Rée's disposition brusquely and broadly separated thought from sentiments. Nietzsche's genius sprang from the exuberant fire behind his thoughts . . . logic alone could not have brought on his illuminations. Rée's intellectual strength was based upon a cold, undeviating, lucid logic of scientific thought. Its danger lay in a one-sided and closed circuit of thinking, deficient in suggestive and fine-tuned nuances. The danger for Nietzsche resided in his unlimited capacity for empathy and a dependence upon stimuli and excitations for his moods. Even when his particular mode of thinking seemed to slip momentarily into contradictory and private wishes and emotional longings, he fought them and gained in strength of perception. Rée, on the other hand, rejected every intrusion of sentiment into quests for knowledge, to avoid distortions. The objective thinker within Rée looked searchingly and probingly at the human in Rée and, so to speak, drained off some of his energy as well as his egoism. That egoism was replaced in his character by a deep, lucent, unlimited goodness whose formulations stood in gripping and interesting contrast to the cold sobriety and hardness of his thinking. Nietzsche, on the other hand, possessed an exaggerated love of self, which eventually became interchangeable with knowledge-ideals; these he presented to the world with the enthusiasm of an apostle and proselytizer.

Despite theories held in common by these friends, the difference between their sentiments, covered by husks of thought, was great. The same ideals, however, were expressed distinctly because of their individualistic personalities. Nietzsche prized, even overprized, in Rée that which came hardest to himself. . . . "What a splendid year, 1881! You, my dear friend and perfect achiever, give me unlimited contentment . . . and I would like to create for you a *sun* that glows over your garden. Things would not be tolerable for me if from time to time I did not liken my nature to a metal heightened to purified form. I resemble a broken fragment and a figure of wandering misery, and can only hope for rare 'good moments' that allow me to glance into a *better landscape* where integrated and fully fashioned people wander about" [letter, end of August 1881].

Such thoughts accompany his new views as he refashions alien modes of being and thought into something original. Periods of suffering create the birthpangs for renewal. And so, Nietzsche's development during such a transition is the story of his inner life and struggles. The phase discussed here encompasses *Human, All-Too-Human* (an offspring of suffering) and takes us into the deeply moving and joyous mood of *The Gay Science* which to a certain degree already leads into his later intellectual period. In all the works during that phase, he had wished to construct a series of aphoristic collections—an ideal image of the free spirit—wherein the freely inquiring spirit of his thoughts would explore all areas of life and knowledge and, even more freely, the fullness of his own experiences. The titles of the works express his basic inclination. Never are Nietzsche's book titles arbitrary, indifferent, or cut from abstractions; they are accurate echoes of inner events and consist entirely of symbols. In that fashion he also summarized, briefly, the contents of his lonely existence as a thinker at the close of the seventies. For instance, on the title page of *Human, All-Too-Human* he wrote, "The Wanderer and His Shadow" (1881). It characterizes his turning from the heat of the battle to the loneliness of the self; the warrior became a wanderer who replaced attacks on an abandoned "homeland" with a searching examination of the land to which he had voluntarily exiled himself. He explored that barren soil to see if it would permit cultivation and if he could possess a rich piece of the land. The persistent split between the wanderer and his opposing shadow dissolved in a silent inner dialogue: the hermit listened to his own thoughts as if they belonged to the conversation of many voices and he lived in their presence and their accompanying shadows. They appear to him as gloomy, uniform, and ghostly, and indeed as threatening, overtowering, and as shadowy figures might when the sun goes down. But this feeling does not last long, for it also strips away, slowly, everything that was shadowy; instead of pure thought and colorless theory, there are resonance and sight, form and life. Here then is the internal process of his acclimatization and of his shaping the new and unfamiliar into a fullness of life. One could say that Nietzsche chooses the most gloomy thoughts in order to nourish them with his own blood and to transform them painfully into another self, his double.

To the extent that he absorbs surrounding thoughts, with which he gradually becomes satiated, his mood becomes progressively more elevated and consoled. One senses that here Nietzsche moves step-by-step toward himself and begins to feel at home in his new "skin". . . . He no longer aims for the same goal as his colleague Paul Rée; he strives toward his own goal. We gather that from his letters in which he still admires the theoretician: "By the way, I always admire how well armed your arguments are from a point of logic. Indeed, this is something of which I am not capable; at most, I can do a bit of sighing or singing, but proving something to one's heady satisfaction, that you are able to do and that is a hundred times more opportune" (letter to Rée, after mid-June 1877).

But it was precisely through "singing and sighing" that the genius of his consciousness forced to the surface his gift for magnificent lamentations and hymns of victory over warring ideas; he had the creative gift for transposing even the most sober or ugly thought into an inner music. The musician within him linked a basic beat to a new and great melody of the whole.

In fact, this gives his work and thoughts of that time a very special meaning since the newly-won unity of self had also made all of his drives and talents useful in the great quest for knowledge. The artist, the poet, and the musician in Nietzsche had been forcibly pushed back and repressed; these talents again clamored to be heard, but now are subordinate to the thinker and his goals. That tacit relation enabled him to "sing and sigh" in a fashion that raised him to the position of premier stylist of the age. One might note some aphorisms which Nietzsche put to paper for me [August 8 to 24, 1882, in Tautenburg]:

Toward the Teaching of Style

1

Of prime necessity is life: a style should *live.*

2

Style should be suited to the specific person with whom you wish to communicate. (The law of *mutual relation.*)

3

First, one must determine precisely "what-and-what do I wish to say and *present,*" before you may write. Writing must be mimicry.

4

Since the writer *lacks* many of the speaker's *means,* he must in general have for his model a *very expressive* kind of presentation; of necessity, the written copy will appear much paler.

5

The richness of life reveals itself through a *richness of gestures.* One must *learn* to feel everything—the length and retarding of sentences, interpunctuations, the choice of words, the pausing, the sequence of arguments—like gestures.

6

Be careful with periods! Only those people who also have long duration of breath while speaking are entitled to periods. With most people, the period is a matter of affectation.

7

Style ought to prove that one *believes* in an idea; not only thinks it but also *feels* it.

8

The more abstract a truth which one wishes to teach, the more one must first *entice* the senses.

9

Strategy on the part of the good writer of prose consists of choosing his means for stepping close to poetry but *never* stepping into it.

10

It is not good manners or clever to deprive one's reader of the must obvious objections. It is very good manners and *very clever* to leave it to one's reader alone to pronounce the ultimate quintessence of our wisdom.

To examine Nietzsche's style for causes and conditions means far more than examining the mere form in which his ideas are expressed; rather, it means that we can listen to his inner soundings. The style of these works came about through the willing, enthusiastic, self-sacrificing, and lavish expenditure of great artistic talents . . . and an attempt to render knowledge through individualized nuancing, reflective of the excitations of a soul in upheaval. Like a gold ring, each aphorism tightly encircles thought and emotion. Nietzsche created, so to speak, a new style in philosophical writing, which up until then was couched in academic tones or in effusive poetry: he created a *personalized style;* Nietzsche not only mastered language but also transcended its inadequacies. What had been mute, achieved great resonance.

* * *

NIETZSCHE'S TRANSFORMATION of mere thought into something really experienced was like no one else's in its creative mode: his thoughts formed, exclusively, the characteristic events in his solitary life. He could only find a pale and lifeless lament for those events: "Alas, my written and painted thoughts, what are you anyway! Not long ago you were so lively, young, and malicious, and so full of thorns and secret spices that you made me sneeze and laugh . . . and now? . . . Well then, what is it we write or paint, we mandarins with a Chinese brush? We immortalize things which *lend* themselves to writing. What is it actually then that we are able to copy with our paintings? Alas, always only that which tends to wilt and just begins to lose its fragrance. Alas, always only departing and yellowed, belated feelings! Alas, always only birds who have exhausted themselves with flying, and as they stray we can snare them with a hand—with *our* hand! . . . And it is only for *your afternoon* and only for it that I have my written and painted thoughts, perhaps too many colors, varicolored tendernesses and fifty yellows and browns and greens and reds; but no one can guess from all that how you appeared at dawn, you sudden sparks and wonder of my solitude, you, my old beloved *wicked* thoughts!" (end of BGE, 296).

It is essential that one visualizes Nietzsche during his quiet and solitary peregrinations as carrying with him a number of aphorisms which have resulted from long, mute monologues rather than from writing with pen in hand and bent over a desk:

I write not with my hand alone;
my feet, co-partners, give things tone.
Firm, free, and brave, my feet
run across fields and over my sheet.

("Joke, Cunning and Revenge," GS, 52)

The background of mountains and the nearness of seas provide the effective settings for Nietzsche's lonely figure. In Genoa's harbor he dreamt of a new world rising from the shrouded horizon during the redness of dawn, and his Zarathustra observed, "From such abundance, it is lovely to look out at distant oceans." In Switzerland's Engadine mountains he recognized himself, however, through the interplay of cold and heat, a mixture out of which came all his battles and changes. "In many of nature's settings we rediscover ourselves, with pleasant horror; it is the most beautiful case of doubleness," Nietzsche said, ". . . as part of the total character of these highlands, encamped here near the frightfulness of eternal snow, which Italy and Finland seem to share as the homes of all silver color-tones in nature" (WS, 338). Of this Engadine locale with its "small out of the way lakes" from which "the eyes of loneliness itself seemed to peer" at him, as he wrote in a letter, "its nature is like mine; we are not surprised by each other but have mutual trust." On the surface it would seem that his headaches and eye problems certainly had forced him to work with purely aphoristic means rather than detailed research, but more and more his intellectual peculiarity refused to fashion a continuously linked chain of thoughts, as in systematic writing; instead, one listens to a dialogue of thought that breaks off and then picks up specific strands. With "ears attuned to the extraordinary" ("Prologue," Z, 9), he captured silent words as if they were spoken.

"Although I would gladly write, I cannot. Alas, my eyes! I don't know how to help myself; they keep me forcefully at a distance from research. And then, what is left! Well, one could say that I still have my ears" [from a postcard, January 1881 to Rée]. But he was painstaking in his listening and overhearing of things, and there is no sentence in his books which is not applicable to what he wrote in one of his letters to me: "I am always busy with finely honed language; a final editorial decision about the text forces me to a scrupulous 'listening' to word and sentence. Sculptors call such final polishing *ad unguem*" (June 27/28, 1882).

When Nietzsche finished his third work founded upon positivism[36] in 1881, *Daybreak,* he concluded the process of individualizing adopted theories. This work (and the next one—*The Gay Science*—to an equally great extent) appears to me as the most meaningful in his intellectual middle-period. Here he has actually succeeded in overcoming the exaggerated intellectualism to which he had subjected himself by voluntary self-martyrdom in *Human, All-Too-Human . . .* without loosening the rigor of his search for knowledge. Nietzsche's own nature helped him to refute the partiality and narrowness of his practical philosophy and to fashion a more fulfilling kind of knowledge during his last years. That was to be made possible through a process we have already seen: the subordination of the emotional life to thinking meant a tremendous sacrifice to an ideal, so that precisely here it dawned upon him how significant was the life of the emotions for that of thinking. Along with this realization, the main accent shifts unobtrusively from a purely intellectual process to the power of feelings at the service of even the most sober and ugly truths, simply because they are *truths*. And so began all over again the placement of rationality with the power of the spirit, determining the quality of the thinker as a human being. And it is easy to see how in this manner Nietzsche had to realize gradually the value of a completely new way of thinking through a philosophy that was averse to rationality.

In *Daybreak*, as in no other of his books, we can trace the delicate transitions from his positivistic phase of intellectuality to a mystical philosophy of will. The transition itself from the old to the new, like that in *Human, All-Too-Human*, forms the charm and value of the book. . . . In *Daybreak*, on the other hand, every possibility for a change of theories was still rejected vehemently . . . while one's own spirit reaches out longingly and gropingly no matter how forbiddingly reason blocks that search. And so, quiet and isolated vacillations punctuate a deeply aroused life of the spirit. From these disturbances, we anticipate the future because this mood possesses an unwanted naïveté and immediacy, which Nietzsche had been avoiding completely. Without realizing it Nietzsche betrays himself constantly in that he tests and reprimands every prompting for experimentation; he reveals the hidden side of his inner life, so that we think we see how his past and future life exchange confessions of secret hopes and demands. He resists them with an aphorism, "Do not make passion an argument for truth!—Oh you good-natured and even noble enthusiasts, I know you! . . . With hatred you carry on against criticism, science, good sense! . . . Sensible reasoning is needed rather than colored pictures! Glow and power of expression! . . . You know how to illuminate and to obscure things, as well as to obscure them *with light!* . . . How you humans thirst for self-justifying passions whose conflagration will light your flames: It is blasphemy against the intellect!" (D, 543).

Only during Nietzsche's last philosophic phase does one understand completely how he hews to the admonition, "Nothing would be more wrong than to wait for science's final discoveries about the first and last things. . . . The urge to possess absolutely *only certainties* is a residual religious drive, and nothing more" (WS, 16).

But in the midst of many such objections that he raises against himself, there also erupt some instances of surfeit with his strict and imposed dichotomy between reason and knowledge and with "the tyranny of truth": "I could not see why the sole dominance and omnipotence of truth should be something to be desired . . . one must, from time to time, escape from truth into untruth in order to *recuperate,* otherwise truth becomes boring" (D, 507). And with longing, he even calls out to artists he has despised: "Oh that poets would only become what they once were—*prophets* who tell us something about possibilities! . . . That they would give us a foretaste of future virtues! Or of virtues which will never appear on earth although they could exist somewhere in this world—made of crimson-glowing galaxies and a Milky Way of beauty! Where are you, astronomers of the ideal?" (D, 551).

In *Daybreak* we not only see how he fights against secret desires that arise but also how he already yields to them in his devoted longing for something new in his anticipation of a higher knowledge. Fight and longing are characteristically mingled. . . . *"This is the sun's circuit of an idea,"* as he portrays it autobiographically: "When an idea rises on the horizon, the soul's temperature usually is cold. Yet the idea unfolds its warmth slowly, and it reaches a peak of heat . . . when one's belief in an idea again is on the wane" (WS, 207). Farther on, he characterizes himself in these words: "Persons who begin slowly and stolidly to accustom themselves to something, experience now and then a steady acceleration, so that finally no one knows where a stream can propel them" (331).

The power of the slow and stolid but ever more fateful and enflamed inwardness—a brimming fullness—had to estrange him finally from positivism and lead him into new distances of thought. In complete contrast to the "unemotionality" he glorified earlier, he then found his ideal in the following: the knowledge seeker is "a human of lofty feelings and the embodiment of a single great mood . . . and of a continuous movement between high and deep" (GS, 288). For the "seeker of knowledge," that which formerly meant danger now assumes an air of enticement: "To leave the ground below, only for once! To soar! To stray! To become utterly mad!" (46). And in *Daybreak* one of the aphorism headings, *"The celebrative mood,"* suggests that "precisely for those people who most fiercely strive for power, it is indescribably pleasant to feel themselves *overpowered!* Suddenly and deeply to find themselves sink into a feeling as one would into a whirlpool! To allow the reins to be torn out of one's hands and to look on as one is driven who knows where!" (271).

A celebrative mood, rising above sober reflections, broke the magical tension and brought release from daylong work. With it, Nietzsche glided into a world of mysticism. His self-conquest was the kind of victory which vanquishes the victor. He sought the "happiness of contrast," the contrast to the cool, strict sensibleness of positivistic ways of thinking; he sought knowledge founded instead upon the enthusiastic yielding to feelings, the life of emotions, and to the creative drive of the will.

This "daybreak" is no longer a pale, cold, retrospectively illuminating work of instruction; behind it already rises a life-giving sun. . . . "There are so many crimson dawns which have not as yet shed light," Nietzsche said in the words of the *Rig Veda* that form the motto for the title page of *Daybreak*. He did not dare to believe that he himself might have the calling to enflame the heavens of knowledge. The book's subtitle, "Thoughts on the Prejudices of Morality," gives the impression of a link with the earlier works of a fragmenting and negating spirit. But over the work there already hover dreams and hopes of breaking through set *prejudices* and creating new value judgments. "When finally all traditions and customs upon which the gods, the priests, and redeemers had leaned for power are destroyed, when morality, in its old sense, also will have died, what happens then, yes, what will happen then?" (D, 96).

The breakup and fall of the old are not exactly ends in themselves; rather they herald an outlook, a beginning, and an appeal to all of Nietzsche's best mental energies: Something is coming, indeed; the main thing is still to come! as promised by the dawn of day.

A year after the publication of *Daybreak*, Nietzsche wrote to me about his new hopes for philosophy and his future plans [probably on June 12, 1882]:

Well, dearest friend, as always you have a good word ready for me; it gives me great happiness to please you. I must endure the terrible life of *renunciation* which is as hard as any ascetic constriction of life, but it has a few consolatory elements that make life something to be treasured above not living. A few great perspectives on the spiritual-moral horizon are my *mightiest* sources of life. I am very happy about the fact that precisely on *this ground* the roots and hopes of our friendship will thrive. No one can be more happy from one's heart about what you are *doing* and *planning*.

Loyally, your friend

F. N.

And he exclaims at the end of another letter:

Even I have crimson dawns about me now, and none of them depressing! That which I never thought would come true— [to find a friend for my *last good fortune and suffering*—] that now appears possible, like the *golden* possibility on the horizon of all my future life. [I am deeply moved whenever I think of the brave and richly intuitive soul of my dear Lou.][37]

When Nietzsche completed his book *The Gay Science* in 1882, he was already sure about his India: he believed that he had landed on the shore of a strange and as yet unnamed and monstrous world of which nothing was known except that it had to lie beyond all that which could be disputed and destroyed by thoughts. A broad and shoreless ocean seemed to lie between him and the possibility of a renewed and comprehensible philosophical criticism, yet he believed that he had found a firm footing.*

---

*This mood had the force of a yearning to conjure up a new world of the spirit on the far horizon, so that it would offer a substitute for everything which had been destroyed by doubt and criticism; it rings out most clearly in the final words of *Daybreak* in whose critical and negative lines of thought themselves Nietzsche attempts to find a road-guide toward

A heady jubilation about this certainty is again heard in the verses he sent to me along with a gift copy of *The Gay Science:* "Friend, spoke Columbus, do not trust/ a Genoese anymore!/ He always stares into the blue,/ the distant draws him on too much!/ The one he loves, he gladly lures/ far into space and time./ Above us each star shines,/ while eternity whirls around us."[38]

But he was mistaken about the complete newness and the otherworldness of that land; it was the parallel of Columbus' mistake: searching for the old he found the new. Without being aware of it, Nietzsche in his circumnavigations approached the coast of that land from the opposite side but returned to his point of origin from which he thought he had departed, just as he thought that he had turned his back upon metaphysics. In the works of his later intellectual phases, we shall see how they grew out of the old soil, despite the experiences and influences during his last years. Without doubt, the main value of Nietzsche's positivistic line of thought consisted in a truly wide range of free play within defined boundaries; positivism held his attention because it offered a spaciousness within which transitions of mood and thought could occur. Unlike metaphysics, positivism did not chain him to a knowledge system. For that reason, emancipation from positivism could take place gradually and smoothly, unlike his sudden and violent break with Wagner. . . . But somewhere along the way, Nietzsche had to go again beyond the essential limitations of experience and an empirical view of his problems. He could not renounce at length the philosophy about the "last and highest things" nor could he renounce his intrinsic disposition. And so, his return to things metaphysical was unavoidable; it was only a question of which silent bypaths he would take in order to sneak back to the abodes of the gods and superior humans.

Nietzsche wrote to Rée on October 20, 1878: "Alas, dearest

---

new ideals: "Why exactly in that direction in which up until now all the suns of humankind have *gone down?* Will it be said of us perhaps some-day that we too have steered to the West in the hopes of reaching an India but that it was our fate to shatter ourselves against infinity? Or, my brothers? Or—?"

and good friend, I read with most painful regret the news about your illness. . . . What will become of us if we fade away so lamentably during our best years? . . . Does not fate intend to save us for a ripe old age because . . . our manner of thinking views that as most natural, like the laying on of a healthy skin? But would we not have to wait too long for that? The danger here would be to lose patience. . . ."

But Nietzsche lost patience completely. "Already, my skin bends and cracks!" he said in an awkward verse from *The Gay Science*, and under the hoary skin of the emotionless knowledge-seeker there stirred a powerful drive toward rejuvenation; even during his later decline, he wrote hymns in praise of life, an eternal life. Fate did not save him for an old age. . . .

For a time, Nietzsche was prompted to translate the forces of his inner life into new and rounded world views. Thus, during the summer of 1882, Nietzsche planned to devote years to the study of natural sciences, which he thought would underpin a systematized philosophy of the future. He was prepared to leave the south and attend lectures in Paris, Vienna, or Munich. Rée too, somewhat later, felt the need to become familiar with the natural sciences, with the aim of stepping out of the narrow confines of his specialty. And so, he turned to medicine, renewed his studies, passed the state examinations for physicians, and had in mind the practice of psychiatry; eventually through this detour, he hoped to return to the humanities. Although both friends seemed to share common goals, they had never been so far apart as at that point: they had reached opposite personal and intellectual poles. A lovely passage in *The Gay Science* marks Nietzsche's farewell to his companionship with Rée.[39] The plans Nietzsche had set in motion for a ten-year cessation of writing in favor of studies changed, and those years turned into a decade of his greatest creativity. Rée, on the other hand, had not reached the point where his old researches would unite with new learning to stimulate heightened activity.

Nietzsche's plans were obstructed by his head pains. Already at the onset of winter in 1882, he again inhabited his "hermit's cell" in Genoa. But even had he been in better health, the earlier plans would not have been feasible because he was in that state of intellectual gestation which would hardly brook any foreign intrusion. . . . He needed to test the conditions of his existence anew and to question them. . . . He needed to create space about himself for the sovereign play of his inwardness, which spontaneously transformed the image of the world into a cradle for his creativity.

In that regard, it may seem paradoxical to say that from then on all of his teachings take on a more personal character; the more they seem to be generalized, the more they gain greater specific meanings. Ultimately, their last secret sense is hidden under so many masks that the theories he expresses emerge almost only through images from his inner life. Absent finally is any desire to reconcile one with the other: "My judgment is *my* judgment to which hardly anyone else has a right" (BGE, 43), and yet, that judgment is turned into a universal imperative, a command to all of humankind. So completely fused have Nietzsche's inner inspiration and outer revelation finally become that at the end he imagined all of the world to be encompassed in his own inner life; he was to imagine that in a mystical way his spirit contained the epitome of being and was its womb. "As far as I am concerned, what is there except my self? There is no externality!" ("The Convalescent," Z, III, 2).

Nietzsche's last creative period consisted through and through of an interpretation of his own spiritual life. In line with that, he calls *The Gay Science,* a work which serves to introduce this period, "the most personal among my books," and he lamented that "the manuscript, in a curious way, is uneditable. This stems from the principle of *mihi ipsi scribo!*"[40]

Indeed, he had never written so completely for himself as during the time when he was ready to subordinate his view of the world to his own self and to interpret everything from that vantage point. And so, the mysticism of his new teachings is already contained here but is not as yet hidden within the purely personal element out of which it emerged. Subsequently, these aphorisms form monologues, more so than anything else in Nietzsche's works, and are like barely audible asides; yes, often, like thoughts in a stony facial mask they wish to disguise far more than to reveal. They already preview his "philosophy of the future"[41]

and surround us like shrouded figures whose gaze rests upon us
ambiguously. . . .

But it is difficult for him to speak about these things without
reservation because in this case his confession is once again a
confession of pain, making the struggles and renunciations during his positivistic period seem innocuous by comparison. At first
glance this appears to be a contradiction . . . as indeed he begins
his last change with an air of jubilation and gaiety. But one should
not forget that this extreme retreat into himself and this attempt
to construct the world in his own image allow his sufferings to
reach daylight. Up until then he had sought to escape them by
pitting one part of himself against another . . . but when he no
longer castigates himself or forces matters and gives his longings
the free rein of expression, then we fully understand the tortures
he endured and we finally hear the outcry for *release from himself*
and for a final and transforming change of the entire inner man.
Desperation makes him reach for a redeeming ideal shaped from
things opposite to his being. It was predictable therefore that
once Nietzsche freely altered the content of his spirit in favor of a
worldly content . . . his philosophy had to portray a tragic world
image: he had to conceive of humanity as suffering "of itself" and
from its hybrid nature, and whose justification for existence did
not lie in itself but in a superior human genus, as such, and
toward which it only had to construct a bridge. Humanity's
ultimate objective was decline and self-sacrifice on behalf of an
opposite ideal set before it.

Only when we enter Nietzsche's last phase of philosophy
will it become completely clear to what extent the religious drive
always dominated his being and his knowledge. His various
philosophies are for him just so many surrogates for God, which
were intended to help him to compensate for a mystical God-ideal
outside of himself. His last years, then, are a confession that he
was not able to do without this ideal. And precisely because of
that, time and again we come upon his impassioned battle against
religion, belief in God, and the need for salvation because he
came precariously close to them. Here Nietzsche reveals a hatred
of fear and love, with which he wishes to convince himself of his
own godly strength and riddance of human helplessness. We

shall see by what means of self-delusion and secret cunning Nietzsche finally resolved the tragic conflict of his life—the conflict between the need for God and the compulsive need to deny God. At first he fashioned the mystical superior-human ideal through self-intoxicated fantasy, dreams, and rapture-like visions; and then, in order to save himself from himself, he sought to identify himself with them through one tremendous leap. Finally, he became a dual figure—half-sick and suffering; half-saved; a laughing and superior human. The one is like a creature and the other a creator; the one assumes a reality and the other a mystical sur-reality. Often however, as one listened to his talking about these matters, one sensed with horror that he placed on the altar of worship what in truth did not even exist for him. And one remembers his words, ". . . who knows if during all great events of the past the same thing had not occurred, namely, that the herd had prayed to a god and that this 'god' was only a poor sacrificial animal!" (BGE, 269).

"The sacrificial animal as God" is truly a title that could be placed over Nietzsche's last philosophy and which most clearly reveals his inner contradictions: an exaltation, mingling pain and bliss. We have seen earlier how Nietzsche's last frame of mind slipped into a celebrative, dream-filled mood of intoxication. We now see the point at which the force of inner stimulation turns into pain. Even in his daily life at that time, he was overwhelmed by a soulfulness in which boisterousness was also possible, since quivering nerves can easily lead to joking and laughter. The immersion in bliss and agony, enthusiasm and suffering, always led Nietzsche toward a spiritual rebirth. . . . The wounding of self and its uprooting from any sense of "home," were conditions within which his spirit luxuriated before they discharged themselves in new creations.

It is characteristic therefore that in the jubilation of his heart he named his book *The Gay Science;* at the same time, he titled his closing aphorism [342] with the dark, riddlesome words, *"Incipit tragoedia:"* the tragedy begins.

This composite of profound turmoil and playful high spirits, the tragic and the gay, typical of his last works, is also in keeping with the sharpest contrast between the dark secret of the closing words and the book's prelude in rhyme, "Joke, Cunning, and Revenge." Here for the first time we see verses in Nietzsche's works; they increase to the extent he believes himself to be nearing his personal decline. His spirit rings out in song. The verses are surprisingly uneven in value, and are completed only in part; and in part they are thoughts whose beauty and fullness turns them into poems so curiously incomplete, as if moved by a caprice to break the reins. There is something gripping about all of them, as if a solitary person strews flowers upon his road of pain, deluding himself that it is a road of happiness. They are like fresh and broken roses upon which he wishes to tread, while at the same time he is already braiding a crown of thorns for his brow.

Nietzsche's thoughts sound like a prelude to the shattering drama of his highest ascendance *and* his downfall. Nietzsche's philosophy does not completely lift a curtain on the drama, but its folds show flower threads and, half hidden, the large, sad words—

"Incipit tragoedia."

III NIETZSCHE'S "SYSTEM"

"Yet you wish to create a world
before which you could kneel"

"MIND? What is 'mind' to me? What does knowledge matter? I treasure nothing except *impulses,* and I would dare say that we have them in common. Look straight *through* the phase in which I lived during the past years—and look behind them! Do not let yourself be deceived about me. Surely you don't believe that 'the free spirit' is my ideal?! I remain—Pardon me! Dearest Lou, [be what you must be]."—*F. N.*[42]

* * *

IN THIS MYSTERIOUS FASHION Nietzsche's letter breaks off. It was a letter written between the publication of *The Gay Science* and his mystical work *Thus Spoke Zarathustra.* In the few lines cited, the essential features of Nietzsche's last philosophy are indicated: a decisive move away from his purely logical ideals of knowledge and from the strict theorizing of reasoned "free spiritedness" up until then; and, as far as the philosophical realm of ethics is concerned, he displaced negating criticism with a search for knowledge rooted within the world of the psyche's impulses as a source for revaluations. Further, it suggests a kind of return to Nietzsche's first phase of philosophical development (before his positivistic "free spiritedness"), namely, to the metaphysics of Wagner's and Schopenhauer's aesthetics and their teachings about the suprahuman genius. And here, finally, the central kernel of the new philosophy of the future is crystallized: the mystery of a tremendous self-apotheosis which he still is too timid to express in the hesitant phrase, "I am. . . ."

The notion of a "system" in Nietzsche's works relies more upon an over-all mood than a clear-cut unity of defined deduction. The aphoristic characteristics preserved in his last works appear, therefore, as an undeniable lack of form in his representations and not, as before, like an idiosyncratic preference.

Through the mastery of the aphoristic form, Nietzsche was able to reproduce fully each idea, along with its delicate inner meaning. But this would not suffice for a systematic construction of personal theories; here and there, though, intelligence is at play with dazzling hypotheses. Because of his eye ailments and his habit of thinking in leaps and bounds, Nietzsche was forced generally to keep to his old manner of writing, but he always attempted—as we note in *Beyond Good and Evil*, as well as in *The Genealogy of Morals*—to go beyond the purely aphoristic and to order and present his thoughts systematically. Also, that which he visualized in his mind had become a complete unity.

For these reasons we find, for the first time, a kind of theory of knowledge which impelled him to come to grips with those theoretical knowledge-problems that he had avoided, like other problems approachable only by purely conceptual routes. Without further ado, he confronted some of the perennial problems in epistemology and broke through them on the way toward his own hypotheses. Fairly detailed comments about this are strewn throughout his works. Yet it appears highly characteristic that he discovers his hypotheses only when he becomes an enemy of the "abstract logical" realm and cuts through all difficult and knotty conceptual problems: he deals with the theory of knowledge only to subvert it completely.

During the time of his association with Wagner, Nietzsche was a disciple of Schopenhauer and the master's well-known interpretations and modifications of Kant's theories, namely, that questions about the highest and ultimate things find their answer not through reason but through inspiration and illuminations in the life of the will. Later, Nietzsche vehemently protested against Schopenhauer's metaphysics. . . . This fanatical protest itself became wearisome to him, and he sought new ideals. Within positivism he found something he had not noticed before, and that is the perception of the relativism of all thought and a return of all rational knowledge to the purely practical ground of human impulses from which it derives and upon which it constantly depends.

That path had already been designated by his own philosophical colleagues and he only needed to follow his usual exuberance in order to return to the original value he placed upon the emotions. . . . In the meantime, though, only his *mood* and *emotional perception* of the state of affairs had changed, but this says everything about Nietzsche because that change was a point of departure toward a new view of the world.

This sequence typifies the origins of all basic thoughts in Nietzsche's "philosophy of the future": first, an association with modern research into knowledge, then a dramatic turn in his emotional moods and perceptions as he drove his findings to extremes, and finally a deriving of his own new theories from that about-face.

Two aspects then need to be differentiated: on the one hand, their factual philosophical content and, on the other, the purely psychological mirroring in them of Nietzsche's deepest being. Such self-mirroring leads us back to the portrait drawn of Nietzsche in the first section of this book. The thought content, however, of his new teachings shows itself to be an artistic combination of both phases in Nietzsche's intellectual development, a model of separate skeins woven together with an ingenious hand: the Schopenhauerian teaching of the will and the rational teachings of the positivists.

Nietzsche's theory of knowledge, with its fight against the meaning of logic and a return willy-nilly to the unlogical, comes most into view in his book *Beyond Good and Evil*; several of its sections could just as well have been titled *Beyond Truth and Falsehood*. For it is here that he explicates in great detail the unjustified opposition of such values as "true and untrue," which in respect to their origin are no less expendable than the contrasting values of "good and evil." "The problem about the value of truth confronts us. . . . Just what is it in us that wishes to 'approach truth'? . . . Granted, we want truth, but *why not* untruth instead?" (BGE, 1). "Indeed, what compels us, anyway, to assume that there is a basic difference between 'true' and 'false'? Is it not enough to assume that there are degrees of semblance . . . like different shades of 'values' in painters' perceptions?" (34). "In what a strange state of simplification and falsification do humans live! . . . Until now science was allowed to rise only from a foundation of ignorance, a foundation no longer of granite nor firm; it is the will to knowledge arising from a much greater will, the will not-to-know, the will to uncertainty, to untruth! Not as its opposite but as its refinement!" (24). "Consciousness is not in any decisive sense the opposite of the instinctive; the most conscious thinking of a philosopher is secretly guided by his instincts and forced into certain channels" (3). All logic ultimately is nothing other than a mere "sign of convention" (TI, III, 3). All thinking is a kind of "sign language of the emotions" since "we cannot step up or step down to another 'reality' except to the reality of our drives, for thinking is only an interaction of these drives" (BGE, 36). And consequently, "the *more* emotions we allow free play and the *more* angles of vision we aim at the same thing, the more complete will be our 'conception' of that thing; herein lies our 'objectivity.' Should it be possible to eliminate will and emotions altogether, would this not result in the castration of the intellect?" (GM, III, 12).

At this point, Nietzsche's ideas turn away from earlier ones and lead in an opposite direction. Earlier, he had warned against trusting any kind of emotion because it was a "grandchild" of old, forgotten, and probably erroneous judgments; now, he summons the primeval source from which all judgments stem and demotes *them* now to unstable and dependent "grandchildren" of emotion. For both conceptions, he then finds validation not only in the world view of positivism but also in the peacefully co-existent realm of relativistic thinking and its emotional aspects. Two irreconcilable contrasts came into view: on the one side, Nietzsche stands at the sharpened extreme of intellectualism, to which he had wanted all thought and reason to be subservient; on the other side, was a heightened feeling of exaltation that took its revenge upon its long repression by turning into resplendent life and culminating in a fanatical expression of *fiat vita, pereat veritas!*[43]

In that connection, he says further, "The falsity of a specific judgment does not in itself constitute an objection against it; the real question is to what degree does this judgment preserve and sustain life . . . rejection of false judgments would mean a rejection of life, a negation of life" (BGE, 4). "Despite all the value placed upon the true, the truthful . . . it is nevertheless possible to attribute a higher and more fundamental value to appearances, the will to deception, and to avarice. It is even possible that the value of those good and venerable things consists precisely in their being insidiously related, intertwined and knotted up with those wicked and seemingly opposite things; perhaps these opposites are identical in essence" (2). "From time immemorial, basically, we have become habituated to *lying*. Or, to express things more hypocritically and therefore more pleasantly: we are far greater artists than we realize" (192). And it is the life-preserving element of the lie which raises the artist far above the scientific person and his quest for knowledge; "within art, the lie sanctifies itself and the will to self-deception boasts a good conscience" (GM, III, 25). . . .

Nietzsche's renewed glorification of the artist, and metaphysics even, tells us how far he has turned towards a new and opposite type of seeker and how far he has already distanced himself from the positivistic "reality-philosophy babblers."[44] They regarded thinking as an act independent of human drives. This reductiveness was their contribution to enlightened thinking, but Nietzsche came to believe in the need for heightened human drives. His insight into the relativity of thinking prompted him to break out of narrow and absolutistic confines and to proclaim a new, limitless horizon for the pursuit of knowledge. Because Nietzsche needed to worship new ideals upon which to exhaust himself, he let the old ideals of logical truth diminish and he sought remedy through a limitless and heightened life of the emotions. Just as he had wanted to strip his search for truth of all illusion, so now in his new relativistic orientation he opened the way to new illusions, entering the realm of emotional stimuli, to which the will subordinated itself. With that, all inhibitive and limiting dams are broken, allowing the life of the emotions to flood the scene ruthlessly. Nowhere is certainty and yet certainty is everywhere, as the belief in independent rational knowledge is swept away. As tool and toy of inner dictates and hidden drives, Nietzsche is tossed from the farthest distances and into the profoundest depths . . . into a labyrinthine wilderness, dark and impenetrable, which surrounds the intelligible world. In this labyrinth are no discernible paths and no masters and laws, but the will has room to assert itself with every type of creativity. Such a dangerous adventure seemed to assure Nietzsche of a direct path into the power of an inner life. Zarathustra therefore calls his disciples "the riddle-intoxicated, twilight revellers . . . whose souls are lured by flutes to every brink of madness; no cowardice keeps you from taking a guideline in hand, and when you can *guess* its destination, you hate to *decipher* it" ("On the Vision and the Riddle," Z, III, 1).

For a long time, Nietzsche's cold and sober thinking calmed and kept in check his aroused emotions. Now he experienced what he had warned against, premonitorily, in *Human, All-Too-Human*: "If one uses one's intellect to become master over the unlimited emotions, it may produce a sorry and diversionary effect upon the intellect" (HATH, II, 275).[45] To avoid such temptation, he swerves wildly and newly adapts the motto "Nothing is true, everything is permitted" (quoted by Nietzsche, GM, III, 24) and praises the value of illusion—the deliberate fiction of the alogical and the "untrue"—as the essentials of life-creating and will-supporting powers. He conceived a representation of the world as a world built and created by us and which contains our psychic idiosyncrasies; and he began to feel that our knowledge ultimately is nothing more than a "humanization of things." He luxuriated in these thoughts until the universe seemed to him an evanescent dream picture conjured up by the solitary thinker. "Why could not the world *which matters to us* be a fiction?" he asks himself in *Beyond Good and Evil* (34). And behind this lies the thought and question about forcefully reconstituting the world that matters to us.

What becomes pertinent here is a short and interesting chapter in Nietzsche's *Twilight of the Idols*. Chapter four is entitled "How the True World Finally Became a Fable: The History of an Error," and it contains a sketch of philosophical developments from the ancients to the moderns. Naïvely though, the old philosophy apprehended the knower and his picture of the world, as well as the person and the truth, as identical. This culminated in the rewriting of the sentence "I, Plato, *am* the truth." The "true world," in contrast to an untrue and illusory one in which the unaware live, "is achievable for the wise one because he lives in it and *it is he.*" In Christendom the idea of the "true world" separates itself progressively from that of "personality" in that it becomes dehumanized and a sublimated promise for the future, a promise that is imposed upon humans. Finally after a series of metaphysical systems, the true world finally is reduced by Kant to a pale shadow—unreachable, unprovable, unpromisable; and with the final departure from all things metaphysical, it completely evaporates into nothing: "Gray morning. The first yawn of reason. The cock-crow of positivism." And so, the price of the world, hitherto denigrated as illusory and untrue, rises because it is the only world left: "Bright day; breakfast; the return of good sense and gaiety; Plato's embarrassed blush; the devil's din of all free spirits." But along with insight into the origin of the fable of the "true world," we have been able to observe how the world picture of our knowledge came to be. Now that we are no longer consoled by a belief in a mystically "true" world behind one created by illusion and error, what is left for us? Since we have done away with the "true" world as well as its opposite and illusory world, what remains? Again, the human being is thrown back upon himself as the creator of all things.

Again the old formulation has been made possible: "I, Plato, *am* the world." It stands firmly as the final wisdom at the beginning of all philosophy, but no longer with a naïve identification of person and truth, subject and object. Instead, the statement stands as a conscious and willed act of creation by one who has perceived himself to be the bearer of the world: I, Nietzsche-Zarathustra, am the world; it exists because I am, it exists as I will it. This kind of formula one may extract from the suggestive, mysterious, and concluding phrases of chapter four: "Mid-day; moment of the briefest shadow; end of the longest error; high point of humanity; *INCIPIT ZARATHUSTRA.*"[46]

Here we can already see clearly how his new ideas loop into mysticism and also become entwined with modern theories of knowledge. And so the point has been reached upon which his new teachings are constructed; he is no longer concerned with mere exaggerated notions of certain commonly accepted ideas. From the limitation and relativity of human knowledge and from the priority of human drives, Nietzsche imperceptibly and unconsciously gains a sense of the new type of philosopher: he is the bigger-than-life picture of a solitary whose will power decides between the true and the untrue and in whose hand the viewpoint of mere human reason becomes a toy. One could say that the element which forces one's intellect toward self-limitation, together with external pressures and influences, becomes personified for Nietzsche in the image of an unchecked omnipotence projected onto a superior solitary person. Life's quintessence and energy become so unified in that person that he is capable of reshaping the norms of knowledge. However, this does not occur through contemplation but through creativity, and as action and command addressed to the world: "Indeed, the *real philosophers are commanders and lawgivers* and say, '*This* is how things *shall* be!' They determine the direction and rationale of humans. . . . With creative hands, they reach for the future. . . . Their 'knowledge' is *creation*, their creation is legislation, their will to truth is *will to power*" (BGE, 211). Their philosophy always creates "the world in their image; they can do no less. Philosophy is the tyrannical drive of the most spiritual will to power, to the 'creation of the world,' and to the '*causa prima*'" (BGE, 9). "The Caesar type and dictator of civilization" (207) occupy Nietzsche's elucidation and description of his philosophy of the future. Through his theory of knowledge, a foundation is prepared for them in Nietzsche's ethics and aesthetics, and from which they grow ever higher into religious mysticism within which God, world, and humanity meld into a single, tremendous superior being.

It may readily be seen how close Nietzsche's image of this creator-philosopher comes to his earlier metaphysical views, but also how he will modify it through his later theories. The "ideal" truths of metaphysics, with their elevating and comforting interpretations of the world's riddle, are not taken up again; and so he makes room and substitutes lost ideal truths, and reasons for consolation, with scepticism by declaring that "everything is untrue," eliminating altogether the possibility of truth. Through a declaration of power and an act of will, Nietzsche injects into things a meaning which they have not possessed. Formerly a *discoverer* of truth, the philosopher now has become, so to speak, an *inventor* of the truth, whose sheer abundance of will is able to turn expressed untruths and deceptions into convincing realities. "Whoever does not know how to project his will into things, may at least project meaning into them" ("Maxims and Arrows," TI, 18). With that he turned against the philosophers of metaphysics, but like them assumed the right to reinterpret and re-create things through the inspiration of mood, thereby going beyond mere intellectualism.

With this personally-conceived superiority of the emotional over the intellectual life—in which ultimately the truth is considered inessential as compared with the emotion and will of a perception—Nietzsche's intellectual manner and his inner longings are uninhibitedly mirrored. In reaction to his long subservience to the disciplined search for knowledge . . . he was drawn into a frenzy of mysticism. . . . Even so, he attempted to grasp intellectually the power of moods. He does not rest until the triumph of his unchained life's will becomes a self-mockery of the mind. In an uncanny way, and through the discarding of all logical knowledge, the thinker is "secretly enticed by his own cruelty and is pushed forward by the dangerous thrill of that cruelty directed against himself"; he must reign as "artist and transfigurer of cruelty" (BGE, 229). The human spirit finally descends voluntarily into its own destruction because only then does it receive its greatest enlightenment; he dives into the limitless and the measureless, which close over him; only in this fashion does he fulfill his goal.

In the aesthetics and ethics of Nietzsche's last philosophizing, we find again the pervasive theme that a decline through excess is the necessary precondition for a highest and new creation. And therefore, Nietzsche's theory of knowledge culminates in a kind of personal thrall in which the concepts of madness and truth are inextricably entwined. For that reason the idea of the "humanly superior" comes like a lightning stroke which annihilates the spirit, a madness, which ought to inoculate his sense of truth: "I would wish that you possess a madness that destroys you! . . . Truly, I would wish that your madness were called 'truth'! . . . And the happiness of the spirit consists of this—to be anointed and sanctified through tears as a sacrificial animal; did you already know this? And the blindness of the blind person and his searching and groping, as before, will be proof of the sun's power, into which he looks; did you already know that?" ("Of the Famous Wise Men," Z, II).

But this last mystery, like Nietzsche's image of the creator-philosopher, can only become fully clear to us as we continue to explore further his ethics and aesthetics. Abstract lines steadily gain concrete features until finally Nietzsche's mystical explanation of his self allows us to see him as an individual.

The ethics of Nietzsche's theory of knowledge . . . reflect his view of the systems of philosophers: "the moral intentions . . . form the true kernel from which the entire plant has always grown" (BGE, 6). This close connection between the philosopher and life, as such, and with its most human and personal ends should have set him apart decisively from all those who view life with hostility and pessimism. Nietzsche should have been a natural apologist for life and his philosophy its affirmation for life can always only affirm itself. In reality, however, almost always the opposite was the case: "Throughout time, the wisest among us have rendered similar judgment about life—it is worse than useless. . . . Always and everywhere, one has heard the same sound—a sound full of desperation, full of melancholy, weariness with life, resistance to life" (TI, II, 1). After all, this weakened will-to-life was a consequence of the refinement and sublimation of their human and animalistic essence, as well as the intellectual and contemplative components of their nature. It was also, according to Nietzsche's former conception, a sign of their nobility, which so to speak set them apart from the spiritually coarse mob and which entitled them to a role of leadership. With such works as *Twilight of the Idols,* Nietzsche's conception had changed to the point of no longer placing emphasis upon the spiritual invigoration of life but on the weakening of life. Persons of intellect from then on appear as the ill and enervated, as the apocalyptic types of that age. The philosopher Socrates, who had originally been so loved and extolled by Nietzsche as representing among the Greeks the teaching of reason's dominance over natural instincts, now appeared to him transformed into the dangerous and opprobrious seducer that he had been during Nietzsche's Schopenhauer period. Among the distinguished and well-fashioned Greeks, the ugly and misshapen Socrates appeared as the first great decadent; he corrupted and maimed the natural Hellenic life-instinct, taming and subduing it to the teachings of rationality. Nietzsche discusses all this in the section "The Problems of Socrates" in his *Twilight of the Idols*. Socrates is pictured there as the archetype of all thinkers who wish to master life through rational thought. In his testimony against life and the instincts, Socrates unwittingly only demonstrated the emptiness of pure intellectualism, without disproving the fullness of life. Philosophers who have contributed to the denigration of existence and life-sustaining instincts failed to see life's values and fell into sickly contradictions. Herein lies the explanation why arrogant intellectuals, who have turned away from the life source which has nourished their minds, are decrepit, weary, and decadent; they come to birth in late phases of declining cultures. Worse still, they no longer possess the triumphing, healing, and transforming strength which conquers sorrows and depressions of life; they cannot shape life into a higher form. We harbor suspicions about these "wise men": "Were they not unsteady on their feet? tardy? wobbly? decadents? Does their wisdom appear on this earth as a raven perhaps who is enthused by the rankish odor of a cadaver?" ("Socrates," TI, 1).

But this question concerns us all, for it represents no less than the extreme point of humanity's historical development. Forcefully torn from their dank and brooding animal-consciousness, humans, because of their more highly developed mental capabilities, came into conflict with that essence of nature in which their strength is rooted. That conflict diminished man and produced a hybrid being who evidently could not draw upon inner resources for enlightenment and justification for existence; he is the embodiment of a transition to something as yet not discovered or not yet created, and as such he is the sickliest, "the *not yet stabilized animal*" (BGE, 62). And so, the characteristics of decadence fastened upon every aspect of humanity.

Accordingly, we find the earliest signs of decadence and the end of self-contained life already at the beginning of every culture, at the point where the "predatory human animal" with his untamed freedom feels himself constricted and hemmed in by the first imposed social restrictions. "These terrible barriers, with which organized society protected itself against the old instincts of freedom . . . , induced all those instincts of the wild, roving man to be turned back *against man himself.*" "All instincts which do not discharge themselves *turn inwards*—this is what I call the *internalization* of man; only in that fashion was something developed which later was called 'his soul.' The entire inner world, originally thin and tensed as if between two membranous walls, . . . expanded in depth, breadth, and height as discharges were blocked from moving outward." "The inventor of the bad conscience was the man who, lacking external enemies and barriers, impatiently tore himself apart when he found himself forced into narrow confines and the conventionality of customs; he persecuted, gnawed, startled, and mistreated himself and wounded himself against the bars of his cage. . . . But through him the greatest and most sinister illness was introduced, and of which mankind has not been healed as yet: man's self-directed suffering in consequence of his forcible break with his animal past . . . a declaration of war against the old instincts which up to then had been the source of his strength, joy, and awesomeness" (GM, II, 16).

In that regard, if the sickliness of man is, so to speak, his normal condition or his specific human nature itself, and if the concepts of falling ill and of development are seen as almost identical, then we will naturally encounter again the already mentioned decadence at the culmination of a long cultural development. Only the appearance of decadence has changed. During times of long and peaceable habituation, decadence takes on new shapes. . . . "Whether variations are deviations (into things higher, finer, and rarer) or deteriorations and monstrosities, they suddenly appear on the scene whole and splendid; the individual dares to be unique and detached" (BGE, 262).

If in the portrayal of the original form of decadence man's passions turned against himself and threatened and mauled him because there was no defense or outward vent, now for opposite reasons they war against each other because no longer are there conditions against which man must defend himself. There is nothing outside himself that requires a deflection outward of his combativeness. In the calm of an ordered life, the strongly internalized person has, in the meantime, become his own battleground for inner and contrary drives. As soon as these begin to stir, he suffers from his own being, "thanks to the wildly exploding egotisms turned against themselves simultaneously." Having developed into a highly complicated being, a person slowly relinquishes his earlier wholeness. During this phase, a human being becomes the final link of a single and enormously long chain of development, a chain in which the individual links are part of him and form the total sum of slowly acquired intellectual, moral, and social "humanness," beside the varied, all-too-active, memories of instincts that reach back to the antiquity of animalness.

But if these two forms of decadence have sprung from the compulsion of human nature and are unavoidable stages of transition toward their growth into something higher, there is also a third kind of decadence which threatens to make the conditions of the described illness incurable and threatens the possibility of recovery. And that form of decadence is embodied in a false interpretation of the world, an incorrect perception of life encouraged by that suffering and illness. The call to asceticism appears variously as a turning away from life and its pains and a yielding to tiredness which stems from the continual "warfare of which one consists." Not only do all religions and moralities preach such an ascetic ideal, but also every kind of intellectualism extols thinking at the expense of life and supports the ideal of "truth" at the expense of a heightened sensation of living. The genuine cure for this spreading infection consists at once in a full turn toward life, so that a new, superior state of health will be born from the rich chaos of contending contrasts.

"One's fruitfulness is the price of rich, inner contrasts" (TI, V, 3), provided that one has sufficient strength to carry them and to *endure* them. Thus, apparent dissolution and decadence, and every so-called corruption, are "only abusive names for the *seasons of harvest*" (GS, I, 23), namely, the seasons when leaves as well as the ripened fruit fall. In this sense may decadence and progress refer to one and the same thing—"Nothing helps: one *must* go forward, step by step, further into *decadence*. . . . One can indeed *block* this development and stem degeneration; one can pull it together and make it more vehement and *sudden:* one can do no more" (TI, IX, 43). Such an end—a tragic knotting of the forward and downward—is explained by the fact that the human being cannot find fulfillment in himself but must push out toward something higher than himself. "The phenomenon of an animal 'soul' turning against itself . . . displayed to the world something novel, profound, paradoxical, and rich with future possibilities," giving rise to the confident hope for a superior form of human being. With that, it seems as if man were not a goal but a harbinger, a pointer, an interim, a bridge, and a great promise" (GM, II, 16). "The human being is a rope tied to the animal and the superior being—a rope over an abyss. . . . Admirable about a human is his being a bridge and not an end; what one may cherish about him is his being a *transition* and a *decline*" ("Prologue," Z, 4). At times of impending decline, humanity could as little have been spared the announcement of a new birth; it is like "the unpleasantnesses and marvels attending pregnancy, of which one must forget the pains in order to enjoy the offspring" (GM, III, 4).

The insight into the transitory "all-too-human" drives, which Nietzsche had so strongly emphasized earlier, is not abandoned but, if possible, even sharpened in favor of his new theory about humanity. With cool intellectual insight, his theory escalated into an emotional mood through which it gathered such great significance that it plunged all his psychic and intellectual strength into turmoil; through anger, grief, and horror he gained new "wings and elementary power" and rose above his mood. From the emphasis he placed upon his erstwhile insight and the extreme consequences he drew from it, there poured forth an overwhelming desire for his new theory which strove for a sacrifice of the all-too-human to something superior.

The sections on theories of knowledge in Nietzsche's new teachings mirror the dependence of the logical upon the psychic and the life of ideas upon the life of emotions. Such a passionate over-abundance which furthers a new birth Nietzsche sees at work as well in humans: the self-sacrifice of embattled drives leads to the highest creative power. From the ever-present feeling of sickliness and personal sufferings, Nietzsche derives his teachings about decadence. As with all the theories of his last phase, decadence meant the following: the painful psychic events which hitherto were for him the *cause and accompaniment* of different thought processes, now became the *content* of knowledge itself.

The idea of a humanity that had become super-charged with emotion and self-sacrifice became in Nietzsche's retrospective review an idea which makes the entire process of human development intelligible. For that development, the long and painful taming of innate animal spiritedness was necessary, even though it cultivated decadence in humans, which they ultimately outgrew again. The meaning of it all was to enrich every human with the fullness of an inner life and to make him master of that richness and of himself. That could only occur through long and hard discipline by which his will, like that of an adolescent, was brought to maturity with a teacher's rod and punishments. And so, humans learned to acquire a more durable and deep-seated will than the fleeting will to which the animal's impulse is subjugated. He learned to stand up for his demands; he became the animal that *can promise*. All of human education is basically a kind of mnemonic technique: it solves the labor of how to *incorporate memory* into the unpredictable will.

"The ability to vouch for one's self and proudly to say *yes* to one's self, that . . . is a late fruit; this unripe and sour fruit hung interminably upon the tree! . . . Let us imagine ourselves as viewing the end of the tremendous process when the tree finally offers its ripe fruits, when a communality of creatures, with its morality-producing customs, finally shows us why it was only a means to an end. And so we see the ripest fruit, the *sovereign individual* who resembles nothing except himself and who again is freed from the morality of custom, an autonomous individual who transcends custom (for 'autonomous' and 'moralistic' are mutually exclusive) . . . in short, the man possessed of a personal, independent, and long-lasting will and who is *competent to make promises*" (GM, II, 1–3). This sureness of self-knowledge by the emancipated individual who has become the master represents a new kind of conscience. He has outgrown the moral representations and concepts of the ideal that belong to his antecedents and to his strict educators who now have become superfluous; abandoning all these, he has discarded as well the old conscience and its roots and justification.

Nietzsche's theory of the will points to a merging of his former metaphysical views with a scientific determinism. During his earlier days as a disciple of Schopenhauer, he made the distinction between the mysterious "will-in-itself," which formed the basis for Schopenhauer's metaphysics, and the will that makes its appearance in our human perception. He called the will "free," insofar as its deepest sources lay beyond our total world of experience, beyond its laws of causality; he called the will "unfree," insofar as the isolated appearances of will only become perceptible within the indestructible net of general causality. After that, Nietzsche paid years of tribute to a rigid determinism and clung to the view that the "will" first earned its name, so to speak, when it was tied to the apron strings of the decisive influences that shaped the will. But, as a determinist, what he denied in regard to the mysterious past and origin of the will, he asserted to be the objective of the development of the will. . . . The world of reality in its accessible and intelligible development was treasured by Nietzsche during his positivistic phase, and he turned against differently inclined metaphysics, saying, "Everything that is perfect and completed is admired; everything in gestation is undervalued" (HATH, I, 162), simply because one can no longer test or understand the causes and origins of the perfect. Now, he was able to admire equally whatever was perfect and seemingly completed, and everything evolving which seemed valuable to him to the extent that it was on the road to completion. He admitted the dependency of all things, but only because at some time the mystical meaning of all things, transcending dependency and experience, would be revealed. This "significance" depends upon the power of a liberated will because it is to be *built into* all things. For that reason, Nietzsche wants to replace the "free" and the "unfree" will of the determinists with the expressions "the *strong* will" and "the *weak* will" (BGE, 21) and he wishes to have all of psychology understood "as the morphology and evolutionary doctrine of the will to power" (BGE, 23).

The possessor of "will" is then, at all times, to the highest degree, the "untimely one," the one in whom genius blossomed during humanity's long preparation. What was learned during humanity's slavery, then streamed freely from his genius. Geniuses are "like explosives in which a tremendous power has accumulated; their precondition always is a long accumulation, hoarding, and preservation, historically and physiologically. . . . Their appearance in time is coincidental, and that they become master of their time is attributable to their being stronger, older. . . . Relative to them, an age is always much younger, thinner, more immature, less assured, more childish." "The great person is a climax . . . genius—in work and deed—is necessarily a squanderer: *his lavishness is* his greatness. . . . The instinct of self-preservation is suspended as well; the overwhelming pressure of outflowing powers prevents him from any such care and caution" (TI,IX, 44). . . .

The birth of a superior human being was intimated in Nietzsche's portrayal of genius. Within the superior being, all of the past is evident and is epitomized; indeed, within him is contained "the entire continuous line of man up to his own contemporary being," and so, quite suddenly, there would have to be revealed to him the future goal of mankind. Through the will to power of such a herald, the development of mankind—its direction, goal, and future—gained an inner and valid significance. Briefly, for the first time, there came into view Nietzsche's vision of the philosopher as a creator. Nietzsche thought of him as a master of his will, the genius who understands the life within. "In fact, it is not so much a matter of discovering than it is recognizing again and remembering again—regression and returning home to a distant and most ancient, common household of the soul, out of which concepts grew. From that perspective, philosophizing is a kind of atavism of the highest order" (BGE, 20). Everything highest as a form of atavism is an idea that contains the curious *reactionary* aspect of Nietzsche's entire philosophizing of his last phase, sharply distinct from his earlier ones. It is an attempt to replace metaphysical glorification. He only takes up the ideas of "remembering again" and "recognizing again" (not in Plato's sense) because he intended to understand them as transcendent constants during the enormously long evolution of human thought. Of all things nobly constituted, Nietzsche regarded only the most ancient as relevant determinants for the future.[47] The worth and dignity of things are exclusively tied to the remotest age: only at the end do they reveal their treasure: power, freedom, and emancipated strength. "Whoever *has* these good things is different from one who *acquires* them. Everything that is good is inherited: whatever is not inherited is imperfect and only a beginning" (TI, IX, 47). Dignity resides in "whatever disallows improvisation." Nothing is actually more uncouth and undignified than the emergent and the bearer of the emergent and the novel: modern man and the modern spirit, completely conditioned by the times, represent a spirit of slavery. A superior, master spirit can only come about after many centuries of biological transmission produce the "untimely" and the "timeless" genius.

"Democracy has been at all times a form of decline in organizing power. . . . For institutions to exist, there must be . . . a will, instinct, and an imperative that are anti-liberal, even to the point of malice—the will to tradition, to authority and responsibility for ages ahead, and to the *solidarity* of infinite links of generations into the past and future" (TI, IX, 39). It is interesting to compare the relevant passages in Nietzsche's previous works and to see the changes in theoretical conceptions produced by an emotional turnabout and to perceive, therefore, how irreconcilably the contrasts appear sharpened.[48] He now excoriates the "uncouth leveling" of all men and the taming influences of peace that prevent raw, barbaric powers from emerging, powers which the healthy force of older times could infuse into a devitalized present. Barbarians are "the more whole humans, who are commonly called 'more whole beasts' at every stage" (BGE, 257). These "more whole humans and beasts" are considered by a mediocre society as evil and dangerous and are stamped as criminals and treated accordingly. Indeed, because of their stronger natural drives, they are born criminals and lawbreakers. "The criminal type is typical of the strong human being under unfavorable conditions. . . . He feels the absence of a wilderness, a somehow more unrestricted and dangerous environment and mode of existence, where everything that is weapon and defense is *justifiable* throughout the instinct of the stronger man. His *virtues* are put under constraints" (TI, IX, 45). The conception of freedom that provides a certain freedom for *everyone*, even for the weakest and lowest, stands opposed to that of the criminal type: his ruthlessness and restlessness always demands the ravaging of others, while his power expresses itself instinctively and necessarily through his trampling upon every visible weakness. The reason why the instincts break out so strongly in him is the fact that he stems from an older stage of culture and represents an older form of humanity: like the man of overpowering will and the genius, he is most atavistically inclined.[49] Even if this oldest and vital instinct for power is ignoble, it is noble nevertheless in that it represents a break-through of long-accumulated fullness that represents strong explosive material with which the past fructifies the future. Where the criminal forcefully becomes a genius of his kind and a possessor of free will, he sometimes succeeds in bending the dominant and uncongenial trends of his time to his own tyrannical will. Napoleon is such an example for Nietzsche, similar to the view of the historian Hippolyte Taine. For Nietzsche, too, it seemed of greatest importance that Napoleon inherited the tyrannical spirit of the Renaissance and transplanted it to Corsica where it could be preserved intact in the wildness and age-old customs derived from forebears; with its primal energy, it finally emerged to subjugate modern Europe, which provided it with a different kind of space than Italy had offered for the release of energy. To Nietzsche's last phase belongs his admiration for the great Corsican as well as for the Italian Renaissance which he had viewed quite differently earlier in his life.*

For Nietzsche, the ideal image of a born master-nature, as it ought to be and which would serve Nietzsche's time, was embodied in the primal health and violence of Napoleon's instinct for power; that power would serve to extirpate whatever has been

---

*In *Daybreak*, 549, Nietzsche explains the ruthless egotism of Napoleon's drive for action as grounded in his epileptic disposition; later, Nietzsche attributed that drive to an outbreak of Napoleon's "superabundant health" that embodied all the forceful instincts of a past culture [a synthesis of the primal and superior]. *See also* HATH, I, 164 and 237. . . .

extolled by the slave-nature of modern man because of his moral considerations and sentimental inclinations. With that, we come to Nietzsche's much discussed and much over-rated differentiation between master and slave morality. Here too, at first, Nietzsche followed positivistic suggestions.

As mentioned earlier, Rée's work in progress at that time [*The Origin of Conscience*] prompted Nietzsche to discuss thoroughly with his friend all the material for that work, including the etymological and historical connections among concepts: noble-strong-good and inferior-weak-evil as understood within the oldest morality or, so to speak, within pre-moralistic stages of culture. The fashion in which these conversations and mutual studies were once again revived by the friends was characteristic of the relation to which Nietzsche still stood in regard to positivistic views: once more he listened to those ideas patiently, and selectively took those items that were inclined toward his own thinking but then, with hostility, turned against his erstwhile companion.

Rée, in his work, interpreted the historical shift in value judgment toward benevolent and egalitarian impulses as a natural and gradual transition toward more highly developed societal forms: the original glorification of animal rapaciousness and selfishness yielded increasingly to the introduction of milder customs and laws, until finally the Christian morality of sympathy and neighborly love appeared as the highest religion-sanctioned law.[50] In his personal assessment of the moral phenomenon, Rée meanwhile was far from putting himself on the side of the English utilitarians, though he was closest to them in his scientific views. For Nietzsche, on the other hand, as a consequence of his changed conception of morality, the historically-given differentiation between the two valuations of what "good" meant sharpened into two irreconcilable contrasts: a battle between master morality and slave morality, which remains unabated into our own time. The uncommonly great significance of the powerful will and instinct, as seen by Nietzsche, led him to perceive them as the only possible source of a healthy morality. In contrast, he saw the sanctioning of benevolent feelings as a grave error which caused man to become sick and remain sick. Nietzsche regarded as erroneous his earlier attribution of all moral valuations to utility—that is, custom and the forgetting of original causes of utility. Such origins could at best be suitable for a slave-morality, but for the master morality, a more noble origin must be found. It is an act of sensibility to call a thing good or bad without consideration for its utility; and so it is with a master nature: it senses within itself and all its impulses, the "good," and looks down on everything outside as weakness, dependency, fearfulness, almost unconsciously and contemptuously referring to them as "bad." In an entirely different manner does the slave morality of the inferior and "the bad" arise: it does not arise spontaneously but out of resentment and a kind of revenge; slave-morality regards everything "bad" to be despicable and as belonging to the ruling class, and deriving from that view the conception of "good" as consisting of the opposite—namely, the weak, the oppressed, the suffering. On the one side, therefore, stands the beast of prey, conscienceless and free of a sense of guilt, a strong, "rejoicing monster" which commits even the most terrible deeds with boisterous and spirited equanimity, as if these were student pranks (GM, I, 11), while on the other side stand the oppressed—practiced in hate, whose soul helplessly thirsts for revenge—and who seem to preach the morality of pity and pathetic neighborly love. Christianity fully developed this type of the ideal, which Nietzsche unhesitatingly conceives as an enormous act of revenge by Jewry upon the self-satisfied world of antiquity. That the Jews [actually, Roman soldiers under orders from Pontius Pilate—ed.] crucified the founder of Christianity and rejected his religion was really part of a finessed plan of revenge whereby the other nations would unthinkingly "take this bait."* But it is not necessary to follow all of Nietzsche's explanations and earlier speculative

---

*In contrast to Nietzsche's later scorn for the Jewish character, one should note his Aphorism 205, in *Daybreak*, headed, "About the People of Israel": "the psychological and spiritual resources of today's Jews are extraordinary. . . . Whereto then shall stream this abundance of great, accumulated impressions . . . this abundance of passions, virtues, decisions, renunciations, struggles and victories of all kinds, whereto shall these flow if not ultimately into great-spirited humans and works! Be-

interpretations of history because the essential significance of his philosophical views lies elsewhere. In his need to generalize and to establish everything scientifically, Nietzsche attempted to place something into the development of history, something whose significance for him lay within a hidden psychic problem. For that reason, it is regrettable that Nietzsche's unique manner of thinking has been obscured by a false emphasis upon his "objectivity." Especially his hypotheses ought not to be taken as abstractions, if one is to draw from them the original kernel. For him the basic question was not the psychic history of mankind but how his own, personal history might be perceived as belonging to all of mankind. In sharpest contrast to the philological preciseness with which he began his career—and through which he earlier also interpreted history and philosophy—diligent academic study no longer played a role in his brilliant inspirations and ideas; moreover, rigorous research could no longer play a role due to his eyesight.

All studies which he still could touch upon relate to the fact that "we always remain only in the confines of our own company" (GS, 166), even when we allow entrance of what is foreign: "All my peculiarities also exist in nature and history and praise me, drive me forward, and console me: everything else I fail to hear or I forget it immediately." "The limit of our sense of hearing: One only hears those questions for which one is capable of finding an answer" (GS, 196). "However great my greed for knowledge, I can extract from things nothing other than what already belongs to me" (GS, 242).

With this kind of arbitrary selection of materials in favor of his philosophical hypotheses, he further distances himself from objective observation and factual bases; he became more subjectively oriented in his conclusions than in those years when he

---

cause when Jews are able to point to such precious stones and golden vessels as their works—works which European nations of a briefer and less profound experience cannot produce—and when having transformed its eternal vengeance into an eternal blessing for Europe, then every seventh day will be here again on which the ancient Jewish God . . . may rejoice in his creation and in his chosen people—and, we all, all of us shall rejoice with him!"

still confined himself consciously to what he experienced inwardly. Now, the inwardly meaningful became the outer determinant and legislator, while he himself became the "great lord of force," the "cunning fiend, who forces and forges the past into a prefiguration and bridge" to the future ("On Old and New Tablets," Z, III, 11).

In respect to Nietzsche's own psychic problem, it is of less interest to determine correctly the historicity of master morality and slave morality than it is to ascertain the fact that in man's evolution he has carried these contrasts, these antitheses, within himself and that he is the consequent sufferer of this conflict of instincts, embodying double valuations. If we recall Nietzsche's description of decadence, we find in it a person with the characteristics of a born master, that is, of natural and untamed strength and savagery, but made subservient and reduced to an obedient slave through social compulsion exerted during the beginning of a culture. *Every* culture as such, for Nietzsche, is founded upon this kind of reduction to illness and enslavement of man; he expressly remarks that without this process and without being turned violently against oneself, man's soul would have remained "flat" and "thin": man's original master-nature is still nothing more than a magnificent example of the animal creature that is only enabled to develop further through the wounds inflicted upon its power. For in the agony of these wounds, it must learn to tear itself to pieces and to take revenge upon itself, and to relieve its helplessness through inward-turned sufferings: *all this exclusively on the soil of slavish* ressentiment [a desire for vengeance]. "The essential thing, it seems, to say it once more, . . . is that there be a long and durable *obedience* in one direction. . . . Something will come of that and make it worthwhile in the long run to live on this earth" (BGE, 188).

Nietzsche's condition of decadence, above all, is not all conquerable but is the necessary precondition for breeding a human being who can tame the will and become emotionally strong and self-confident. But one would note well that this completed person with his deepened and individualized master-nature ought not to live out his naïve egoism or discard preconceptions and slavery's chains only in order to become his own reason for being;

on the contrary, he must become the first in a line of a higher human type and sacrifice himself while giving it birth, because, as we have seen, the peak of development also represents the decline of mankind in that it only serves as a transition to something higher and only forms a bridge and a means. Therefore, the greater the man and his genius, and the greater he is as a pinnacle, all the more does he become an end, giving of himself with outpouring powers: "Ready to be destroyed within victory!" ("On Old and New Tablets," Z, III, 30). He would become "something completed and a fully fashioned end, mighty and triumphant" and "ready for even newer, heavier, and future tasks" like "a bow tensed ever more tightly by the force of necessity" (GM, I, 12), a bow whose arrow targets the superior being.

And so, Nietzsche became the battleground of conflicting and contentious drives, out of whose painful abundance alone came development. Through this turmoil—the will to mastery and the need to serve, the rape of one by the other—we see in Nietzsche a replay of the origins of all culture and the struggle from which a superior culture was to evolve as the very summit of creation. Never a person at peace with himself nor one who takes pleasure in himself, Nietzsche is a fighter who invites his own defeat. Although he is free-spirited and completely individualistic, he places demands upon himself that are similar to the age-old *external* pressures used by society to educate people for slavery. In Nietzsche we find self-imposed norms against which he always rebels. He describes this process as "this secret ravaging of one's self, this cruelty of the artist, this passion to shape one's self out of suffering and refractory materials, as well as to instill criticism and contempt and to brand the self with a 'nay'; this is the sinister and horrifyingly passionate work of a soul which wills its own split and inflicts pain upon itself out of a desire for creating pain" (GM, II, 18). Inexorably, the most complete and comprehensive soul must express clearly and irrevocably life's fundamental law: "I am *that which must always conquer itself*" ("On Self-Overcoming," Z, II).

One must not underestimate how greatly Nietzsche submitted his own psyche to these theories, how strongly his own being is mirrored in them, and how he ultimately derived from their deepest necessity the fundamental basis of life. His pained "multiplicity of soul" and his enforced "dividedness" into a self-sacrificing, self-worshiping being, and as a dominating deified part of nature, all underlie his total picture of human development. Whenever he speaks of master and slave natures, one must remember that he speaks about himself, driven by the longing of an inharmonious nature to seek its opposite and the longing to be able to look up to its god. He images his own "I" when he says of a slave, "His spirit *squints* and loves hiding places, devious paths, and backdoors—everything hidden seems to him to be *his* world, *his* security, *his* balm" (GM, I, 10). Its opposite picture is portrayed by Nietzsche in the active, joyous, instinctual, and carefree master-nature of the man of deeds. But while Nietzsche allows that one is the precondition for the other, as human nature becomes the arena for these contraries which attempt to subdue each other, he also perceives them as *stages of development within the same creature*; historically considered, they remain contrasts, but psychologically considered they constitute a split within each individual who is capable of development. For that reason, the total significance of Nietzsche's interpretation of the historical battle between master and slave mentalities is nothing less than a radically simplified illustration of what transpires in the superior individual and what must split him into a sacrificial god and a sacrificial animal.

At this point we may now see the meaning of Nietzsche's "revaluation of all values," and of all the old conceptions of morality and ideals, as well as their relevance to the *ascetic ideal* in which all religious and moral ideals are, contrarily, not gathered, according to Nietzsche. This revaluation of values *begins*, above all, with a canonization of the "human, all-too-human" in humans, something which had formerly been despised and suppressed because the natural and the physical senses had stood in the way of the supernatural and the suprasensual that were believed to be unassailable and given facts. Nietzsche's philosopher of the future no longer believes though that any kind of superior humanity is a given certainty; it must be created by the human being, and for that he has recourse to no other material than the elementary life-force of nature as it is. It is no longer valid to consign the here-and-now to a higher beyond, but it is only valid to draw the entire abundance of an unimaginably magnificent beyond out of the midst of the here-and-now.* And with that, Nietzsche restores the right to existence to the despised, feared, mistreated drives and passions of the "natural man" not as yet cut to size by any morality. Then follows the conviction that a separation of good and bad powers is immaterial to the important question of strengthening and heightening life's inner powers so that life can convert its highest purpose to reality. It is evident that the worst in man is necessary for his best and most creative: "man must become better and more evil" ("The Convalescent," Z, III, 2).

As an advocate of life, man should lavishly spend his virtues. . . . Although at first glance egotistic free-play and virtue appear to be the same, in reality they remain widely separated from one another. . . . Excess is the path to the overhuman. . . : "Where is the lightning which licks you with its tongue? Where is the madness with which you must be inoculated?—See, I teach you the overman: he is that lightning and that madness!" ("Prologue," Z, 3).

For that reason one ought not to confuse Nietzsche's path toward his ideal goal with the goal itself; he regarded the sovereignty of the "terrible instincts" only as means toward the highest end. Unjustifiably and with gross misunderstanding, he has been saddled with the accusation that his "overman" bears the features of a Cesare Borgia or some other blasphemous monster, rather than those of a Jesus. In truth, the primal man is not a

---

*For the free-wheeling life of man as an individual, Nietzsche found the most beautiful expressions in his Zarathustra composition, which could be called the "Song of Songs" of modern individualism. The following sayings may be regarded as characteristic:

"If you are the willer of the will and make of this needed turn a necessity: that is the origin of your virtue."

"Like myself, lead far-straying virtue back to earth; yes, lead it back to body and life, so that it will give meaning to the earth, a human meaning."

"At the end, all your passions become virtues and all your devils become angels."

model but only a pedestal for the superior man; he represents, so to speak, the raw block of granite upon which a godlike statue is to be fashioned. And this godlike statue of the superior man is the very opposite of a monster. That difference is more profoundly perceived by Nietzsche than by the most ascetic of moralists. Every morality strives only to improve and cosmetize the human, while Nietzsche proceeds from the assumption that a new and completely different species of a superior kind must be created. What in the past has been regarded as a transition from the lower to the higher and a retention of the characteristically human in an idealized image, Nietzsche sees instead as a necessary and radical break fostered by the battle of contending opposites. What was up to then only a degree of difference between the "natural" and the "moral" within humans became for Nietzsche an absolute contrast between the man of nature and the superior man. Therefore, one may say that Nietzsche's *moral approach* is anti-ascetic; within his tropic wilderness, he found untroubled self-satisfaction. Nevertheless, if one looks more closely at Nietzsche's moral aim, it turns out to be completely ascetic in that it wants not only to uplift the human being but to transform him radically. On the one hand then, Nietzsche fights common morality because of its ascetic character and its denigration and condemnation of the animality which Nietzsche values so highly as a source of strength; on the other hand, he fights the reigning morality because it is insufficiently ascetic. He turns thoroughly against its optimistic beliefs . . . for man cannot be brought into the range of an ideal goal . . . and therefore, all so-called ennoblement rests upon sheer weakening of the elementary life force. "I had once seen them naked—the greatest and the insignificant person, both all-too-similar: even the greatest is all-too-human!" ("Of Priests," Z, II).

The attempt of all morality to ascribe a similarity to human essence *and* ideal essence results only in an unreal imitation at the expense of true strength, and therefore all moral change is only a kind of aesthetic veiling of the weakened, but otherwise completely unchanged, human essence. "A great man, you say? What I see though is always an actor who only dramatizes his own ideals" (BGE, 97). "I searched for great human beings but always found only the *apes* of their ideals" (TI, I, 39).

This pessimistic perception of the human is the source of the extreme ascetic fundament of the ideal goal in Nietzsche's philosophy, and that is only achievable through the decline of man. And this fundament consequently emerges all the more emphatically, the more Nietzsche is occupied with denying and rooting out everything ascetic. At the start, Nietzsche demanded an exclusive heightening of egotistical powers, which makes it all the more astonishing that at the end he demands the giving up of one's self to make room for the superior man. Although at first he deemed man a creature who must become evil, wild, and gruesome, he finally concluded that man is a creature who must be conquered: every acquired gruesomeness and wildness accrues only for the purpose of turning man against himself and destroying him.

These two aspects of Nietzsche's ethics are quite irreconcilable, although they are yoked together in the first and only moral injunction engraved on the new tablet of values: "*Become hard!*" ("The Other Dancing Song," Z, III, 29; TI, end line). The phrase "become hard!" indeed glows with the antithetical features of Nietzschean morality, comprised of tyrannical fierceness and ascetic renunciation. For to become hard means to turn one's power of resistance, at once, against all soft and benign impulses and against habituated self-pleasuring egotism. In brief, he calls for hardness against others and for a graciousness in the performance of duties that attend sovereign power; however, at other times it calls for a hardness against one's self, a declining self, which must be chiseled away in the same way that a sculptor shapes his stone into a lofty work of art. One may yield to everything except the danger of being fragmented while the sculptor works, otherwise those fragments—though highly treasured in the eyes of the old morality—are worth no more than the junkheap that is swept away; they are spoiled materials. The most discardable of all are the anxious softness of the emotions and hesitant reflectiveness in facing the terror of what is decisive. That is the hymn sung by the creator of the future, Zarathustra, ". . . my devout, creative will drives me ever again toward man, as the hammer is driven to the stone. O men, an image sleeps in the stone, my image of images. O, that it must sleep in the hardest, ugliest stone! My hammer now rages ruthlessly against the prison of the image. Pieces dust down from the stone: what does it matter to me?" ("Upon the Blessed Isles," Z, II).

And so, we confront the riddle and secret within Nietzsche's teachings: how is it at all possible for the superior man to develop from the inferior, if both are to be thought of as irreconcilable opposites? The answer to this question reminds one suddenly of an old moralistic healing recipe, which goes somewhat like this: "In order to get rid of a failing, yield to it and exaggerate it until its exaggeration and excess will have a repelling effect." The moralistic recipe which Nietzsche wrote for humanity bears resemblance to it because he knew of none better tested on himself. Indeed, he wanted the unbound, wildest drives to bring humans to a condition where egotistical self-satisfaction through exaggeration and excess become suffering attributable to the self. From the torment of such suffering was to develop a boundless, overwhelming yearning by the strong and intemperate impulses for the tender, measured, and mild; the yearning, dark desire on the part of coarseness for beauty and lucid purity is the yearning of the tormented for their god. Nietzsche thought it possible that from this mood its opposite could indeed emerge with the help of an overpowering emotion. Some time earlier, Nietzsche characterized the magnanimous man "as a person possessing an extreme thirst for revenge, who finds satisfaction close at hand and drinks it up so fully and thoroughly to the last drop—*even in his anticipation*—that a tremendous and rapid disgust follows this rapid orgy, but then, however, he 'rises above himself,' so to speak, and forgives his enemy and even blesses and honors him. With the ravaging of his self and his mockery of the so recent and mighty drive for revenge, he merely yields to the new urge, a powerful disgust. . . . Magnanimity and revenge possess the same amount of egotism, though egotism of a different kind" (GS, 49). . . .

Since neither gradual development nor transition brings opposites closer together, their inherent characteristics keeping them apart, an eternally unbridgeable abyss remains. On the one hand is the force of human drives heightened into the terrifying and chaotic; on the other is a false picture, a superficial reflection of life, and to a certain extent a divine mask without an independent inner substance. In the light of all this, the same objection can be raised strongly against Nietzsche's criticism of conventional morality, namely, the belief that it is sufficient for humans to resemble a projected image of the ideal. Critically put, the effect of this would simply result in an aesthetic veneer but not in a thoroughgoing change, so that man would sink to the level of an actor who merely dramatizes his own ideal. Here we meet precisely the same thing that surprised us in Nietzsche's attitude toward the ascetic. That which Nietzsche seems to combat most strenuously, is what he fully incorporates into his theories, with extreme consequences and meanings. . . . Indeed, we can assume with certainty that when Nietzsche denigrates and pursues something with special hatred, he harbors it deep in the heart of his own philosophy or in his own life. That holds true of his attitude to people he knew, as well as of his theories.

Most of the time in cases such as this, Nietzsche himself admits that the object he has attacked has a type of value as a "moment" in the development toward a new conception. In regard to the instance discussed, he admits to the following: human beings have first gained a capacity for superiority gradually through their development within a reigning morality, art, and religion.

Only when this view permitted Nietzsche to believe in the possibility of a change in man's essence did he also think that man "becomes so much a work of art, surface, and play of color . . . that one no longer suffers when one looks at him" (BGE, 59).[51] "Artists and playwrights have taught us to treasure the hero who is hidden in the everyday man and how, in a simplified and transfigured way, one can from a distance view oneself as a hero. The art of staging allows one to see oneself acting and being 'placed within a scene.' Only in this way can we overlook some base details about ourselves!" (GS, 78). The difference between the man of the past and the one Nietzsche wished for consists therefore in the latter's refusal to yield to faith; his essence has been transformed since he developed moral, artistic, and religious features. He knows, so to speak, that only when he creates as a poet or playwright does he bring the ideal to the surface. But he only gains this insight when he has reached the measure of strength anticipated by Nietzsche and when he has become "hard enough, strong enough, and artistic enough." Otherwise he could not endure the truth that his essence is unchangeable, that his ideal of the superior man is only a visualized image, and that his highest ethical work is only a *work of art*. It therefore is understandable that Nietzsche said, ". . . among artists, one might count the *homines religiosi* and assign them highest rank" (BGE, 59). For it is the artistic principle out of which flow the living, highest ethical and religious value judgments and Nietzsche's *Beyond Good and Evil*. . . . The superior man is only possible and conceivable as man's *work of art*. And if we wish to find an illustration of this, we can perhaps find none better than in Nietzsche's *The Birth of Tragedy From the Spirit of Music* where he speaks of the connection between the Dionysian and the Apollonian within the creation of art. There he notes the Apollonian visions which originated from the life-enhancing powers of the Dionysian, those optic illusions that arise from staring into the full volcanic sea of the sun as dark-colored flecks are produced like balm before our dazzled eyes, a phenomenon active in one's transformation. With the submersion into the painful darkness of unbounded excess and of self-devouring primal powers, there emerges with similar healing effect a tender and illuminating image of the superior man. In Greek tragedy, upon which Nietzsche centered his comparisons, the Apollonian symbols of light or the heroic figures of the Hellenic stage are basically only the masks of a single Dionysus. Just so, the image of the superior man engendered in the excess of creativity is basically only a divine illusion, a symbol, in the sense of art. Behind him, deep, as in an abyss "in purple darkness," rests his Dionysian self, the elemental power of life, which he always draws upon for renewal.

And so we see that in Nietzsche's philosophy, ethics unobtrusively merges with aesthetics—into a kind of religious aesthetics—and that his teaching about the good is made possible through the divinity of the beautiful. The fine boundary-line where appearance must be wedded to reality, in order to fashion the ideal, makes the world of the beautiful and its fantastic self-delusion a "real womb for ideal and imaginative happenings" (GM, II, 18), toward which the deepest impulse strives, precisely because the "happenings" remain eternally unrealizable and because no yearning can lend them substantive truth and reality. The same situation is pictured when Nietzsche says about the artist that he derives "much more from his ultimate incapacity than from his ample strength. . . . A tremendous lust for this vision [of what he would like to see come about] remains in his soul and from that he takes his equally tremendous eloquence of yearning and craving" (GS, 79). One then needs to think of the rise of the overhuman illusion—the mystery of a sudden self-renunciation and self-uplifting, this ascetic conception toward which Nietzsche's ethics flow—as an *aesthetic phenomenon* and as an intensive immersion into the suffering of excess. From this phenomenon arises a longing for an opposite, a communicated and experienced vision. "From no one more than from yourself do I demand beauty, you powerful one," as Nietzsche characterized the human weighed down with strong and powerful moods, "but precisely for the hero *beauty* is the heaviest to bear of all things; despite every intense will, beauty is unobtainable. . . . For this is the soul's secret: only when the hero has abandoned her does the superior hero (the superior man) approach her in a dream" ("Of Those Who Are Sublime," Z, II). Caught up in blissful dream, the soul stammers, ". . . a shadow approached me once—the most silent and weightless came, to me! The beauty of the superior man came to me as a shadow" ("Upon the Blessed Isles," Z, II). For "everything godly runs with tender tread. . . . Would anything be beautiful if its opposite had not itself come into consciousness or if the ugly had not said to itself: I am ugly?" In the ugliness of that chaotic excess . . . "a *hatred* seethes up . . . he hates out of the deepest instinct of his species; in this hatred there is a shudder, caution, depth, a splendid view—it is the deepest hate possible. For its sake, art is deep" ("Skirmishes of an Untimely Man," TI, 20). It is deep because hate teaches man a boundless yearning for the beautiful and so makes possible the begetting of a beautiful appearance out of the unconfined abundance of a true existence; it is deep because it awakens a tremendous urge toward idealization and through its vision of beauty stimulates man's will to its "fathering," so that he weds himself with passionate enthusiasm to his very opposite. . . . "The essence of this passionate enthusiasm is the feeling of increased power and fullness. We impose these feelings upon things . . . and violate them; one calls this process *idealizing*" (TI, IX, 8). "One enriches this from one's own fullness: one sees what one wishes, sees it swelled up, taut, strong, and overloaded with power. A man in this state transforms things until they mirror his might. This *need* to transform things into perfection is—art" (TI, IX, 9).

If Nietzsche's ethics have a predominantly aestheticizing character in that the transformation into perfection only yields a beautiful illusion, then all the more does his aesthetics approach very strongly the religio-symbolic: his aesthetics arise from the urge to deify humans and things and to dissolve them into something divine in order to endure them. Not only did Nietzsche construct a theory which is interpreted in scattered aphorisms, but he made the effort as well to lay the groundwork upon which the abundant creativity of man would, for the first time, bring the superior to fruition. This creative work is his *Thus Spoke Zarathustra*. The Zarathustra figure represents Nietzsche's own transformation, mirroring the transformation of his vitality into a godlike photograph; this is analogous to his dream about the birth of the superior man from the human. Zarathustra is, so to speak, Nietzsche's superior man; he is the superior Nietzsche. Consequently the work possesses a deceptive double character: on the one hand, it is a work of literature in the aesthetic sense and can be judged from that perspective exclusively; on the other hand, it is a work of literature only in a purely mystical sense—an act of religious creation through which the highest demands of Nietzsche's ethics find their fulfillment for the first time. This explains why Nietzsche's *Zarathustra* has remained, at best, the most misunderstood of all his books, and all the more so since it has been commonly assumed that this poetic work contains in *popularized* form that which had been previously rendered in stricter philosophical form. In truth, however, of all his works it is the least intended for popularization. If ever there was an esoteric philosophy which would not be accessible completely to anyone, this was it.

The work reflects Nietzsche's psychology and the peculiar mysticism of a believer who yearns for his god. This tremendous wish—and demand—forced itself toward satisfaction: it created a god or a superior godly being in which a counter-image of Nietzsche's own being was exteriorized and transformed. The twin representation by Nietzsche, through which he observed himself as his double, is embodied in his Zarathustra; they walk in the same shoes. Through isolated spots of the writing, there shimmers strangely the secret admission that Zarathustra has no existence in reality and is only a creature of the poetic imagination, a poet and a poetizing figure: ". . . what did Zarathustra once tell you? That poets lie too much? But Zarathustra also is a poet" ("Of Poets," Z, II). Yet, already in Nietzsche's conception of the highest ideal, illusion has the right to declare itself to be essence and being—indeed, the highest truth resides in the *effect of the illusion* and its effect upon others. The human being in his mystic transformation seeks to become that maturing illusion: "Whoever is a teacher through and through takes all things seriously only in regard to his students—even himself" (BGE, 63).

With all this, in a very conscious way, a justification of the "holy deception" is rendered. And not in vain does Nietzsche say repeatedly that he had most persistently pursued the uncanny problem of *"pia fraus."*[52] Even honesty, as a relatively late virtue of modern man in quest of knowledge, had to be conquered by the "untimely person" within himself for the sake of his purposes that could not tolerate a tender conscience. Significantly, we already find this in The Gay Science: "Whoever is unbowed nowadays will often suffer pangs of conscience because of his honesty; for inflexibility is a virtue that belonged to a period of the past, while in ours the virtue of honesty prevails" (GS, 159). However, the clever hunchback, who listens to Zarathustra and reads his mind, says, "Why does Zarathustra speak one thing to his disciples and another to himself?" ("Of Redemption," Z, II). And Zarathustra himself cried out to his disciples, "Truly, I give you this advice: leave me and resist Zarathustra! And better still, be ashamed of him! Perhaps he has deceived you. . . . You venerate me; but what if your veneration were to collapse some day? Beware lest a statue smash you!" ("Of the Gift-Giving Virtue," Z, I, 3).

The more completely, however, reality and truth disappeared in that process and the more consciously the ideal was thought of as an illusion, all the greater became Nietzsche's desire to lend it truth in a religious sense and to turn it into mystic self-deification. And here we see how his thought curiously encircles itself: in order to escape the ascetic self-destruction of all morality, he dissolves the moral phenomenon into an aesthetic one in which the basic nature of man remains unchanged while juxtaposed to its image; however, in order to give this image a positive meaning, he elevates it to the mystic-religious and then is forced to portray basic human nature as darkly and as anguished as possible in order to highlight the contrast. So that the redeeming superior being becomes believable, the contrasts would have to be sharpened to differentiate it as much as possible from the natural-human. Every mediating transition would have destroyed the mystical illusion and would have thrown man back upon himself; the superior being would then have become a mere development of being-in-itself. The shadows on the human side would have to be deepened as much as those on the other, the overhuman side, so that a light would appear all the more brightly and compel the belief that it was of a completely different sort. And so originated the teaching that the unhuman was necessary for the breeding of the superior human and that only out of the excess of the wildest greed would come the longing for one's own contrast.

An objection may be raised against this mystic creation of God, the same objection Nietzsche had raised against the Christian-ascetic creation of God: in this creation resided the *will* of humans "to erect an ideal—that of the 'holy God'—in the face of which man's absolute unworthiness would appear quite palpably certain." And further, "All this is limitlessly interesting but also of a dark, unnerving sadness. . . . Here is *sickness,* and without doubt the most terrible sickness that has as yet raged within a human being: whoever is still able to hear . . . in the night of torture and unreason, the resounding cry of *love* and the cry of blissful ecstasy and redemption through *love,* he will turn away, gripped by an irrepressible horror! In man there is so much that is horrifying! For too long has the world been a madhouse!" (GM, II, 22).

This hidden trend toward the ascetic and mystical—a trend within his battle against the ascetic and mystical—shows most clearly a return to his first philosophical world view, that hybrid of Schopenhauer and Wagner. But insofar as he resists, in principle, all mysticism and asceticism up to the present, he yields just as readily to the old influence of the positivistic quest for knowledge. The mystical and ascetic significance of the aesthetic is as important in Nietzsche's system as it was in Schopenhauer's; in both, they converge with the deepest ethical and religious experience, and not in vain does Nietzsche reach back to *The Birth of Tragedy* for ideas and images. But Schopenhauer had conceived of the aesthetic view as a mystic penetration into the background of things and into the essence of "the thing-in-itself," and to a certain extent the discarding of everything earthly. With Nietzsche, however, the psychic presupposition is exactly *opposite* because there is an absence of metaphysical background; a substitution therefore has to be *created* out of the midst of an excess of life-forces: the beautiful was to stimulate the will to life in its depth, it was to unleash all the forces, "to bring about rutting and then stimulating birth," for what is involved is not the metaphysical revelation of something existing eternally but the mystical creation from something not at hand; Nietzsche's "mystical," therefore, is always much like a life force escalated into something tremendous, and consequently into the overhuman. Just as the supernatural resulted from the destruction of the ascetic by Schopenhauer, so with Nietzsche the mystical overflowing of life is only possible as a consequence of the decline of everything human and given, and through excess. Here lies the main contact between both views: through the *tragic* both enter into the bliss of their mysticism. *The Birth of Tragedy From the Spirit of Music** has transformed itself into a Birth of Tragedy from the Spirit of Life. Life as "that which must always conquer itself" constantly demands as a precondition an ever increasing effort toward a decline. What appears tragic from the standpoint of such a determined decline is, on the other hand, experienced as a full life

---

*Schopenhauer interpreted music as the resounding expression of the "thing-in-itself."

from the standpoint of existence itself, or that with which one identifies in order to conquer one's self by rising to excess. In characteristic fashion, this changed interpretation of the tragic is evident in *The Twilight of the Idols* in which Nietzsche once again discusses his old problems of *The Birth of Tragedy*, namely, the meaning of the Dionysian mysteries and the Greek sense of the tragic.

Originally, Nietzsche thought of the Dionysian orgy as the means for release of the emotions whereby a requisite calmness of soul would be presented by means of the Apollonian images; now however, for Nietzsche, frenzy and torment in themselves are the necessary conditions for the creative act out of which one shapes the luminous and godly.** Originally, also, the Dionysian was for Nietzsche evidence, in Schopenhauer's sense, of the deeply pessimistic nature of the Greeks because their innermost life, as revealed through the orgiastic, was one of darkness, pain, and chaos. Now it appears to him to be the life-thirsting Hellenic instinct which could only satisfy itself though excess and which even in pain, death, and chaos gloried in the inexhaustibility of life: ". . . in the Dionysian mysteries, the *fundamental fact* of the Hellenic instinct is expressed—its 'will to life.' Of what does the Hellene assure himself through these mysteries? The *eternal* life, the eternal return of life, just as the future is promised and sanctified in the past; the triumphal 'yes' to life carries beyond death and change. . . . In the teachings of mysteries, *pain* is declared holy: the 'pangs of the woman giving birth' assuredly sanctify pain . . . so that there may be an eternal lust for creativity; so that the will to life affirm itself, there must also always be the 'agony of the birth-giving woman'. . . . All this is signified by the word Dionysus. . . ." ("What I Owe to the Ancients," TI, 4).

**A related thought is echoed in *The Gay Science* (84) where Nietzsche regards the effects of orgiastic cult-ceremonies as the calming of humans, releasing them from their passions when "giddiness and the wantonness of their emotions were driven to extremes, making the raving ones mad and the vengeful ones drunk with lust for revenge: all the orgiastic cults want to discharge the *ferocia* of some deity all at once into an orgy, so that the deity would then feel more free and calm and leave man in peace."

"What induces beauty to give birth" ("Skirmishes of an Untimely Man," TI, 22) is the religious aspect of art because it teaches creative fulfillment. The highest or the most religious art is the tragic because within it the artist delivers *beauty from the terrifying.* "What does the tragic artist tell us about himself? Does he not precisely demonstrate fearlessness in confronting the terrifying and questionable? . . . Bravery and freedom of feeling before a mighty enemy, before a lofty calamity, before a problem that awakens dread—that *triumphant* attitude is chosen and glorified by the tragic artist. The combative in our soul celebrates its Saturnalia in the presence of tragedy. Whoever is accustomed to sorrow and whoever searches out sorrow, to him alone the tragedian offers a drink from this sweetest cruelty and the heroic human extols his own existence through tragedy" (24).

"The psychology of the orgiastic as an overflowing feeling of life and strength, within which even pain still works as a stimulant, gave me the key to an understanding of *tragic* feeling: The affirmation of life—even in its most strange and difficult problems; the will to life that rejoices in its own infinitude and in the sacrifice of its highest types—*that* is what I called Dionysian, *that* I guessed to be the bridge toward the psychology of the *tragic* poet. *Not* in order to be rid of terror and pity, and not to purge oneself of a dangerous emotion (as Aristotle would have it) through violent discharge, but in order to follow the eternal lust for becoming oneself—beyond terror and pity—that lust which yet harbors within it the *lust for destruction*" ("What I Owe to the Ancients," TI, 5).

This interpretation of the tragic and its corollary and conditioned feeling toward life made it possible—precisely through a return to Schopenhauer's philosophy of pessimism and asceticism—for Nietzsche to teach the celebration of life—to teach the *eternal recurrence of all things.* However much Nietzsche's system philosophically and psychologically called for the recognition of basic ascetic features, it also called even more strongly for the recognition of its opposite—the apotheosis of life; for in the absence of a metaphysical belief there was only the suffering and anguished life itself which could be apotheosized. Nietzsche's teaching of the eternal recurrence has not yet been sufficiently emphasized and acknowledged, although it constitutes to a certain degree the foundation and coping stone of his ideas; this idea emerged from his conception of the philosophy of the future and is an idea which he uses to round it out fully. It is mentioned at this point because it becomes understandable only within a total context; in fact, Nietzsche's logic, ethics, and aesthetics must be regarded as building blocks for his teaching of the eternal recurrence. The thought of a possible return of all things through an eternal cycle of being already occurs as a conjecture in Nietzsche's aphorism (341), "The Heaviest Burden," in *The Gay Science:*

> Suppose a demon were some day or night to creep into your loneliest loneliness and were to say to you, "This life, as you live and have lived it, you will have to relive once more and even countless times more. And nothing new will be added; instead, every pain and every pleasure and every thought and sigh and everything inexpressibly small and great of your life must return to you, and all in the same series and sequence—and even so this spider and this moonlight among the trees, and just so this very moment and I myself. The eternal hourglass of existence is ever again turned over— and you along with it, you speck of dust."
>
> Would you not throw yourself down, gnashing your teeth and cursing the demon who spoke in this fashion? Or have you ever experienced a tremendous moment during which you would answer him: "You are a god and I have never heard anything more divine!" If this thought would take hold of you, it would change you, as you are, or perhaps crush you. The over-riding question, "Do you desire this once more and uncountable times more?", would lie like the heaviest burden on your dealings! Or how would you need to come to terms with yourself and life, in order *to yearn for nothing any more* except for this last, eternal confirmation and sealing?

Nietzsche's basic thought stands out clearly here, much clearer and less entangled than anywhere later; Nietzsche could not bear to be completely silent about that which filled and stimulated his spirit. But still, he was so stirred by this new insight that in speaking of his thought about the eternal recurrence, he inserted it unobtrusively, like something harmless, among other ideas, so that whoever might lightly gloss over the reading would not notice the connection with the serious, concluding observation, "*Incipit tragoedia*," which is "so secretive that all the world ignores it, that all the world ignores *us!*" ("Preface," D, 5). And so, this thought stands amid the others, altogether the most enshrouded among the shrouded. Here is a clever jesting with masks, for nothing can be hidden better than by being placed in view quite openly and nakedly. Rich in secretiveness and joyous in secretiveness, Nietzsche enjoyed his prank, despite the deep disturbance in his soul.

Indeed, Nietzsche even then carried around with him an inescapable fate that wished to "change and crush" him; he wrested up courage in order to confess its invincible truth and far-reaching implications for himself and others. Unforgettable for me are those hours in which he first confided to me his secret, whose inevitable fulfillment and validation he anticipated with shudders. Only with a quiet voice and with all signs of deepest horror did he speak about this secret. Life, in fact, produced such suffering in him that the certainty of an eternal return of life had to mean something horrifying to him. The quintessence of the teaching of eternal recurrence, later constructed by Nietzsche as a shining apotheosis to life, formed such a deep contrast to his own painful feelings about life that it gives us intimations of being an uncanny mask.

Nietzsche was to become the harbinger of teachings that could only be endured by way of a love that outweighs life and would only be effective at the point where the thought of man soars up to a deification of life. In truth, all this must have been in contradiction to his innermost perceptions—a contradiction that finally destroyed him. Everything that Nietzsche thought, felt, and experienced after the origination of his eternal recurrence concept arises from his inner split. Everything then moved between two poles: "to curse, with gritted teeth, the demon of eternal life" and the awaiting of that "tremendous moment" which lends power to the words, "you [demon] are a god and I never heard anything more divine!"

The higher he rose as philosopher toward the full exaltation of life, the lower he fell into suffering as a human being, all in consequence of his own life's teachings. This contention within his soul was the true source of his later philosophy. That can only be intuited partially from his books and declarations, but perhaps most grippingly it comes through in Nietzsche's music to my poem "Hymn to Life"; he composed the music when he stayed with me in Thüringen near Dornburg. In the midst of his work on the music, he was disrupted by one of his attacks of illness, and once again for him the "god" was transformed into the "demon" and his enthusiasm for life was transformed into the anguish of living. "To bed. A violent attack. I despise life. F. N." (August 25, 1882). That was a message he sent to me in one of his notes when he was confined to bed. And the same sentiment is voiced in a letter [of September 8, 1882, written in Naumburg] shortly after the completion of that musical composition:

My dear Lou,
Everything you[53] report does me good. At any rate, I need whatever is comforting! . . .
My Venetian art critic [Peter Gast] has written to me about my music for your poem; I am enclosing the letter. . . .
As always, it costs me the greatest effort to come to a decision to *accept* life. I have much ahead of me, upon me, behind me. . . . Forward, my dear Lou, and upward! . . .

At that time, as mentioned, the recurrence idea had not as yet become a conviction in Nietzsche's mind, but only a suspicion. He had the intention of heralding it when and if it could be founded scientifically. We exchanged a series of letters about this matter, and Nietzsche constantly expressed the mistaken opinion that it would be possible to win for it an indisputable basis through physics experiments. It was he who decided at that time to devote ten years of exclusive study to the natural sciences at the University of Vienna or Paris. Then, after ten years of absolute silence, he would—in the event that his own surmise were to be substantiated, as he feared—step among people again as the teacher of the doctrine of eternal recurrence.

As is known, things took a different turn. Inner and outer circumstances made his planned work impossible and drove him

Retouched photograph of Nietzsche included in the 1894 Vienna edition, along with the caption: "Friedrich Nietzsche, formerly professor and now a wandering fugitive."

back again to the South and into isolation. The decade of his intended silence became instead the most eloquent and fruitful period of his entire life. Even a cursory study of the problem soon showed him that a scientific foundation for the recurrence teaching based on atomistic theory would not be tenable; and so he found that his fears about the fateful idea would not be validated nor be irrefutable. With all that, he seemed to be freed from his prophetic mission and from a fate he had anticipated with horror. But then, however, something characteristically strange stepped into the picture: far from being able to feel himself released through this gained insight, Nietzsche took an entirely opposite position toward it. From the moment when his frightening surmise became unprovable and untenable, it became hardened for him—as if through a magic formula—into an irrefutable conviction. What was to have become a scientifically proven truth assumed instead the character of a mystical revelation and furthermore gave Nietzsche's philosophy its final and fundamental principles. Instead of finding a scientific basis, Nietzsche's philosophy found an inner inspiration—his own personal inspiration.

Despite this resistant horror, on the one hand, and an insufficient proof, on the other, what influence was it that exerted such a change? Only a solution to this riddle will allow us an insight into the hidden spiritual and mental life[54] of Nietzsche and into the originating source of his theories. A new and deeper significance of things, a new searching and questioning aimed at the ultimate and highest problems, all these Nietzsche had pursued as a metaphysician but had sorely found missing as an empiricist, driving him into the mysticism of his recurrence[55] teaching. No matter how closely this teaching may have been allied to his new torments of soul, even threatening to destroy him, he preferred to shoulder life's sufferings rather than persevere and remain within a despiritualized world, one that was shorn of the gods. With all other sufferings, except this one, he could come to terms; not only did he endure them but indeed he knew how to incite and prick his mind through these means. At the same time, they inexorably taught him to seek and explore the *sense* of life and its deepest secrets: "If one has a sense of life's *why*,

134

it will be possible to come to terms almost with every *how"* [without striving for pleasure] ("Maxims and Arrows," TI, 12). But Nietzsche's *why*, as a fundamental desire in his life, also strove for an extensive response and tolerated no self-denial. The philosopher in Nietzsche, even here, did not wish to be saved from the pain of a teaching he feared, but he wanted to become fruitful through it, to learn from it, and become its prophet; and he wished for this so fervently that—even when scientific proof fell by the wayside—his inner resources possessed enough power to escalate vacillating surmises into enthusiastic convictions.

For these reasons, the theoretical outlines of the recurrence ideas are never actually drawn with clear strokes; the outline remains pale and indistinct and retreats completely behind practical conclusions—the ethical and religious consequences—that Nietzsche seemingly derives from them, while in fact they serve as an inner precondition for him.

In one of his earliest works, the second of his *Untimely Reflections* (*On the Advantage and Disadvantage of History for Life*, 1874), Nietzsche mentioned in passing the "eternal return" philosophy of the Pythagoreans [the chain of transmigration by which the soul enters a new body] as a uniquely suitable means "to depict each fact in its precisely structured individuality and uniqueness" (Section 2) and lift it toward a lasting meaning, but he adds the comment that such a teaching has no place in our thoughts or probably at least not until astronomy again becomes astrology. Certainly, in his later years, the theoretical difficulties of a modern revival of this old idea did not appear less than during an earlier time when he followed Schopenhauer's metaphysics. At that time though, Schopenhauer's metaphysics interpreted for Nietzsche the things of this world in such lofty terms as to make any mystical ruminations superfluous. The eternal existence behind the tremendous process of becoming, which constitutes the world of illusion and objectifies itself through a higher sense in every one of its manifestations, did not awaken in Nietzsche a longing to ascribe more than an ephemeral meaning to the process of becoming through a cyclical repetition of being. Nietzsche had put aside a metaphysical explanation of the world but involuntarily desired a substitute for it. Only later, the thought of eternal repetition forced itself upon him again. Apparently, this thought sharpens rather than weakens the pessimism of the positivistic perception of life. . . .

Nietzsche, characteristically, gained a new redemptive philosophy from the pessimistic views of positivism and Pythagorean philosophy. A sober look at the sorrowfulness and oppressiveness of life coupled with the inevitability of an eternal return to the human condition could serve to spur the human spirit to its highest activity. The human spirit needs to be whipped by frustration and horror to produce a mighty will which imposes meaning and goals upon a meaningless and random process: if indeed there are no inherent life-values, values will have to be created through one's own efforts.

And so, one may say that instead of turning away from the pessimism of his "free-wheeling spiritedness" or returning to a more consoling metaphysics, Nietzsche heightened his pessimism to the extreme, only in order to use his emotional surfeit and life's pain as a springboard from which to plunge into the depths of his mysticism.

In fact, his recurrence theory seemed to be particularly suited to create such an effect insofar as it is pertinent to the actual life of every individual and not only to philosophical thinking (and particularly pertinent to the creative will). To confront all of life as a meaningless, random totality, and to view it thoughtfully, means something different from only having to repeat it individually and senselessly, without ever being able to escape from it. Here, a purely abstract way of viewing acquires a personal direction, and philosophical theory is pressed into the sensitive, living flesh, like a pain-inflicting spur which is intended to create, at all cost, a new hope, a new sense of life and its goal.

In regard to this optimism, Nietzsche's last philosophy is the complete opposite of his first philosophical world view, or of the Schopenhauerian metaphysics with its glorification of the Buddhistic ideals of asceticism, denial of the will, and abdication from life. The old Hindu teaching of reincarnation through the migration of the soul, a curse to which everyone is heir until one has achieved an extinction of the self, is completely turned upside-down by Nietzsche. Not *release* from the duress of the recurrence cycle but a joyous *conversion* to it, becomes the goal for the highest ethical striving; not Nirvana but Samsara is the name for the highest ideal. This correction of the pessimistic in favor of the optimistic is the real difference between Nietzsche's initial and later thinking; in the development of this solitary sufferer, this correction portrays for us the heroic victory of a conquest over the self. . . . Caught in the cycle of life, and unremittingly and eternally bound to it, we must learn to say "yes" to all its configurations in order to become reconciled and to endure it joyously and with strength by means of our identification with that cycle of life. . . . An unrestrained *love of life*, therefore, is the one and divine moral dictate of the new lawgiver; Nietzsche's near-intoxication and unbounded exaltation of life assumed *religious edification*, becoming divine god-cultism.

Of this turnabout from pessimism to optimism, and of the new ideal which calls for an affirmation of the world, Nietzsche has this to say:

> Like myself, whoever has concerned himself at length with some enigmatic desire to probe into the depths of pessimism and to rescue it from the half-Christian and half-German narrowness and simplemindedness with which it is represented still, namely, in the guise of Schopenhauerian philosophy, or, whoever has intently looked into the most world-negating ways of thought—beyond good and evil . . . , has involuntarily perhaps also opened his eyes to the opposite ideal: the ideal held by the most exuberant and world-affirming human being who has not merely learned to come to terms with all that was and is but who wants everything *as it was and is* back again and repeated for all eternity, insatiably shouting *da capo*[56] not only for himself but for the entire spectacle and performance, and not only for a performance, but basically shouting at him who precisely has need of this performance and makes it necessary: because he always needs himself and makes himself necessary. How else could it be? Is this not the *circulus vitiosus deus*?[57] (BGE, 56).

These words not only give an inkling of how decisively for Nietzsche his optimism developed through a sharpening and exaggeration of pessimism, but they also indicate to what extent his new philosophy possesses an indigenous religious character. The human being, in one way, feels mystically expanded into a cosmic totality of life, so that his own decline, as well as his own tragic sense of life, no longer matters; and, in another way, the human being spiritualizes and personalizes symbolically the meaningless and random processes of life, raising himself to the status of divinity. World, God, and I melt into a single concept from which the individual may draw, just as well as from any metaphysics, ethics, or religion, a norm for activity and for highest worship. Behind these formulations lies the premise that cosmos and world are man-made fictions, created by his godlike essence, wholeness, and the richness of life; he knows that conceptual representations rely upon his own creative will and his own minting of values. With this in mind, Nietzsche's mysterious phrases in *Beyond Good and Evil* (150) become clear: "Around the hero everything turns into a tragedy," meaning that the human being as such, and in his highest development, is exactly a declining and sacrificed being; "around the demigod (everything turns into) a satyr-play," meaning that in man's full yielding to life's totality, he smiles down upon his own fate, like one who has been uplifted; "and, around God everything turns into—what?— perhaps into 'world?',", meaning that through the complete identification of the human being with life, not only will he be taken up into life's totality—reconciled—but also life's totality will be absorbed absolutely by him, so that he becomes a god out of whom the world flows, and who subtly changes his being through the creation of the released world.

And here again we encounter the basic thoughts in Nietzsche's philosophy, which, like all his teachings, had given rise within him to the recurrence theory. We encounter the tremendous deification of the philosopher-creator. In him reside the origin and conclusion of the recurrence philosophy, and one can say that even the most abstract aspects of this "system" are attempts to sketch the features of his dominant superior-man . . . combining divine and human essence. For Nietzsche, the recurrence philosophy finally fused everything into a single, unique, gigantic figuration; because the world's course is *not infinite* but one which within its limitations constantly *repeats itself*, it was possible to construct a superior mode of existence within which the entire world's course resides and rounds itself out. Only through such a process does sense and goal gain a direction toward redemptive creation of the superior being; only in this fashion does this creation become more than a hypothesis—it becomes a *fact*. We also see that Nietzsche does not deliver his most fundamental philosophy and mystical teaching in his own name, so to speak, but in the name of Zarathustra; hence, not the thinker and human being was to deliver that teaching but the one upon whom power is bestowed to translate teaching into blissful redemption.[58] In Nietzsche's aphorisms, whenever he glancingly touches upon the recurrence thought he falls into silence, with a gesture of horror and awe: "But what am I saying? Enough! Enough! At this point it behooves me only to remain silent, otherwise I would trespass on a domain open solely to someone younger, someone who belongs more to the future and is stronger than I am—a domain open to Zarathustra alone, to *Zarathustra the godless*" (GM, II, 25).

And the spiritual significance of the Zarathustra figure for Nietzsche also becomes evident here, fully for the first time, when that figure appears as the carrier of his recurrence teachings. Inwardly, Nietzsche retained thoughts of this figure as resembling a mystical being, but distinguishable from his own human form. Nietzsche believed that chance had brought him to birth in a variable and temporal present which then conditioned him biologically and mentally. He regarded himself as one of the decadents but, unlike the others, he felt himself fit and destined only for decline. Yet he also believed himself to be the fated, though sickly, medium through which humans would solve the riddle of existence and would become conscious of their essence and potential future. . . . Embodied in himself, Nietzsche thought, was that which he had pictured as the highest meaning of human decadence. He felt himself ill with the pangs of giving birth to a superior being; he felt himself to be sinking and breaking down under the stress of a new creation that was to save the world: "The creating person must himself be the child who is newly born, and he must also wish to be the mother who gives birth and be the suffering that comes to the woman who gives birth" ("Upon the Blessed Isles," Z, II).

Zarathustra, then, is also the child, as well as the god of Nietzsche, the act or created art-form of an individual, linking this individual with the whole lineage of man and with the *essence of man*. He is "the created as well as the creator," the "stronger person of the future," and the one who towers over the suffering, human Nietzsche-manifestation—he is the "over-Nietzsche." What is expressed by him is therefore not the experiencing and understanding of a single individual but human consciousness itself from its most ancient origins: "I do not belong to those who may be asked about their 'why.' Is then my experience confined to yesterday? It was long ago that I experienced the reasons for my opinions. Must I not be a barrel of memory if I even wanted to carry my reasons with me?" ("Of Poets," Z, II).

A wondrous play of thought develops, in that Nietzsche and his Zarathustra incessantly merge and then seem to pull apart again. This becomes obvious to those who know in how many small and purely personal ways Nietzsche has secretly nested himself in his Zarathustra and what visionary rapture this whole mystery brought him. With this we find an explanation of the incredible self-confidence with which he speaks of his book . . . "A book so profound, so strange, that six sentences understood in it, and therefore experienced, raise things to a higher order of being!"[59]

If his Zarathustra composition meant for him the work through which the human gave birth to the superior man, so he may have thought of his unpublished and partially completed major work *The Will to Power*[60] as having been created by the Zarathustra figure, that is, by an eternal and free-spirited figure who alone could succeed in bringing about a "revaluation of all values" because he stood outside of all time and influence, absolutely independent, all-knowing, and all-encompassing. Only in this fashion is Nietzsche's assertion in *Twilight of the Idols* to be understood: "I have given mankind the most profound book it has ever possessed, my *Zarathustra*; soon, I shall give it the most independent" ("Skirmishes of an Untimely Man," 51). In the first instance, the superior human was to have arisen from Nietzsche's humanness and, in the second, it already hovers over things, with free rein.

However mystically and mysteriously this Zarathustra figure has been conceived in its meaning for the world, it still is closely tied, with strict logic, to Nietzsche's expositions of the nature of genius, free will, and the atavistic, as preconditions for the future. Reflecting upon these theories, one notes that all of them are directed toward the possible creation of a superior human; and it is interesting to pursue the clues that lead to similar thoughts which much earlier stimulated Nietzsche and which were transferred to his later philosophical periods through his positivistic view of the world. During his final period, these thoughts were awakened to a new life. The spirit of ethics and aesthetics already included the meaning of the essence in Schopenhauer's philosophy . . . but in it, eternal existence, or the metaphysical thing-in-itself, is completely divorced from the actual history of mankind's and the world's development. Nietzsche took account of these metaphysical representations but he required the introduction of "genius" in whose sole, isolated superior being a totality of world and mankind is conceived.

In *Human, All-Too-Human* he says in retrospect of the Schopenhauerian ideas which he modified in a positivistic sense, ". . . a striving for knowledge about the entire range of historical development . . . is a striving to discern the entirety of human genius. A thought-through history would be a cosmic self-awareness" (II, 185). Alongside this quote, one may place the following comment from the aphorism *"Historia abscondita"* (GS, 34): "Every great human being has the power to reassess the past: for his sake all of history is again put on the scales and a thousand secrets of the past crawl out of their hiding places—into *his* sunlight." Further:

> Anyone who knows how to experience the whole of man's history as *his own history* will feel in a highly generalized way all the grief of a sick person who is robbed of health, of the graybeard who reflects upon the dream of his youth, of the lover who is robbed of his beloved, of the martyr who sees his

ideal collapse, of the hero at nightfall after an undecided battle which has brought him wounds and the loss of a friend. But [it is extraordinary] to be able to carry this enormous accretion of griefs and to be the hero who at the outbreak of a second battle still greets his dawn and fortune as one whose horizon stretches ahead thousands of years and reaches back into the past and who is heir to all things noble and all the spirit of the past—the responsible heir of an aristocratic line; the likes of him was never seen before nor even dreamt before. To take all this upon one's self—the oldest of things and the newest, the losses, the hopes, the conquests, the victories of humanity—to contain all this finally in one soul and compress all into one emotion, this must yield a happiness never before known by man—the happiness of a god full of power and love, full of tears and ringing laughter, a happiness which like the sun at evening lavishly and continually gives of its inexhaustible richness and pours into the sea, and like the sun feels most luxuriant when even the poorest fisherman rows as if with golden oars. Let this divine emotion be called—humanness! (GS, 337)

But human genius, as far as Nietzsche is concerned, is released always to a lesser extent through knowledge or an acquired empathy by someone matured by history, because maturity already lies in humans themselves and can be brought to the surface by diving deep into the self and then bringing it to consciousness. Already in *Human, All-Too-Human,* he points to the quality of the emotions that retroactively can awaken whatever slumbers in us and which belongs to earlier conditions of being: "All *stronger* moods bring with them an echo of related sensations and moods; at the same time, they dredge up memory" (I, 14). This occurs not only in regard to one's individual past with its effects but simultaneously, also, through thoughts and sensations discarded during the course of human development, for the individual is their offspring and continuously contains their various phases. That is taken into account in the aphorism "The Consciousness of Appearance" (54) in *The Gay Science*:

How wonderful and new and yet at the same time how horrible and ironic do I feel myself positioned by my insight toward the whole of existence! I have *discovered* for myself that all of ancient man and animality—indeed, all of the primeval and the past—all sentient being continues in me to poetize, to love, to hate, to reason. In the midst of this dream, I suddenly awoke, but only to the consciousness that I merely dream and that I *must* continue dreaming so that I do not perish: just as the sleepwalker must continue dreaming in order to avoid a downward plunge. What now is the meaning of "appearance"? Certainly not the opposite of some kind of essence. What can I say about any kind of essence except merely to call it by the attributes of its appearance! Truly it is not a dead mask that one can place upon or remove from an unknown quantity! To me, appearance is the effectuating and living thing itself, which goes so far in its self-mockery as to let me feel that here is appearance and will-o'-the-wisp and ghost dance, and nothing more—that among the dreamers even I, the "knower," dance my dance, that the knower is a means for stretching out the earthly dance, belonging to existence's masters of ceremonies, and that the lofty consequence and inter-relatedness of all knowledge perhaps is and will be the highest means for *preserving* the universality of day-dreaming and its all-embracing understanding among these dreamers, as well as preserving *the duration of the dream* intact.

Already here, Nietzsche had made a turn that formed the transition toward his later mysticism. In it, the world has become for him the fiction of the "knower" who, when he awakens as if from a somnambulistic dream and becomes conscious of its fiction, can well feel himself to be a lord and creator, imperiously fixing the sense of this appearance, this dream. A transformation takes place through the mystical idea that awakening from the dream of cosmic totality is at the same time a creative and world-redeeming act; the same thought returns later, in wonderfully poetic dress, in the "Old Growl-Bell" song ("The Other Dancing Song," Z, III, 3) which in deep midnight announces the beginning of day for the awakener by sounding twelve strokes:

One!
Oh man, take care!

Two!
What does deep midnight say?
Three!
"I slept, I slept—
Four!
"From a deep dream have I awoken—
Five!
"The world is deep,
Six!
"And deeper than the day could fathom.
Seven!
"Deep is its woe—
Eight!
"Joy—deeper still than the heart's anguish:
Nine!
"Woe speaks: 'Pass away!'
Ten!
"Yet every joy strives for eternity—
Eleven!
"wants deep, deep eternity!"
Twelve!

The ultimate formulation of this representation again contains strong echoes of Nietzsche's Schopenhauer period and of Hindu philosophy, although always with the characteristic modification that the ultimate goal, as well as the road which leads to it, does not eventuate in an *ending of life* but is to be sought in the *heightening of life*. But nevertheless, however much these two emotionally interpreted conceptions of the problem of existence near each other, it is all the more evident from his newer conception that the Hindu turning away from life—an extreme ascetic expression of a world-negating philosophy—is actually not a release from life but only the redemption from an "ever and again having to die" in consequence of the migration of the soul. Here, after all, is nothing less than another form of the fear of death, which has given to other religions the motif of the belief in immortality; it is fear whose conciliation can just as well be achieved by one's being lifted into hands which keep eternal life and by means of the full identification of the individual with the power and fullness of life's totality, as well as by a stripping away and volatilizing of all those life-drives deeply associated with death, extinction, and dissolution.*

But the charm which a mystical exposition of dream situations, and the concept of cosmic consciousness and dream consciousness, held for Nietzsche, also possessed a personal significance. In fact, more is involved than an equivalence or analogical reasoning, for he was convinced that especially during conditions of intoxication and dream, a fullness of the past could be revived in the individual's present. Dreams always played a great role in his life and thinking, and during his last years he often drew from them—as with the solution of a riddle—the contents of his teachings. In this manner he employed, for instance, the dream related in *Zarathustra* (II, "The Soothsayer"),[61] which came to him in the fall of 1882 in Leipzig; he never tired of carrying it about him and interpreting it. A clever interpretation or one that suited the mood of the dreamer had the effect of making him happy or positively bringing him relief. And so, it becomes evident that quite early on he had occupied himself with these matters, but he rejected bold interpretations in the same degree as he later preferred them.

---

*Coincidence would have it that one of the probably last academic studies thoroughly read by Nietzsche was the work of a Schopenhauerian, with rigorous observations about Hindu philosophy, which brought back to Nietzsche his own earlier world-views. It is a superb book by Paul Deussen, *Das System des Vedânta nach den Brahma-Sûtra's des Bâdarâyana und dem Kommentare des Çañkara über dieselben* (Leipzig: Brockhaus, 1883), in which the author objectively portrays the subject but interprets and judges it from his own perspective. It is impossible to ignore the influence of this work upon Nietzsche's own writings since 1883, especially in his deifying the creator-philosopher and placing him on the highest level of the all-encompassing life-principle, as well as Nietzsche's conception that he harbors in himself all of mankind's past history—so to speak, within his spiritual juxtapositions—within a spatial rather than a time-determined migration of the soul. When one reads Nietzsche's scattered assertions about individual psychological dispositions with their half-mystical meanings, one is tempted to write explanatory notes in the margin—"ātman" [the World Soul or breath from which all souls derive and return] and "Brahmān."

In various passages of *Human, All-Too-Human* he spoke about dreams. Compare for example the aphorism "Dream and Culture" (I, 12), and "The Logic of the Dream" (I, 13). In those aphorisms he still believed that the muddle and disorder of representations in the dream, as well as the lack of clarity and logic and causal connection, . . . remind one of mankind's earliest conditions which, even as today, aborigines act out in their lives as we act them out in our dreams. In contrast, however, Nietzsche no longer speaks in *Daybreak* with this sort of an analogy but addresses straightaway the possibility of the *reproduction* of a slice of the past in dreams. And here and there in *The Gay Science*, dream for him is heightened furthermore into a positive copy of life and the world's past within the individual. From that view, it took only one step to reach a third thought that incorporated the previous ones which held that the past is reproduced in the dream or that the totality of the world and developed life are to be compared philosophically with dream-fiction. Nietzsche's unifying thought then emerged: under certain circumstances, dream is the revivication of everything lived in the past, while life, on the other hand, in its deepest essence is a dream whose spirit and meaning we must determine for ourselves as awakeners. The same is true of all dream-related conditions and of all that which could lead far down into the chaotic, dark, and inexhaustible underground of life—not only into that of past mankind but even farther down to the source from which even it developed initially. And yet, the tranquil dream is insufficient for that quest. What is needed is a much more real, effective, and even more terrible experiencing, namely through orgiastic Dionysian conditions and the chaos of frenzied passions—yes, *madness* itself as a means of sinking back down into the mass of entwined feelings and imaginings. This seemed for Nietzsche the last road into the primal depths imbedded within us.

Quite early Nietzsche had brooded over the meaning of madness as a possible source for knowledge and its inner sense that may have led the ancients to discern a sign of divine election. In *The Gay Science* he says, "And only the person who can cause fright, can lead others,"[62] and in *Daybreak* we find the following strange words that remind one of the representation of the future genius who incorporates the collective history of mankind: "In the outbursts of passion, and in the fantasizings of dreams, and in madness, man rediscovers his own and mankind's prehistory: . . . his memory reaches back far enough, while his civilized state evolves from the forgetting of primal experiences, from an easing up of that memory. Whoever has most extensively forgotten and remained far from all this does *not understand humans*" (312).

At that time, however, Nietzsche wished that he could be a "forgetter" because he still thought human greatness lies in "unemotional knowledge," which is born from reason alone. At that point, he still called it a ghastly confusion when back in older times madness was often considered to be inseparable from great and new acquisitions of knowledge,

> when nevertheless new and deviating thoughts, valuations, and drives always broke out again, it occurred with a gruesome accompaniment: almost everywhere, madness prepares the way for a new idea which breaks the spell of a venerated custom and superstition. Do you understand why it had to be madness which was at work? Something in voice and bearing that was so chilling and incalculable? . . . Something which so visibly carried the sign of complete involuntariness . . . that seemed to characterize the madman as the mask and ear-trumpet of a divinity? . . . Let us go one step further: If all those men of superior thought, who were
> . irresistibly drawn to breaking the yoke of any sort of morality and to provide new laws, *were not really mad*, they would have no choice but to pretend madness or to drive themselves to madness. . . . "How can one make oneself mad without being mad. . . ?" These dreadful lines of thought have been pursued by almost all significant men of ancient civilizations. . . . Who dares to cast a glance into the wildness of the most bitter and superfluous needs of the soul in which apparently the most fruitful people of all time have languished! One hears the sighs of the lonely and disturbed: "Alas, if I could finally believe in myself! Give me delirium and convulsions, sudden lights and darknesses, frighten me with frost and heat as no mortal has ever experienced them, with alarm and prowling figures, and let me howl and whim-

per and crawl like an animal—all so that I may find faith in myself! Doubt gnaws at me and I have killed the law; the law makes me as anxious as a corpse does the living. If I were to be no *more* than law, I would be the most depraved of all men. . . ." ("The Meaning of Madness in the History of Morality," *Daybreak*, 14).

In *Daybreak*, Nietzsche frequently explained or refuted ideas that secretly had already made an impact upon him. But later, these ideas formed the very evidence for his belief that states of intoxication are signs of having been uniquely chosen. During this transition, Nietzsche caricatured positivism and gained a distorted picture of existence as one of hopelessness and horror. He wanted to *replace* that dismal picture with something new and glorious. Replacement called for the creation of something not hitherto in existence. Such a creation depended solely upon his vacillating self-confidence. Therefore when his mood sank downward even for a moment, his tormenting doubts must have risen alarmingly. As a human being, Nietzsche, in his doubting and vacillating moods, felt a relentless need to differentiate himself from the self-confident and omniscient Zarathustra figure. No matter how terrible the lot heaped upon Nietzsche in his temporal self-decline, for Zarathustra, on the other hand, it remains a sign of election and elevation. If Nietzsche, in a horrifying and chaotic mood, had to decline into animality, for Zarathustra it only represented an encompassing of the lowest and profoundest.

That is why in *Twilight of the Idols* (I, 3) the highest type of philosopher is a kind of joiner of animal and god. A related thought [about the merging of contrasts] is found in Nietzsche's assertion about the knower as creator-philosopher (*Beyond Good and Evil*, 101): "Today the man of knowledge may readily feel himself to be like the god who becomes animal." Indeed, the mask of the lowliest could present to man the most suitable form for representing the highest, because within the mask one does not shame it and, at the same time, one effectively hides one's glow: "Above all, might it not be *contrast* which is the proper disguise into which the modesty of a god enters?" (BGE, 40).

Here we encounter Nietzsche's last attempt to hide himself

and his longing for the mask. Apparently that mask was to veil the god in all-too-human clothing, while in fact Nietzsche's longing was grounded in a shattering need: to reinterpret his terrible fate, which threatened his human spirit, and give it the aspect of the godly in order to endure it. In the aphorism "Here the view is free" (TI, 46), he offers the intimation that it could be the nobility of one's soul that allows one to meet and not to fear "the most unworthy": "A woman who loves, sacrifices her honor; a knower who 'loves,' sacrifices perhaps his humanness; a god who loved became a Jew."

And so we see how self-sacrifice and self-ravaging not only heightened his self-induced inner conflicts to the extremity of his spirit but also how these infused even the most personal aspects of Nietzsche. In ever more pronounced fashion, his entire line of thought peaks to a self-destructive *deed* through which, by continuing to act and endure, his redemption was to be completed. Just as it is possible to pursue clearly the way Nietzsche's inner life expresses itself philosophically through his recurrence teaching, so we may note the point at which his philosophy retransformed itself into a most personal kind of experiencing as expressed by the words, "I drink back into myself the flames that shoot out of myself" ("The Night Song," Z, II). And if the basic features of his thinking were only tremendous lines which rounded out the drawing of a god-figure, a mystical self-apotheosis rather than some abstract system, the bliss of self-deification drastically takes a turn into the *purely human tragedy of life.* Zarathustra's redeeming world-action becomes at the same time Nietzsche's decline; Zarathustra's divine right to interpret life and to revaluate all values is only achieved at the cost of entering into that primal ground of life that in Nietzsche's human existence reveals itself as the dark depth of madness. "Whoever is of my kind," says Zarathustra (III, "The Wanderer"), "does not escape such an hour, an hour which tells him: Only now do you follow your way to greatness! Peak and abyss—they now join as one!" And so, Zarathustra's shudder at the prospect of this limitless sinking into the abyss is therefore also Nietzsche's shudder in the face of his personal fate; indistinguishably, things melt into the imaging of Nietzsche's transfigured life—the superior Nietzsche realm.

"And then, everything called out to me in signs: 'it is time!' But I did not listen, until finally my abyss stirred and my thoughts bit me. Alas, abysmal thought—which is *my own* thought! When will I find the strength to hear you digging, without shuddering any longer? My pounding heart jumps up to my throat when I hear you digging! Your silence wants to choke me, even now, you abysmally silent one! Not yet do I dare summon you: it is quite enough that I carried you with me!" ("Of Involuntary Bliss," Z, III). These shattering words should be remembered when one reads in Nietzsche's writings the description of the "stillest hour," in which life itself commands him to experience his thoughts and to proclaim life which glides with joyous laughter over the torments of the individual, because bliss lies in its own fullness:

> Fright takes hold of him down to his very toes, so that the ground under him yields and the dream begins. Let me tell you a parable. Yesterday, in the stillest hour, the ground under me gave way—the dream began. The pointer moved, the hour of my life drew its breath—never have I heard such silence about me: my heart then took fright. Then it spoke to me without voice: "Zarathustra, *you know* it?" And I cried out with fright at this whisper and the blood drained from my face. . . . Laughter ensued about me. Oh, how this laughter tore at my innards and cut my heart open! . . . And it laughed again and fled: then silence surrounded me like a twofold silence. But I lay on the ground and sweat flowed from my limbs. . . . ("The Stillest Hour," Z, II).

Passages from the chapter "The Convalescent" (Z, III) link up with all these portrayals:

> One morning . . . Zarathustra jumped up from his resting place and like a madman roared with a terrifying voice, behaving as if *some other* [Nietzsche-Zarathustra] were still lying down and not wanting to get up. . . . But, Zarathustra spoke these words:
>
>> Up, abysmal thought, up out of my depth! I am your crowing-cock and morning dawn, you sleepy worm—up, up! . . . Here is enough thunder to make even graves learn to listen! [The graves of the past and all past beings.]

Now wipe away sleep and all idiocy and blindness from your eyes!

Listen to me also with your eyes: my voice is a healing means even for those born blind.

And once you are awake, be awake for me eternally. It is not *my* habit to awaken great-grandmothers from sleep only to tell them to sleep on.

You are stirring, stretching, gasping? Up! Up! Do not gasp, but speak to me! Zarathustra, the godless, calls you!

I, Zarathustra, the advocate of life, the advocate of suffering, the advocate of the circle—I summon you, my most abysmal thoughts!

Hail to me! You come—I hear you! My abyss *speaks*; I have turned my ultimate depth inside out and have led it into the light!

Hail to me! Come near! Give me your hand . . . ha! Let go! Haha! . . . Loathing, loathing, loathing . . . woe is me!

The picture of madness stands at the end of Nietzsche's philosophy, like a shrill and terrible illustration of theoretical knowledge and of the conclusions drawn from it for his philosophy of the future, because the point of departure is formed by dissolving everything intellectual and letting drive-like chaos dominate. Nietzsche's theory of knowledge, however, goes beyond the decline of the knower and conceives a revelation by life, inoculated by madness: "Spirit is that life which itself cuts into life: with its own torment, it increases its own knowledge. Did you know that? And the happiness of the spirit is this: to be anointed and to be consecrated through tears, like a *sacrificial animal*. Did you know that? And the darkness of the blind man and his seeking and groping shall yet bear witness to the power of the sun into which he gazed. Did you know that before?"

Madness was to bear witness also to the power of life's truth through whose brilliance the human spirit is blinded. For no power of *reason* leads into the depths of life in its fullness. It does not permit a climbing into its fullness step by step or thought by thought: "And if, moreover, you have no ladders, you must then know how to climb upon your own head: how else would you want to climb upward? . . . Yet you, Zarathustra, wanted to gaze into the depth of all things and their real background: so, you must ever climb above yourself—on and upward until even your stars are below you!" ("The Wanderer," Z, III).

And here an end seems to have been reached and the development of the whole seems to have necessarily closed: the insatiable and passionate impulse that drove and heightened this spirit finally burned and swallowed it up again. For us, the outsiders, we can see that from then on Nietzsche was shrouded in the total darkness of night; he stepped into the most individual life of his inner experience before which the ideas that had accompanied him had to come to a halt: a profound and shattering silence spreads over these matters. Not only *can* we no longer follow his spirit into the last transformation, which he achieves through self-sacrifice, but also we *ought* not follow it. For in this transformation Nietzsche found proof for his truth, which has become completely merged with all the secrets and seclusions of his inwardness. During his last loneliness, he has drawn away from us and has closed the gate behind him. At the gate's entrance, however, these words radiate toward us: "What hitherto has been your ultimate danger has now become your ultimate refuge. 'You are on your way to greatness, and that must be of greatest courage to you because there is no path behind you! . . . Here no one may sneak after you! Your own foot has obliterated the path behind you, and above that path is written: Impossibility'" ("The Wanderer," Z, III).

And the only indication that even behind the gate lies an inaccessible world of a wandering spirit is a quiet lament that diminishes within: "Alas, my steepest way is still ahead! Alas, I begin my loneliest wandering! . . . My last solitude has just now begun. Alas, there is that black, sad sea below me! Alas, this pregnant, nightly moroseness! Alas, destiny and sea! To you I must now *descend* . . . deeper into pain than ever I have descended, down into its blackest flood! My destiny will have it so: Well then! I am ready."

"'From where arise the mountains?' I once asked. And I learned that they arise from the sea. This testimony is written on their stones and in the stony walls of their peaks. Out of the deepest depth must the highest arise to its fullest height" ("The Wanderer").

In this manner, height and depth, the abyss of madness and the peak of truth's essence, become swallowed up in one another: "I stand before my highest mountain . . . and therefore must descend deeper than ever." And so the highest self-deification first celebrates its total mystical victory in the most profound self-destruction, in capitulation and in the decline of the knower. Of both the symbolic animals at Zarathustra's side—the serpent of knowledge and wisdom and the eagle with an upward-striving, kingly pride—he finds this to remain true: "Might I only be wiser! May I be thoroughly as wise as my serpent! But that would be asking the impossible, and so I ask that my pride always accompany my wisdom! And if ever my wisdom abandons me . . . let my pride, too, fly away with my foolishness!"

"Thus began Zarathustra's decline" ("Prologue," Z, 10).

And so Nietzsche's spirit vanishes before us into the dual secret of decline and elevation and into a darkness encircled by the flight of eagles.

There is something touching and gripping here, as with the return of a tired child to its original shelter of belief that required no understanding in order to participate in highest blessings and revelations. After the spirit has run through all cycles and has exhausted all possibilities, without finding satisfaction, it buys satisfaction through the highest sacrifice, the sacrifice of the self. We are reminded of Nietzsche's conversational reflections earlier in the second part of this book and his words, "When everything has taken its course—where does one run to then? When all possible combinations have been exhausted, what follows then? How would one then not arrive again in belief? Perhaps in a Catholic belief? *In any case, the circle could be more plausible than a standing still.*" Indeed, he describes a circle in his own repetition. And it is interesting that to the degree he nears his original point of departure—and reason appears meaningless when contrasted with a mystic belief-craving superior being—Nietzsche's philosophy always takes on more absolute and reactionary features. This comes about because against his own and earlier individualism, he reconstructs an absolute and determined tradition and expresses a self-deification within a religious absolutism. That may be viewed as especially intriguing because this course of events, despite pathological preconditions, suggests something that is typically psychological: when the religious drive is motivated by free-thinking—living itself out strictly in individual fashion, as with Nietzsche who creates something godly out of his own self—then he forcibly avails himself again of the most absolute and reactionary powers that ever were at the disposal of an objectified god; Nietzsche downgraded reason, so to speak, which originally had given him direction, and he cut off any further arguments raised by reason. Out of the human, a god was to arise, even if one had to make this possible by a return to childhood and adolescence. Only through such a split, which he ruthlessly fostered within himself, does he celebrate his redemption and mystic self-unification within belief:

. . . At noon, one changed into two—
a joint victory assured, we now celebrate
the feast of feasts:
Friend Zarathustra came, the guest of guests!
The world now laughs, the horrid curtain parts,
the wedding then of light and darkness starts.

So ends the wonderful aftersong "From High Mountain," which concludes *Beyond Good and Evil.*

Nietzsche's personal fate fits like a capstone into this entire structure of thoughts in such a fashion that one cannot doubt the influence of his moody intimations about the shaping of his philosophy of the future. With a powerful hand, he forced what awaited him into the plan of the whole and made it serviceable for the last secret sense of his philosophy. From here on in, he looked back over his life and thoughts; he surveyed the alterations in his transformation and gave them, retrospectively, a unifying mystical significance—just as the creator-philosopher does regarding the collective life of mankind. And so, he became a signifying god who—even if somewhat forcibly—turns all things of the past into things intended for the highest goal. Making the past meaningful for the future is now his motto; consequently, it is diametrically opposite to what he had aimed for earlier during his peregrinations, namely, to discard the past rapidly in order to separate it as completely as possible from an evolving future.

The strong influence of his earlier assertions about the future of philosophy is also grounded in all this. At one time, he had seen the evidence of spiritual independence in the ability to free himself constantly from the truths he had seized, and it had seemed to him irrelevant, therefore, if while seizing them he had leaned upon others. Now his all-encompassing independence demanded that one keep in mind the fact that although he had discarded his old ideas, his essential thoughts still reside in them; they had been stimulated by his own self and not by others. Yet, in regard to Nietzsche's last works, in which he apparently, and most independently, constructed an individualistic system, one so often has the feeling that Nietzsche is looking back into the past as if he were returning to the old positions he has abandoned, whereas indeed he is far removed from them by means of the independence of unique, hard-won hypotheses. The solution to this contradiction lies in the fact that he drew from his earlier convictions only that through which his individual essence and his hidden needs are expressed; whatever theories he had drawn from other thinkers were basically prompted by unconscious pretexts and instinctive incidentals, necessarily serving his inner development. Reaching the end of this development, he pulls himself together by integrating his entire inner life; he returns to it and surveys it, only to emphasize the unity underlying all previous changes, doing so retrospectively just as he had earlier emphasized exclusively his capacity for changing. Like someone who is about to take a trip from which there will be no return, and like someone who wishes to bid farewell, Nietzsche gathers up various intellectual elements of the past that belong to him. He undertakes a "real estimate of what has been achieved and what one has desired, a *summation* of life" ("Skirmishes of an Untimely Man," TI, 36); he is certain that "it has just returned, it has finally come home—my own self, and those parts of my self that have for so long been strewn among all things and all coincidentals" ("The Wanderer," Z, II).

This put him at odds with his erstwhile companions and their convictions; he *wanted* to forget how often they had determined the direction of his thinking: "One should dismantle the scaffolding after the house is built" ("The Wanderer and His Shadow;" HATH, 335). That is "the moral for a builder of houses," Nietzsche thought, and he ignored the fact that he ever had any need of scaffolding for his own constructions. This unjust view, then, runs entirely counter to an earlier one which stemmed from the impassioned change of ideas and the energy with which he formerly shed acquired thoughts. Now he does not want to believe that a foreign "skin" could ever have grown upon him. His unfairness particularly against positivism is expressed in the preface to his book *Toward a Genealogy of Morals*, as well as in scattered passages of other writings, and in *The Wagner Case* (published in 1888). This brief book on Wagner impels one to make an interesting comparison between the way Wagner is fought against here and in *Human, All-Too-Human*; it was hate with which he once cast off Wagnerisms and it is the same hate with which he now approaches it again in order to retrieve his spiritual property, without giving up his independence.

Nietzsche's earliest strivings to be independent and self-contained ultimately led him so far as to declare in the preface of September 1886 to the second volume of the second edition of *Human, All-Too-Human* that all of the ideas in his earlier writings should be "dated back" to times before their appearance in those works because they spoke *only* about things overcome and already left behind; he claims that their author, Nietzsche, had stood above them reflectingly and had shown himself in a deliberate disguise. And so, the fourth (and last, 1876) of the *Untimely Meditations (Richard Wagner in Bayreuth)*, instead of having been a glorification of Wagner, is reinterpreted as having been merely Nietzsche's "tribute and gratitude for a part of the past"; similarly, Nietzsche's positivistic writings, influenced by Paul Rée's views, were characterized as only the belated portrayal of something that Nietzsche had already outlived. Nietzsche's attempt to re-mint the sense of his works, and at the same time to stamp them with new dates, calls for an application of his own words (Spring 1886, preface to the first volume of the second edition of *Human, All-Too-Human*, 1): "In this respect, perhaps one could reproach me for all sorts of 'art' and all sorts of finer counterfeitings." "Art" and counterfeiting too belong to the many masquerades of this hermit, even to the point where he finally attributed to himself a mask which he had never worn; but this is understandable and forgivable since even here, in his heart, he intended that mask only for *himself* as the human Nietzsche, in distinction to Zarathustra as the mystical superior-Nietzsche.

During each of his changes, certainly the human Nietzsche could not have known anything about his own masking nature; that was possible only for the superior Nietzsche, the figure which Nietzsche's intuition from the beginning had sensed tc be within himself. Consequently, it would appear that the superior Nietzsche is nothing other than a mystic interpretation of Nietzsche's innermost essence and longing, that hidden "fundamental will" which, as we saw, unconsciously tailored the theories acquired from others in order to direct them finally to his goal, with all his power.

In the autumn of 1888 . . . and in characteristic fashion, Nietzsche in the preface to his *Twilight of the Idols* appropriately called his book "a convalescence." The first title he had assigned to it was "The Idleness of a Psychologist." It is indeed an exceedingly interesting idleness because the *Twilight* is one of those books in which he gives himself away most often and chats at the promptings of his soul's secrets. In that regard, and although it is less substantive, the book resembles *Human, All-Too-Human* and *Daybreak*. In *Human, All-Too-Human* Nietzsche reveals something of his inner life merely in the way he is reconciled with a sudden but final and completed turn of spirit; in *Daybreak*, he permits us to look into his inner self in his analysis of newly-surfacing desires and thoughts, at the same time as he combats them just before he allows himself to be swept toward his new philosophy. In the *Twilight of the Idols* a completely different mood becomes his betrayer: the trembling emotion of a tremendous achievement and an exhaustion mixed with the anticipation of something to come.* We see how with these upheavals in *Twilight of the Idols*, Nietzsche himself, as it were, slides into a spiritual twilight.

---

*His mood is mirrored even more undisguised in the "Dithyrambs of Dionysus," written during that time and added after the fourth part of

Thus Spoke Zarathustra. Particularly noteworthy are the following lines from the poem *"Zwischen Raubvögeln"* ("Amidst Birds of Prey"):

Whoever wishes to descend here,
how rapidly
the depths do swallow him!
But you, Zarathustra,
you love even the abyss,
just like the *fir-tree*? . . .
Now—
at one with yourself,
twosome in your own knowledge,
amidst hundreds of mirrors
and false before yourself,
amidst hundreds of memories
uncertain,
weary with every wound,
cold with every frost,
strangled with one's own ropes,
self-knower!
self-hangman! [. . . .]
Now sick,
made ill by snake poison;
a prisoner now,
who drew the hardest lot:
in one's own well,
bowed, working
entombed in your self,
burrowing into yourself
clumsy,
rigid,
a corpse—
overtowered by hundreds of burdens,
overburdened by yourself,
a *knower!*
a *self-knower!*
the *wise* Zarathustra! [. . . .]
Lying in wait,
cowering
one who no longer stands upright!
You misshape things for me with your grave,
you *deformed* spirit! . . .

The same mood marks also the fourth and last part of *Zarathustra*, originating in 1885, but only generally accessible in 1891. From its "strings" sounds the laughter of the superior man, but here and there with shrill, uncanny dissonances. From the purely personal perspective, they are perhaps the most gripping of Nietzsche's writings because they show him already to be in decline and hiding his decline behind laughter. From this point of departure, the full splendor of irreconcilable contradiction then becomes clear: it lies in his introducing his philosophy of the future with a "gay wisdom," which he called a joyous mission intended forever to justify life, with all its power, fullness, and eternity; and for life's highest thought, Nietzsche held up to view the *eternal recurrence* of life. Here we see the conquering optimism that resides in his last works, like the touching smile of a child, yet who also shows, obversely, the face of a hero who shrouds his features distorted by horror. "Is not all weeping a lament? And is not all lament an accusation? And so, my soul, you talk to yourself and therefore you would sooner smile than pour out your grief," sings Zarathustra ("Of the Great Longing," Z, III), and therefore he comes as "the scarlet prince of every whim" (from the dithyramb "Amidst Birds of Prey"). "This crown of the laughing one, this rose-wreath crown, I myself place upon my head; I myself pronounced my laughter holy" ("Of the Higher Man," Z, IV, 18).

The great thing which Nietzsche knew was that he was going under, and yet with a laughing mouth and "rose-wreath crowned" he parted from life, absolving and justifying and transfiguring it. In the Dionysian dithyrambs, the sounds of his life's spirit faded away, and the intended jubilation of the dithyrambs was drowned out by a cry of pain. They are the last ravagings of Nietzsche by Zarathustra.

("Amidst Birds of Prey" was one of the last poems of Nietzsche's "Songs of Zarathustra," composed between 1883–88. In a letter from Genoa on March 22, 1883, Nietzsche wrote to his friend Peter Gast, ". . . I would rather shake off my extreme malice than to perish from it. I continue to compose, at the same time, Dionysus Songs in which I take the liberty of expressing the most terrible things and saying laughingly: this is the most recent form of my madness"—editor.)

Nietzsche once expressed this paradox: "Laughing means to take pleasure in someone else's discomfort, but with a good conscience" (GS, 200). This kind of meditative *"Schadenfreude"* which is capable of taking pleasure not only in one's own injury but suiting oneself to it, courses like a heroic self-contradiction throughout Nietzsche's entire life and suffering. In his tremendous power of spirit, however, through which he was able to raise himself high above himself, lay—psychologically considered—his own inner justification for seeing himself as a mystical double-being, as well as our seeing the profoundest meaning and value of his works.

We, too, are greeted by a shattering double-sound from his laughter, the laughter of a strayer—and the laughter of a conqueror.

NOTES

1. Philology—as an academic specialization and discipline—entailed research and the rigorous study of rhetoric and texts of antiquity, as well as their relationships, sources, and transmissions. Nietzsche soon unsuccessfully applied for a chair of philosophy that would allow teaching the history of philosophy. But even in that position he would have been unhappy because his inclinations increased markedly toward psychological philosophizing.

2. "*Gifthüttli*"; the young Basel colleagues—Nietzsche, Franz Overbeck, Konrad von Orelli, Julius Kaftan, Carl von Geɾsdorff, Heinrich Romundt—frequently met for lunch at a small, local pub which was then dubbed the "poison hut" by other academics who looked upon them as a group of pessimists. Disapproving Basel tongues of conventional burghers also wagged at such get-togethers by educated young bachelors.

3. Nietzsche, in fact, only met Förster in 1885 when he married Nietzsche's sister. *See* Pfeiffer, *Lou Andreas-Salomé* (1983), p. 305.

4. To Paul Rée, end of July, 1879.

5. The two photographs mentioned by Salomé date from 1882; Nietzsche became insane in January of 1889. *See* the Introduction for a discussion of the photographs.

6. *See* the parallel quote in I Corinthians 15:54: "Death is swallowed up in victory."

7. Walter Kaufmann noted that "this is quintessential Nietzsche. Those who ignore this theme . . . misunderstand him."

8. *See* Nietzsche's own discussion of a person's ethical and egoistic choice in sacrificing elements in his divided self to that element which he loves best in himself: "In ethics, man considers himself a *dividuum* and not an *individuum*" (HATH, II, 57).

9. After the publication of Salomé's study in 1894, several more books written earlier by Nietzsche were published, including *Ecce Homo*, a serious, playful, propagandist, and sometimes romanticized review of his own life and works, as well as *The Will to Power*, a posthumously compiled edition of his unpublished materials from 1883 to 1888.

10. Nietzsche's "*Übermensch*" generally has been translated as "superman" and "overman." Essentially the designation refers to an ideal "superior" person of the future as distinct from the corrupt and morally "inferior" society of the present.

11. In a footnote, Salomé points out that she is not concerned with placing Nietzsche in the history of philosophy, and she rejects the

"noise" of contemporaneous critics who attribute the different phases of Nietzsche's development to the influence of works by other philosophers.

12. In a footnote, Salomé lists Nietzsche's scholarly works and their contemporaneous editions, actually from 1867 to 1873, written in Greek, Latin, and German; only the German works have been translated into English so far.

13. "Mothers of Being": Their names for Nietzsche are *Wahn, Wille, Wehe,* or Delusion, Will, and Woe (BT, 20). *See* also Goethe, *Faust II* for a different view.

14. In BGE, 204, Nietzsche also attacked the "mischmasch" and "reality" of positivist philosophers and he notes with regret that the modern world lacks such regal "anchorites of the spirit" as Heraclitus, Plato, and Empedocles.

15. By "intellectualism" Salomé here refers to Nietzsche's scorn for the pedantic passion to idolize and collect more facts than the compiler knows what to do with. Nietzsche had raised no objection to the German theologian's controversial *Das Leben Jesu,* 1835 (translated in 1846 by George Eliot as *The Life of Jesus Critically Examined*) which rejected supernatural revelations and claims for Jesus' divinity. But Nietzsche attacked the views in Strauss' new book as superficial adaptations of materialism and evolutionism toward a new universal religiosity, a "Straussian Paradise." Nietzsche quotes Strauss as saying, "It seems to me that the time has not as yet come . . . to destroy any Church institution." Nietzsche polemically responds, "But why not . . . ?" Nietzsche also faulted Strauss for imputing moral significance to the nature of the cosmos.

16. The study of history and not the course of events. Here is an idea already broached in *The Birth of Tragedy,* namely that the Greeks created beauty in order "to be able to live"—aesthetic worth is consonant with its "use for life."

17. Nietzsche wrote that "inspired by instinct" he turned to Spinoza's writings and found a *precursor* who had the same tendency as his own to make *knowledge* the *most powerful* affect. "This unusual and loneliest of thinkers is closest to me . . . he denies the freedom of the will, teleology, the moral world order, the unegoistic, and evil. . . . My loneliness is now a twosomeness" (postcard to Franz Overbeck, July 30, 1881). A later letter to Salomé expresses a similar pleasure at finding in her an intellectual *"Geschwistergehirn"* or twosomeness, with a likeminded person. During Nietzsche's last period of creativity, that also marked increasing withdrawal and solitariness, he attributed to himself the capacity for being *"zweisam"* or twosome within his own being. In the poem

"Zwischen Raubvögeln," ("Amid Birds of Prey," DD), Zarathustra is "two-some" in his knowledge.

18. In section 10, *Of the Use and Disadvantage of History for Life,* Nietzsche writes, "With the word 'unhistorical' I designate the art and strength that permits one to forget and to enclose oneself in a limited horizon; 'superhistorical' I call those powers which can divert one's gaze from a 'becoming' and turn toward that which gives existence the character of the eternal and recurring, namely, toward *art* and *religion.*

19. Namely, the historical or monumentalistic, the unhistorical or anti-quarian (also a kind of unselfconscious existence within time as experienced by animals), and the superhistorical—a symbolic or critical view of history.

20. "Untimely" in the sense of "out of season or fashion" or irritatingly new.

21. Salomé will not mention Wagner's "deadly insult" that caused Nietzsche's suppurating wound. *See* the Introduction for a discussion of the troubled situation, with hidden repercussions.

22. The lines in brackets were omitted in the facsimile of Nietzsche's letter which Salomé published; they were restored in Pfeiffer's 1970 edition of letters and documents. The unsubtle demands for Lou's trust are repeated assertively toward the end of the letter, written probably on July 16, 1882.

23. Nietzsche distorted matters here. In full, Wagner's inscription reads "Cordial greetings and regards to his dear friend Friedrich Nietzsche. Richard Wagner (Senior Church Councillor: for kind transmission to Professor Overbeck)." The phrase "Senior Church Councillor" (*Oberkir-chenrat*) was a personal joke Wagner thought the church historian Over-beck would take as such.

24. Middleton (p. 189) quotes a postscript to the letter, in which Nietzsche told Lou Salomé that he values impulses more than mind or spirit and knowledge—the "free" thinker is not "my ideal." If this was a bit of rationalization or meant to explain his personality to Lou, it might have served as a suggestion that his inclinations toward her were becoming more personal than solely intellectual.

25. The excursion took place during the time Nietzsche visited with Salomé and Rée from May 13 to 16, 1882. Other biographically notewor-thy incidents occurred. Nietzsche staged the photograph with Lou Salomé standing in a cart and wielding a whip over himself and Rée [*frontispiece photograph*], a photograph that brought unwanted notoriety. Preceding that, Nietzsche had also arranged a rendezvous with Lou at the Lion Monument in Lucerne's Gletschergarten on May 13, a moment

in time that surfaced again in a drawing he made seven years later when he was engulfed by madness. *See* the Introduction.

26. Salomé knew Nietzsche's private correspondence with Rée, and she used Nietzsche's autobiographical information for her characterizations of him. In a postcard dated April 23, 1879, Nietzsche wrote, ". . . the good dæmon in us is mightier than sickness and pain—by *whatever name* this 'good dæmon' may be called."

27. Trophonius, a master architect, and his brother Agadedes built the temple of Apollo at Delphi. He also stole a treasure, killed his brother, and was swallowed up by the earth. He became an oracle in a Labedean cave, offering dark, truthful, and pessimistic views to those who consulted him.

28. Nietzsche uses the formal address: *Sie*.

29. From a letter written by Nietzsche to Rée, October 31, 1880. They met in 1873, while Rée was working on a doctoral thesis published in 1875 as *Psychological Observations (Psychologische Beobachtungen)*. Lou Salomé's role in the lives of these men is discussed in the Introduction, as is the Wagner-Nietzsche affair.

30. Nietzsche's lines here may seem flowery but they were in the back of Rée's mind in 1882 when Lou Salomé asked "brother" Rée to find a third party who would join their intellectual communality. Already in letters during the years 1870 and 1873, Nietzsche mused about founding a cloister for self-educating recluses; Rée and other friends expressed personal interest in the idea.

"Epicurean garden" refers to a school founded by Epicurus (341-270 B.C.) in a garden outside of Athens' city walls, where he devoted his life to teaching and quiet withdrawal from the world. Information about Epicurus comes from the biography by Laertius Diogenes (third century A.D.). During Nietzsche's graduate student days, those biographical fragments became the source for one of his early historical investigations.

31. "At that time Nietzsche was full of admiration for English scholars and philosophers, which later reversed itself completely. But in *Human, All-Too-Human* (II, 184) he still called them 'the full and fulfilling,' and in a letter to Rée, he said that English philosophers have 'the only good philosophical approach' at present. In that regard during this period, the only thing he still valued about Schopenhauer was 'his hard sense of the real, his will to clarity and reason that often allows him to resemble the English. . . .' (GS, 99)."

These above remarks by Lou Salomé need to be tempered by realizing that Nietzsche's knowledge of writings in English came through German translations or summaries.

32. Rée was at work on a book entitled *The Origin of Conscience* (*Die Entstehung des Gewissens*), published later in 1885 (Berlin: C. Heymons). *See* the Introduction for Nietzsche's reaction to it after the demise of their friendship.

33. Of Rée's book, Nietzsche wrote that it belonged to "one of the boldest and coolest thinkers" who ever analyzed human behavior. He quotes Rée's sentence, "The moral person does not stand closer to the intelligible (metaphysical) world than does the physical man." This "hard and cutting sentence" that stems from a knowledge of history, says Nietzsche, "may perhaps in the future serve as the axe which cuts to the root of the 'metaphysical need' of man—whether this will be *more* of a blessing than a curse to the general welfare, who can say?" (HATH, 37).

Rée often mentioned his gratitude for Nietzsche's encouragements while he was writing his book. He inscribed a copy for Nietzsche with the following hand-written note: "To the father of this essay, most gratefully from its mother." There is controversy about who is actually in whose debt. Kaufmann (p. 48f.) notes that Rée was "conscious mainly of his own debt to Nietzsche" for his second book. However, Nietzsche's frequent acknowledgement of "Réealisms" turns the question into a Gordian knot, especially when one considers how much both men were indebted to others. Rée's book was well received in German and English media (Pfeiffer, *Friedrich Nietzsche, Paul Rée, Lou von Salomé,* pp. 389–90); one reviewer praised Rée as a young Spinoza. But the book itself, published in 1885, carried no dedication to Nietzsche. After the rupture of their friendship, though distant cordiality remained, Nietzsche wrote to Rée in May of 1883 that he wished no dedication. To others, Nietzsche's letters disavowed any debt whatever and warned against confusing Rée's views with his own.

"*Empfindungen,*" in the title of Rée's book, may also be translated as sensations, perceptions, feelings, sensitivities.

34. *See also* the aphorisms in HATH entitled "The cult of genius derived from vanity" (162) and "Danger and gain in the cult of genius" (164).

35. The aphorism reads, "The thing most prone to being wounded and yet most unconquerable is human vanity; indeed, its strength grows with being wounded and finally can become gigantic." Compare this with the motto adopted from Furius Antias of Gallius by Nietzsche: "*Increscunt animi, virescit volnere virtus.*"

36. Positivism, generally speaking, is a philosophical system that seeks verifications through the data of sense experience and rejects metaphysical speculations; for its source of knowledge it relies on the physical sciences.

37. This is part of a letter Nietzsche wrote to Lou Salomé on June 7, 1882. In her Nietzsche book, she gracefully shielded the purely private elements of the letter from public view. The omissions are restored within the brackets.

38. Salomé may not have been aware at the time of variant closing lines to the poem, which Nietzsche addressed "L.": "Courage! for it is you who stands at the helm—/dearest Victoria!" Nietzsche's sister, possessor of the archives, suppressed the information for as long as possible in order to minimize evidence of his deep ardor for Lou.

39. Salomé refers to section 279, "Stellar Friendship," as Nietzsche's valedictory farewell to Rée rather than to Wagner as others believe. The widening difference between Nietzsche's and Rée's philosophical attitudes was not as great a factor as was Salomé's disinclination to remain a disciple or soul-mate of Nietzsche or to change her close life with Rée. Nietzsche begins and ends the passage with the following: "We were friends and have become estranged. But this is as it should be. . . . And so we will *believe* in our stellar friendship, even though we should have to be terrestrial enemies to one another." Only by not quoting these sentiments can Salomé give an impression of a "lovely" rather than a disharmonious parting between friends Nietzsche and Rée, or between Nietzsche and Wagner, as the case may be.

40. "I write for myself" (from a letter to Rée, May 29, 1882).

41. Significantly, "Prelude to a Philosophy of the Future" is the subtitle of Nietzsche's *Beyond Good and Evil*, 1886.

42. From the closing part of a letter written by Nietzsche to Salomé, probably November 24, 1882. Salomé omitted the bracketed material. Nietzsche prefaced the passage cited with the remark, "Do I speak obscurely? Once I sense trust, you will learn that I also have the right words. Until now, I have always had to remain silent."

43. The idea that truth comes from the emotions.

44. Nietzsche's pejorative colloquialism for "*Wirklichkeits-Philosophastern.*"

45. Salomé, in a long footnote, cites other passages in *Human, All-Too-Human* and *The Gay Science* in which Nietzsche warns against indulgence in emotions and madness and calls upon genius not to undermine the sensibleness of science.

46. "*Incipit Zarathustra*" (Zarathustra begins) recalls the conclusion of *The Gay Science* (1882), while in the 1882 prologue to *Thus Spoke Zarathustra* the phrase recurs as "Thus Zarathustra began to go under."

47. Salomé, in a footnote, asks the reader to compare this view with Nietzsche's earlier assertions in HATH, 147 and D, 159 (in which he

attacks art that conjures up the ghosts of the dead), and in HATH 244, 251.

48. In a footnote, Salomé pinpoints contrasts and similarities in Nietzsche's writings: "The Wanderer and His Shadow," 275, 289; HATH, I, 245, 614.

49. For Nietzsche, the man of violence is an atavistic throwback and therefore no leader into the future.

50. In a foreword to his *The Origin of Conscience* (1885), Rée outlines the development of the human conscience as follows: "The elements from which conscience forms itself are (1) punishment; (2) the sanction of punishment through divinity; (3) moral laws and prohibitions. For the historical origination of these elements, we must search really within the individual person."

51. Nietzsche's thought here, in context, is that man who is not as yet ready to possess the truth—which would lead to a profound pessimism—and is in *fear* of it, may adopt piety and the artist's counterfeiting through his will to reverse the truth; piety and artistic counterfeiting only apply cosmetics to man.

52. The pious fraud or holy lie ("The 'Improvers' of Mankind," TI, 5). Nietzsche goes on in that section to express a formula: "*All* means so far whereby one has aimed to make mankind moral were basically *immoral.*" Plato's myths may be considered pious or holy deceptions designed for people's well-being, in contrast to unholy lies. Both types of lies, however, are offensive to the free spirit of inquiry, which has its own "piety" (BGE, 105).

53. Nietzsche here addresses Lou with the formal "*Sie*" and closes with ". . . Your F. N."

54. "*Geistesleben*" can mean spiritual, mental, or intellectual life, or all of these.

55. When Salomé uses the term "*Wiederkunft*," I have translated it as "recurrence" and "*Wiederkehr*" as "return."

56. As in musical terminology, the direction to start all over again.

57. In order of preferred translation, Kaufmann (BGE, p. 68, fn. 17) suggests: "A vicious circle made god"; "God is a vicious circle"; or, least likely, "the circle is a vicious god." In the passage cited, Salomé omitted Nietzsche's phrase that Buddha and Schopenhauer were under the spell of delusion and morality and therefore their thoughts did not rise "beyond good and evil."

58. In a footnote, Salomé quotes extensively from "On the Vision and the Riddle," Part Three of *Zarathustra*, to link up with the thoughts interpreted here. Zarathustra keeps asking the same question, with

variations: "Must we not return eternally?" And says subjectively, "And so I speak ever more quietly because I am afraid of my own thoughts and ulterior motives."

59. The reference here is to a passage in Nietzsche's section in *Ecce Homo: How One Becomes What One Is*, "Why it is that I write such good books": "Once when Dr. Heinrich von Stein honestly complained of not being able to understand a single word of my *Zarathustra*, I told him that this is perfectly natural because to have understood six sentences of the book would mean to have *experienced* it and to be lifted up to a higher level of mortals than 'modern' people could achieve." There are slight variations of style between a few published excerpts read by Salomé and the posthumously published version of 1908, but in both Nietzsche's wry sense of humor is evident. *Ecce Homo* was written in 1888, transcribed by Nietzsche's amanuensis ("my pupil and friend," said Nietzsche), Peter Gast, who used some unpublished materials in his prefaces to Nietzsche's books.

60. *Der Wille zur Macht: Versuch einer Umwerthung aller Werthe* is a collection of some thousand notes written by Nietzsche between 1883–88, a number of which appeared in parallel form in his other works. Nietzsche died in 1900, and the notes were published afterwards in different editions. Salomé based her comments on pre-publication announcements; *see* Pfeiffer edition, p. 354.

61. The enigmatic Nietzsche-Zarathustra dream sees him as a night watchman who guards tombs. The allegorized figure of life, vanquished, looked out at him from glass coffins. Angry sounds rush through corridors, and finally the wings of a gate-vault are torn open. A black coffin is spilled before him, and when it bursts open, it releases mocking laughter and angels, owls, and butterflies as large as children. In fright, he throws himself to the ground, and his own outcries—cries as never before in his life—awake him to consciousness. In another dream ("Of the Vision and the Riddle," Z, III, 2), Zarathustra comes across a young shepherd who is being choked by a black snake whose tail hangs from his mouth. Zarathustra cries out to him frenziedly to bite off the snake's head. That single cry, Zarathustra said, was compounded of dread, disgust, pity— and all that was good and evil inside himself. Once the shepherd did what he was told in the parable and spewed away the snake's head, he became a laughing, radiant, and changed being—"no longer human"— releasing an unearthly laughter that Zarathustra envies and yearns for. Later Zarathustra identifies the snake with the ever-recurring conventional, unimaginative and unheroic "small man" who sticks in one's craw.

62. In context, Nietzsche makes an epigram of the idea: "One who does not frighten *himself* will not cause fright in others. . ." ("Joke, Cunning, and Revenge," GS, 33). Salomé paraphrases this.

Austrian / German Culture Series

- ☐ R. M. RILKE, Poems 1912–1926
- ☐ GOETHE, Roman Elegies
- ☐ LOU SALOMÉ, Rilke
- ☐ LOU SALOMÉ, Nietzsche
- ☐ LOU SALOMÉ, Freud
- ☐ LOU SALOMÉ, Ibsen's Heroines
- ☐ R. M. RILKE, Worpswede Journal
- ☐ M. HAMBURGER, Variations
- ☐ KARL KERÉNYI, Excursions of a Hellenist
- ☐ NIETZSCHE, Dithyrambs of Dionysus